Feeding the WHOLE Family

DOWN-TO-EARTH COOKBOOK and WHOLE FOODS GUIDE

BY CYNTHIA LAIR

Foreword by Annemarie Colbin

San Diego, California

LuraMedia™

Cover illustrations by Mindy Dwyer
Cover design by Tom Jackson (Philadelphia)
Book illustrations by Cynthia Lair

LuraMedia, Inc.
7060 Miramar Road, Suite 104
San Diego, California 92121

Library of Congress Cataloging-in-Publication Data
    Lair, Cynthia (date).
        Feeding the whole family : down-to-earth cookbook and whole foods guide /
    by Cynthia Lair : foreword by Annemarie Colbin.
            p.   cm.
        Includes bibliographical references and index.
        ISBN 0-931055-97-0.
        1. Cookery (Natural foods)   2. Natural foods.   I. Title.
    TX741.L34   1994
    641.5'63—dc20   94-14274
                                                                  CIP

"Freezer of Dreams" by Cynthia Lair and Nancy Rankin originally appeared in *Northwest Baby Newspaper,* July 1991.

"Getting Your Child to Eat Vegetables" by Cynthia Lair and Nancy Rankin originally appeared in *Northwest Baby Newspaper,* November 1990.

"Nutty Carmelcorn" from *Fresh from a Vegetarian Kitchen* by Meredith McCarty, Turning Point Publications, 1989, is reprinted by permission.

"She Knows What You've Been Eating" by Cynthia Lair and Nancy Rankin originally appeared in *PCC (Puget Consumers' Co-op) Sound Consumer,* no. 228, March 1992.

The information in this book has been prepared thoughtfully and carefully. It is not intended to be diagnostic or prescriptive. Please use your good judgment and consult with your health-care practitioner when planning your family's diet.

Dedicated to Michael and Grace,

who light the candle

and eat the food

with me.

Acknowledgments

I am especially grateful to:

Jeff Basom for his incredible creativity with whole foods and for sharing his skills with me. His recipes or adaptations of them are featured as follows: Lemon Basil Potato Salad (page 127), Golden Mushroom-Basil Soup (page 155), Creamy Broccoli Soup (page 156), Sesame Greens (page 191), Cashew-Curry Greens (page 191), Cooked Cabbage Salad with Sweet Sesame Dressing (page 195), Roasted Potatoes and Carrots (page 203), Homemade Whole-Grain Breads (page 210), Pumpkin Muffins (page 217), Poppyseed Muffins (page 218), and Homemade Curry Paste (page 226).

Annemarie Colbin, who remains my most influential teacher on the subject of food and healing.

Nina Petrulis, for her meticulous work on the chapter "Feeding the Whole Foods Baby" and her undying support of the project.

And Nancy Rankin, for her inspiration and work at the beginning of this book. Parts of the book came from our work together in Two Moms Cooking School.

I would also like to thank the following people and organizations for their contributions of recipe ideas and expertise:

Lea Aemissegger, Aunt Cathy, Michael Boer, Minx Boren, Karen Brown, Rita Carey, Goldie Caughlin, Chikai, Mim Collins, Connie Feutz, Susan Wickett Ford, Dr. Bruce Gardner, Terry Kady and Essential Sandwiches, Jack Kelly, Holly Koteen, Margaret and Brad Kulkin, Chris Lair, Buck Levin and Bastyr University, Theresa Lewis, Judy Loebl, Meredith McCarty, Puget Consumers' Co-op, Silence-Heart-Nest Restaurant, Joy Taylor, Jackie Williams, Dr. Louisa Williams, Sherry Willis, and Susan Wilson.

My heartfelt thanks to Jenny Russell, for helping me make sense of a mass of paper, and to Carol Sowell, for her careful attention to details. Thank you to Lura Geiger for her intelligent guidance, gentle encouragement, and willingness to take a risk. I am also grateful to Marcia Broucek for her keen mind, compassionate heart, and dedicated spirit. And, finally, I would never have started this journey without Michael and Grace and their continual support of who I am.

Table of Contents

Foreword

Few of us can look at the state of the world and not feel despair. The breakdown of the family unit seems to lead to the loss of a firm system of values, including caretaking. And when families no longer take care of their own, other social structures must fill the gap. Joseph Chilton Pearce, in *Evolution's End,* says the breakdown of society begins with the severing of the mother/child bond through medicated childbirth and the hospital practice of separating the newborn from its mother — and, it should be noted, by the replacement of the home cook with the factory.

Many of us no longer live in the place where we were born, or in the same town as our parents. The extended family and the stable networks of longtime friends and acquaintances aren't always there to help us along, or to show us the tried and true, well-established traditions. Therefore, we must re-create ourselves anew wherever we live. We must establish our own traditions, and create new connections and relationships with kindred communities, by choice and not automatically by physical proximity. We need to examine our "customs" to see if they have been around for years or if they're recently established. The more recent the custom, the closer we might wish to scrutinize it for efficacy, usefulness, and its effect on our health.

In the past 50 or 60 years, we have established many new customs in our way of eating. Canned, frozen, chemically preserved, irradiated, and microwaved foods are new in the history of humanity; so are refined foods such as sugar and white flour, artificial sweeteners, preservatives, colorings, emulsifiers, and other unnatural ingredients. Is it coincidental or significant that the breakdown of our society is occurring simultaneously with the widespread consumption of refined and artificial foods? Could it be that by our dietary customs — consumption of unnatural foods and large amounts of meat and milk from animals raised on antibiotics and hormones — we are building a new kind of human being, one that has little connection with the healthier ways of the past?

It often seems that there is little we can do to correct the wrongs of our society. However, we can always help ourselves, our families and friends, and our surroundings. Each of us can make an effort to light the darkness around us. As our numbers multiply, so will our little lights. And our first areas of concern can be how we raise our families and what we feed them. We have considerable power over our health through our choices in food. If we are in charge of feeding others, we have a great influence over their health as well — not only in the amount and kinds of nutrients in the food, but also in its quality and the energy and love put into preparing and serving it.

The importance of homemade food cannot be overestimated. To have a real person cook and prepare our meals is a crucial element in our well-being. As many of us have been raised on commercial or processed foods, we need to relearn the skill of nurturing through nourishment. That's why books such as this one are so needed and so helpful.

You'll find here a sensible, workable, effective approach to healthful eating. It relies on well-tested principles, it's fad-proof, and the foods taste great. I brought up my children on such a regime; now that they are in their 20s, I can say with certainty that the system works. Cynthia Lair has put her intelligence, her commitment, and her love into this book, just as surely as she puts those ingredients into her family's meals. You will find here a community of parents serious about their families' health and a connection with a tradition older than that of freeze-dried foods with artificial colors and flavors. You'll find tips and ideas that can help you every day, and recipes that are delicious and easy to make.

As concerned parents, as concerned human beings, we should always remember that the best place to start improving the world is at home.

Annemarie Colbin, CHES
The Natural Gourmet Cookery School
New York, NY

PREFACE: My Journey with Food

When I was a child, I had free reign to eat as much sugar as I liked. Opened bags of candy beckoned from kitchen drawers, and a fresh case of soda pop was delivered weekly to our home. Sugar was present in most of our commonly eaten foods (cereals, imitation orange juice, Jello), and an ever-present bowl of sugar adorned the table. I scooped from the sugar bowl to sweeten my milk, my toast, and my already sugary cereal. I was addicted to the stuff. I have little recollection of eating or wanting any other foods except an occasional burger and fries.

I remember dinner as an awful time of being nagged to eat more, and as something to endure so I could come back later and get my bowl of vanilla ice cream or a bag of chocolate-covered peanuts. You may be wondering if I have any teeth left. Surely I must remove a set of dentures to exemplify the evils of sugar to my whole foods cooking classes. I still have my teeth, though they are full of old fillings. After reading extensively on the subject of refined sugar, I found that my childhood habits had damaged more of my body than my teeth.

When I was 21, my sugar habit caught up with me. I had always had a small body frame and been "thin as a rail." After I left college, I began piling on weight, about 25 pounds in one year. In shock, I put myself on a strict, calorie-counting diet for the next seven years. I wrote down everything I ate in a little notebook and computed the calories and grams of carbohydrates. My obsessive approach never worked. My diligence lost me a few pounds, but I had to refuse all but a few nibbles of boiled chicken, cottage cheese, and green beans and fight off hunger  with liters of diet soda and pots of coffee to maintain any small drop in weight. I was starving, and my body, in its wisdom, held on to every ounce of fat it possessed. I had intense food cravings, I was constipated, my gums were bleeding, and I was a very irritable young woman.

In 1980, my mother began her slow death from cancer. In talking with others about my frustration with "official" medicine and the "treatments" it imposed, I heard about macrobiotics. I began reading and found the subject fascinating. I learned that food was more than calories and grams of whatever. I learned that food has energy, that we eat food in order to take its life force into our bodies. Macrobiotics taught me about *whole* foods via the wisdom of Eastern philosophy. With great fear I threw away my diet sodas and began eating brown rice, azuki beans, steamed vegetables, and a Creamy Ginger-Garlic Dressing I learned to make (page 193). My starved, overweight body told me to give it more and more of these simple foods. I was certain I would gain a hundred pounds. But after one month of eating whole foods, I had a new shape and more energy than I could ever remember having. I studied about these new foods as voraciously as I ate them. The spiritual side of the Eastern point of view on food and health called to me.

I began taking classes from Annemarie Colbin of The Natural Gourmet Cookery School in New York. Blending the Eastern and Western points of view on food, Annemarie taught easy-to-grasp nutritional philosophies with a commonsense approach. And she could cook! Really good-tasting, healthful, whole foods cooking. I studied with Annemarie on and off for eight years, and she continues to be my mentor on the subject of healthy eating.

My appetite for information was ravenous, and I went back to school, studying nutrition. I wanted to direct my studies toward groups of people who would be not only receptive but also excited about improving their diets — pregnant women and families with young children. I focused my research projects on the needs of this population, and after graduation, I began teaching cooking classes. Teaching nutritional information via a cooking class turned out to be practical, fun, and satisfying.

I was humming along with my brown rice, probably driving my friends and family insane with my zealousness about healthy eating, when things changed again. I became pregnant. I was incredibly nauseated during the first trimester. Brown rice and broccoli, my favorite standbys, tasted awful. I craved foods I had eaten as a child: french fries, chili dogs, taco burgers. I craved fresh fruit — a macrobiotic no-no. Something had to give. I began to wonder if macrobiotics, a diet invented and perpetuated by Japanese men, could work for a pregnant German/Scottish/Irish woman from Kansas. The rigid

and controlled regime of macrobiotics contrasted with my need as a parent to become more flexible. I had to change my cooking and my teaching to reflect the healthy eating traditions of many cultures, not just one. I reinvented foods I'd grown up eating, creating healthier versions. I began to realize no single set of rules about food (or anything) works for every individual.

I was lucky to have Grace for a baby. She devoured everything served her with delight. I breastfed Grace for about two years and then chose not to put her on cow's milk. She ate a variety of whole foods by then, and I felt confident that she would grow and develop properly, which she has done. Now she's a kindergartner, dancing out into the world of cupcakes and pizza. My rules may bend and standards loosen, but I always guide her back to the wholesome foods provided at home. I learn from Grace, and she learns from me.

In discovering nutritionally sound, easy-to-make, delicious-tasting food for my family and my classes, I collected many recipes and articles in various computer files, and this book began to emerge. My hope is that by encouraging enlightened food choices for families, through my classes and this book, I can help plant seeds for a better future. Learning to prepare and eat simple, whole foods that the Earth naturally provides can transform lives. When you feed your family whole foods, you make your family more whole.

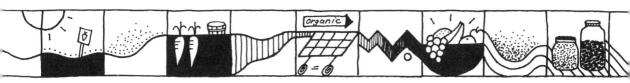

Part I

WHOLE FOODS GUIDE

This guide to whole foods reflects my rock-solid trust in Nature. Thinking about whole foods and their relationship to our bodies reminds me of the life force that inhabits all growing things. This vital force, or "chi," shapes who I am, who you are, what a carrot is like.

If you took all the parts of a carrot — the carbohydrates, amino acids, fiber, water, beta-carotene, vitamin C, magnesium, potassium, etc. — and put them in a jar and shook them up, would you have a carrot? No. Something would be missing. The life energy of the food — the vital force that makes each carrot grow, giving it a unique size, shape, and color — would not be there. I don't know exactly where that life energy comes from. The sun, the water, and the soil seem to play a part. But I am convinced that foods are more than the sum of their parts.

FEEDING THE WHOLE FAMILY

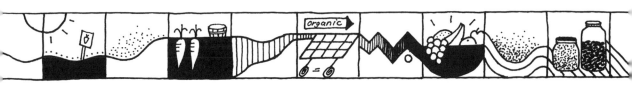

Balancing the Family Plate

I have recently read several books that were set in the late 1800s in this country. Only 100 years ago, our great-grandparents created a dinner plate very different from what is typical today. Food on the table was, for the most part, grown, raised, caught, or shot. The only fresh fruits and vegetables available were what grew in season in one's climate. Often, folks ate the same foods every day. Corn mush and rabbit stew were regular hits on the prairie. Day after day, Laura and Mary, in "Little House on the Prairie," ate corn mush. Reading this book to my child, I felt so relieved when summer came and Laura and Mary got to go blackberry picking!

Each summer I visit Wichita to see my family. My sister's house is near a big suburban supermarket. This place has everything! People push giant grocery carts piled high with packages of every color, shape, and size. Besides a vast array of food, there's a post office, a paperback book section, video rentals, a banking facility, a dry cleaner, a prescription drug counter, and free colon cancer screening tests — all in the same store! The number of choices and amount of stimuli are overwhelming. The question, "What should we eat for dinner?" has 10,000 answers at our fingertips. And there are several thousand more choices of what to do after dinner.

If I don't have my priorities in place, a trip to the grocery store can be like getting lost in the woods. Not only do I function better with a list in hand, but I need a clear concept of what is healthy and wholesome and what isn't. I want our hard-earned family dollars to buy food that will vitalize our bodies, minds, and spirits.

In this book, I have carved out my interpretation of the more-than-ample information available about nutrition. I have used research and data from today, as well as the simple common sense of yesterday. The information here isn't meant to be the final word for you or for me. I encourage you to start your own journey with food and health. Once you understand the power you hold as you stroll down a grocery store aisle, your dinner plate may never look the same.

What Is a Whole Food?

For more than ten years, I have taught whole foods cooking classes. Early in the class, I always ask my students, "What is a whole food?" My favorite response was from a young woman who said, "A food that hasn't been cut."

If you want to know whether a food is whole or not, ask yourself these questions:

- **Can I imagine it growing?** It is easy to picture a wheatfield or an apple on a tree. Tough to picture a field of marshmallows.

- **How many ingredients does it have?** A whole food has only one ingredient — itself.

- **What has been done to the food since it was harvested?** The less, the better. Many foods we eat no longer resemble anything found in nature. Stripped, refined, bleached, injected, hydrogenated, chemically treated, irradiated, and gassed, modern foods have literally had the life taken out of them. Read the lists of ingredients on labels; if you can't pronounce it, don't eat it.

- **Is this product "part" of a food or the "whole" entity?** Juice is only a part of a fruit. Oil is only part of the olive. When you eat partial foods, your body in its natural wisdom craves the parts it didn't get.

Good-bye Basic 4

Much of our information about healthy eating habits comes from television commercials and from our government. Obviously the companies that make and market food products have a vested interest in how the facts are portrayed. The United States Department of Agriculture (USDA), which publishes our national nutrition guidelines, has sometimes had problems with vested interests as well. The USDA was created in 1862 to promote agricultural products (primarily meat and dairy) and to foster public health. As more information is discovered about the relationship between food and health, these two goals have proven to be conflicting at times.

Most of us raised in the second half of the 20th century learned to judge the healthfulness of a dinner plate by seeing if it contained something from each of the "four food groups." The USDA devised the Four Basic Food Groups in 1956. They consist of (1) milk and milk products; (2) meat, poultry, fish, and eggs; (3) fruits and vegetables; and (4) bread, cereal, and flour.

The "Basic 4" was drilled into our heads at home and at school. A typical evening meal centered around a meat dish, and few children's plates were without a glass of milk on the side. School cafeterias followed the Basic 4 as well, and the same guide was taught in the classroom. The dairy industry has provided schools with free educational material on nutrition for years because the Basic 4 helped promote sales of dairy products. These notions of how to create a balanced meal are so deeply ingrained that, without conscious effort to change, we naturally resort to what we learned as children.

Today, we're on the verge of creating a new vision of the ideal dinner plate. Current research shows the Basic 4 to be unhealthfully outdated. The government, as well as other concerned researchers, has been busy drawing up healthier guidelines to reflect the emerging consensus that for a vital future, our bodies require a whole foods, carbohydrate-based diet, in which grains, beans, vegetables, and fruits are emphasized and animal products and other high-fat foods are de-emphasized. These new dietary recommendations better support our current lifestyle, in which most of us earn a living by using our brains while sitting down, rather than by performing hard physical labor. And few of us walk to get places; we drive.

In 1991, a nongovernmental group decided to update the Basic 4. The Physicians Committee for Responsible Medicine (PCRM), a nonprofit organization made up of physicians and consumers, introduced the New Four Food Groups. The new groups are: whole grains, legumes, fruits, and vegetables. These guidelines encourage us to eat several servings a day from each group, choosing a wide variety of foods. Other foods, including nuts, sweets, oils, dairy, and meats, are considered "optional, not essential." PCRM's New Four Food Groups is a bold, sometimes controversial, food guide backed up by impressive, documented data. [1]

The USDA, jointly with the U.S. Department of Health and Human Services, has also developed a teaching tool that promotes updated nutritional research. In 1993, the Eating Right Pyramid was unveiled, replacing the Basic 4, the mainstream guide for nearly 40 years. The pyramid promotes grains, cereals, fruits, and vegetables as the foundation of our diet. The pyramid encourages a moderate intake of protein foods, such as fish, poultry, meat (preferably low-fat), dried beans, eggs, and nuts, and moderate amounts of dairy products, preferably low-fat or nonfat. Fats, oils, and sweets are to be used sparingly. The standard serving sizes are fairly small, and the number of recommended servings is based on activity level and age. The pyramid urges us to choose a variety of foods and to eat moderate amounts.

1   For more information on the New Four Food Groups, contact PCRM, P.O. Box 6322, Washington, DC 20015.

As helpful as the recent research and information are, both guidelines leave unanswered questions for the family cook. The PCRM's New Four Food Groups is a powerful and needed point of view; however, given the wide array of requirements in a growing family, I would prefer a little more information about the optional, not essential, foods. Many of us who continue to eat fish, chicken, dairy products, nuts, and seeds would appreciate guidance on how to include these foods in a healthful way. The USDA's Eating Right Pyramid is specific about serving sizes, number of servings, and calorie requirements, yet it isn't specific enough about the quality of food. For example, it doesn't mention the difference between refined, unrefined, and enriched grains, distinctions worth discussing. A slice of white bread does not contain the nutrients of a serving of brown rice! The pyramid gives no alternatives to dairy products for meeting calcium requirements, yet many exist. And neither chart lends itself well to the daily task of family meal planning. Consequently, I invented my own guide, "The Well-Balanced Plate."

The Well-Balanced Plate

"The Well-Balanced Plate" guide uses the sound nutritional concepts of the New Four Food Groups and the Eating Right Pyramid, emphasizing the fundamental foods — whole grains, vegetables, beans, and fruit. But "The Well-Balanced Plate" goes further, giving specific information about quality and stressing fresh, whole, organic foods. The complementary foods — fish, dairy products, sea vegetables, nuts, and seeds — are given a workable role as side dishes or toppings.

I've also put the information together in a way that active families can easily use. Thinking in terms of main dishes, side dishes, and toppings is a practical approach to meal planning. Grams, serving sizes, and other numbers aren't a major part of "The Well-Balanced Plate." Given simple, whole, nonaddictive foods, our bodies are amazingly accurate at letting us know how much and what kinds of food we need. I've featured a sun and the word "energy" to remind us of the energy link among living things. Our food choices hold more importance when we are conscious that eating is our main conduit for taking in and putting out energy. I've also included exercising and spending time outdoors, activities that improve our relationship with food, with wholesome eating.

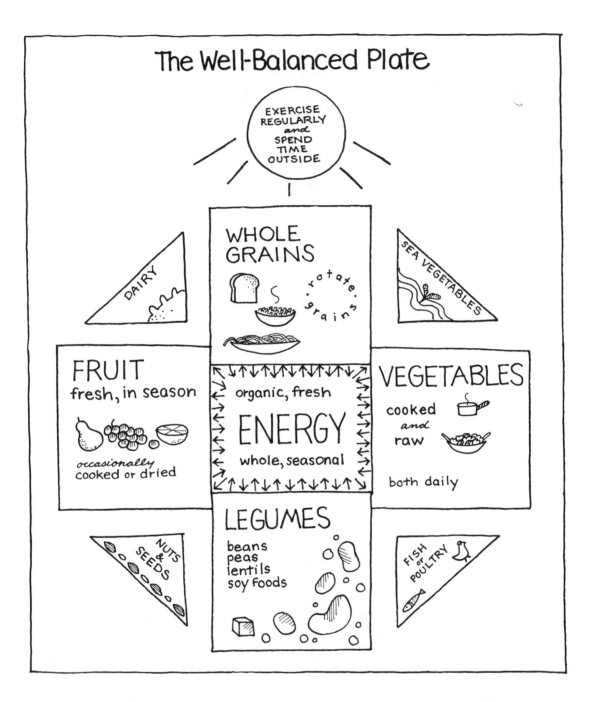

The Well-Balanced Plate

EXERCISE REGULARLY and SPEND TIME OUTSIDE

WHOLE GRAINS

rotate grains

DAIRY

SEA VEGETABLES

FRUIT
fresh, in season

occasionally
cooked or dried

organic, fresh

ENERGY

whole, seasonal

VEGETABLES

cooked *and* raw

both daily

NUTS & SEEDS

LEGUMES

beans
peas
lentils
soy foods

FISH *or* POULTRY

"THE WELL-BALANCED PLATE" focuses on whole foods. Some 75 to 80 percent of the recommended foods come from the *Fundamental Foods* (squares): whole grains, vegetables, legumes, and fruit. Vegetables and fruit are light and active, whereas whole grains and beans are dense and sustaining. You need both. These foods should form the main dishes of every meal you have.

The *Complementary Foods* (triangles) show foods that you can use as condiments, toppings, or small side dishes.

There is an *energy link* among all living things, creating a healthy interdependence. The sun gives energy to the plants you eat; the plants give your body energy; and you give energy to yourself, your family, and your world. You can improve the quality of your energy by eating organic, fresh, whole, seasonal foods. The sun symbol also reminds you to move and to go outside — that's as important as anything you eat.

The Fundamental Foods

Whole Grains

The whole grains include the familiar whole wheat, brown rice, barley, oats, corn, buckwheat, and rye as well as the less familiar millet, quinoa, spelt, amaranth, and teff. For daily consumption, whole grains are superior to refined grains because the whole product contains protein, fiber, B vitamins, calcium, iron, vitamin E, and *life* (the germ of the grain is the live part). Eating grains in their whole, natural form is satisfying and beneficial. Grains can also be ground into flours or cereals, or made into pasta, noodles, and spaghetti. Brown rice has even been made into a milklike beverage and a frozen dessert.

As you discover the benefits of whole grains, keep in mind the familiar advice: Rotate grains in the diet. When you eat the same grain daily, you are more likely to develop an allergy to it. Rotation — choosing a new whole grain every day — helps prevent this. If you have brown rice on Monday, try quinoa on Tuesday. Each grain has something unique to offer your body.

Vegetables

Eat both cooked vegetables and raw vegetables every day. Cooking vegetables lessens some of their nutritional value yet makes the food more digestible and easier to assimilate. Raw vegetables are rich in nutrients and some enzymes that can't be found in cooked vegetables; however, some vegetables, such as broccoli and cauliflower, are harder to digest eaten raw. You need both.

Eat vegetables of all colors. Don't form prejudices. Try dark green, light green, white, purple, red, yellow, orange, gold, black, brown; eat vegetables you've never had before. Lean toward nutrient-dense vegetables: dark green (collards, kale, watercress, spinach, chard) and orange (winter squash, sweet potato, carrot). These are supernutritious vegetables that contain vitamins and minerals you can't get too much of. Give dark green and orange a daily appearance on your plate. Buy organic produce whenever possible.

Legumes

For centuries, many cultures have combined legumes (beans, peas, lentils, and soy products) with whole grains to create delicious daily fare. Beans are rich in protein and complex carbohydrates, high in fiber, and low in calories, and they contain appreciable amounts of calcium, iron, and other nutrients. Beans accept herbs and spices graciously to create hearty, mouth-watering dishes. And beans are inexpensive and can easily be found wherever you shop — what more could you ask from a food?

You can choose from traditional beans such as navy, kidney, lima, pinto, garbanzo, and black beans; the familiar peas and lentils; or offbeat varieties of legumes such as azuki beans, Christmas limas, Swedish brown beans, and calypso beans. You'll find tips for reducing the raffinose sugars in beans, which can cause gas, on page 88. Soybeans are used to make a variety of versatile food products including tofu, tempeh, and soy sauce. The various soy products are discussed in greater detail in the "Glossary of Ingredients."

Fruit

In-season fruit is least expensive and most delicious. It's sometimes hard to decipher what is in season since we import fruit from many parts of the world. Local and/or organic produce reflects what is in season. Buying produce seasonally helps remind you of the rhythm of the passing seasons and keeps you in tune with nature: strawberries every June, plums in September. Eat fruit in its whole, fresh state. Include some cooked and dried fruits in your diet, especially in winter.

Drinking juice is not the same as eating a piece of whole fruit. Juice lacks fiber, which slows the rate of sugar absorption, and juice is not a whole food. Children can get the equivalent of a sugar "high" from straight fruit juice. They may crave juice for quick energy and fill up on it instead of eating more nutritious foods. Avoid serving juice with meals. I recommend diluting juice for children, one-half juice, one-half filtered water.

Include vitamin C-rich fruits regularly, such as oranges, strawberries, grapefruits, melons, or kiwi. Buy organic fruit whenever possible, especially for babies, children, and pregnant women.

The Complementary Foods

Sea Vegetables

These jewels from the ocean are unknown to most American palates. The sea vegetables described in this book include arame, dulse, dulse flakes, hiziki, kombu, nori, and wakame. This is just a sampling of the variety of sea vegetables to be found. Each kind is unique, and offers the cook an array of tastes and textures.

Sea vegetables have a rich and diverse nutritional profile. Ounce for ounce, they're higher in vitamins and minerals than any other class of food because they're grown in seawater where minerals are constantly being renewed. They are rich sources of vitamins A, B, C, and E, as well as calcium and iron. Sea vegetables provide calcium without the fat and cholesterol of dairy products. Many trace elements and some key minerals such as zinc and iodine are difficult to obtain in vegetables today because modern farming methods have badly depleted our soil. Including sea vegetables in your diet is the best way I know to provide ample vitamins and minerals and avoid costly supplements.

The taste may seem strong or unfamiliar at first, so use a good recipe when first incorporating sea vegetables in your diet. Not even my relatives from Kansas shy away from Mim's Hiziki Pâté (page 184). Many sea vegetables (such as nori) can be toasted and crushed or ground into a powder that can be put in a salt shaker and used as a condiment.

You may wonder about the pollution factor in these vegetables. Harvesters of sea vegetables conscientiously seek out chaste waters to grow and forage their crops. As with other ocean vegetation, sea vegetables don't flourish in polluted areas.

Fish or Poultry

You may want to eat fish or poultry occasionally as a side dish with grains and vegetables. Fish and poultry are included in this book for their vitamin B12 value and because you may not want or need to be a vegetarian. Flesh foods are denser and more filling than fruits and vegetables, giving your body a heavier feeling and slower energy. Fish can provide a nice balance to the lighter, quicker energy that results from eating fruits and vegetables. Fish or poultry can be a useful balancing food for children who have consumed too many fruits, juices, and sweets.

Nuts and Seeds

Nuts and seeds are delicious, whole foods that contain many beneficial nutrients. Almonds are rich in calcium; pumpkin seeds are high in iron. You needn't exclude nuts and seeds just because they are high in fat. The added calories can be useful for pregnant or nursing moms and active children. To keep nuts and seeds in proper perspective, think of them as condiments, using only a Tablespoon or so at a time.

Dairy

The question of whether to include or exclude dairy products can be confusing, especially when it comes to children. I have been schooled in the ill effects of dairy as well as the importance of including it. For me, the evidence leans toward keeping dairy intake moderate to minimal.

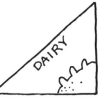

Dairy has been traditionally used as a condiment or garnish. Thinking of it as such will keep this high-fat, high-protein food in proper perspective in your diet. I have used dairy products in small amounts in some recipes in this book for added calcium and for the familiar taste. You'll find a scattering of yogurt, butter, goat cheese, feta, parmesan, and other cow's cheeses in a few recipes. A few farms produce organic dairy products (with no hormones or antibiotics), and I encourage you to seek out those products and purchase them regularly. (For further information about dairy products, see pages 24-27.)

The Energy Link

The sun links all life on our planet. Without the energy from the sun, human life could not be sustained. We depend on the sun for our food, and we depend on our food for life. By choosing food that is organic, fresh, whole, and seasonal, we provide a higher quality of energy for our bodies and stay more in tune with the planet we live on.

I positioned the sun at the top of "The Well-Balanced Plate" to remind you of one of the uses of your energy. Regular exercise can improve your body, mind, and mood. Calcium absorption is vastly improved by regular walking, running, or other weight-bearing exercise. The human body was designed to move, so let it loose.

Spending time outside improves energy, too. Go outside at least 15 minutes a day unless you are ill. Throw on a sweater, slicker, or snowsuit, and soak up some vitamin D and breathe some fresh air. Problems that seem big in small rooms diminish outdoors.

Frequently Asked Questions

The recipes I have used in my many years of teaching and in this book center around whole grains, fruits, vegetables, and legumes. I support a whole foods diet based on plant foods for many reasons. Current research links the overconsumption of animal fats to many degenerative diseases. Also, as a result of the use of hormones, antibiotics, pesticides, and unacceptable or nonexistent inspection practices, the poor quality of our meat and dairy supply makes it desirable to eat items lower on the food chain. Livestock absorb much of this country's crop harvest along with vast quantities of energy and water. Reducing our consumption of factory-produced meat, poultry, and dairy is one of the simplest ways we have of healing our planet's ecological wounds.

You may be aware of these factors but wonder if a whole foods diet provides all the essential nutrients.[2] Here are some of the questions about nutrition most often asked in my classes.

Protein

Q: *Will my family get enough protein from a plant-based diet?*

A: The U.S. Food and Nutrition Board recommends a daily average of 47 grams of protein for adult females; 56 grams for males; 16 grams for children ages 1-3; 26 grams for ages 4-10. You may be unaware of the protein available from plant foods, thinking that only meat, dairy, eggs, fish, beans, or peanut butter contain protein. The following chart shows protein values for various grains, beans, vegetables, and fruit.

Food	**Amount of Protein** [3]
1 cup cooked oatmeal	6.0 grams
1/2 cantaloupe	2.5 grams
1 cup cooked quinoa	10.5 grams
1 cup broccoli	5.0 grams
2 Tablespoons sunflower seeds	4.3 grams
1 cup baked winter squash	3.7 grams
1 cup cooked brown rice	4.9 grams
1/2 cup kidney beans	7.5 grams
1 cup cooked collards	6.8 grams
Total grams	**51.2 grams**

---

2   The scientific study of nutrition is relatively new and constantly changing. To keep abreast of the latest nutritional research, I recommend subscribing to the *Nutrition Action Healthletter* published by the Center for Science in the Public Interest (CSPI, 1875 Connecticut Ave. N.W., Suite 300, Washington, DC 20009-5728). The newsletter is short, unbiased, and readable.

3   Protein amounts from Laurel Robertson, Carol Flinders, and Brian Ruppenthal, *The New Laurel's Kitchen* (Berkeley, CA: Ten Speed Press, 1986)

Q: *Is it possible to eat too much protein?*

A: Most Americans eat more than 80 grams of protein daily. Yet more is not necessarily better. The excess fat usually accompanying a high-protein diet is thought to be a factor in heart disease, weight problems, and certain types of cancer. Studies show that replacing animal protein (even low-fat animal protein) with plant protein can reduce cholesterol.[4] Some researchers believe that excess animal protein in the diet can result in calcium depletion, a factor in the growing osteoporosis crisis.

When you examine foods from an energy standpoint, you see that animal proteins are dense and filling. When you eat these foods in excess, your body craves lighter, more expansive foods to balance the protein, such as sugar, coffee, and alcohol. Centering the diet around grains and vegetables, and diminishing use of animal products, can help you feel more balanced and reduce cravings.

Q: *Do I have to combine foods in special ways to get "complete" proteins?*

A: Current research buries this old notion. Only 20 percent of your protein intake needs to contain a complete protein, that is, a complete set of amino acids. You carry an amino acid pool of some 80 to 90 grams of complete protein in your digestive tract that can be called upon to fill in any gaps. Nevertheless, I often use grains and beans together in recipes, thereby providing ample amounts of complete protein in delicious combinations. As long as you obtain an adequate amount of your calories from whole foods, a protein deficiency is highly unlikely.

Calcium

Q: *If I don't eat several daily servings of dairy products, how can I get enough calcium?*

A: Calcium can be obtained from a wide variety of whole foods. Most cultures do not depend on dairy products to meet calcium needs, yet they appear to suffer no adverse effects on their bone health. Americans practice many lifestyle habits that inhibit the absorption of calcium. The whole picture must be assessed when you're analyzing osteoporosis or any other disease.

---

4   David Schardt, "The Problem with Protein," *Nutrition Action Healthletter.* Vol. XX (5) (June 1993)

Q: *What are some nondairy sources of calcium?*

A: I am often asked this question as more and more parents report that their children are allergic or sensitive to dairy products. Foods high in calcium that you will see used in the recipes in this book include dark greens, such as kale, collards, mustard greens, and watercress; sea vegetables; almonds; sesame seeds; beans; whole grains; and carob. Dairy products are used in small amounts as optional ingredients. Millions of Asian children drink little or no milk and have strong teeth and bones. Remember, there are some very large-boned animals that eat nothing but plants — cows, elephants, and brontosauruses!

Q: *Isn't milk the "perfect" food for growing children?*

A: Don't confuse promotional slogans with nutritional concepts. Cow's milk is the perfect food — for calves. I discourage parents from giving children over 2 years of age more than one glass of milk a day for two reasons. Since milk is a food, not a beverage, it is filling, and may crowd out more beneficial foods. A child using cow's milk as the main source of calories may become deficient in nutrients not found in milk, such as iron.

Perhaps a more compelling reason to decrease milk consumption and incorporate other calcium-rich foods is the questionable quality of today's milk. Pollution of livestock is a problem, not only because pesticides and industrial wastes are found in the food cattle consume, but also because antibiotics and hormones are regularly administered to mass-produce animal products. Toxins accumulate in the fat of the animal and are passed to us in fatty dairy substances such as milk, cheese, and meat. Ingesting a constant, low-level dose of antibiotics in food may compromise the effectiveness of an antibiotic given your child when it is truly needed. The continual low level of hormones passed on to your children (in meat as well as dairy products) is suspected of causing early onset of menses and early development of breasts in girls, creating a physical maturity not matched by emotional growth.[5] Today's milk is vastly different from yesteryear's.

5   John Robbins, *A Diet for a New America* (Walpole, NH: Stillpoint Publishing, 1987) and Joseph Chilton Pearce, *Magical Child Matures* (New York: E.P. Dutton, 1985). Pearce also cites Orville Schell, *Modern Meat* (New York: Random House, 1984).

Q: *How about using nonfat dairy products as my source of calcium?*

A: This is the popular solution for keeping calcium intake high and fat intake low. However, these products are no longer whole, natural foods. Their nutritional composition has been altered, leaving a disproportionately high protein content. I prefer using a wide variety of whole foods to meet calcium requirements and including whole dairy products in the diet in small amounts.

    Parents should be aware that low-fat or nonfat milk is inappropriate for children under 2 years of age. These products are too high in protein and minerals, which can stress young kidneys. The unweaned child needs milk that is high in fat for proper brain development. Breast milk contains ample fat and naturally supports the infant's growth rate. If you have chosen to wean your child from formula or breast milk before age 2, you may want to use whole goat's or cow's milk to supplement your child's diet.

Q: *What lifestyle habits inhibit calcium absorption or deplete calcium stores?*

A: Smoking cigarettes, drinking alcohol, eating refined sugar, failing to exercise, taking a great deal of antacids, and ingesting large amounts of high-phosphate foods, such as luncheon meats and soft drinks, are choices that may lead to poor calcium maintenance. High animal-protein intake may also be a factor. Stress depletes vitamin and mineral stores. It is interesting to note that the United States has one of the world's highest rates of calcium intake, yet also has one of the highest rates of osteoporosis.

Vitamin D

Q: *If my children don't drink vitamin D-fortified milk, will they become deficient in that vitamin?*

A: Not necessarily. The human body produces vitamin D with exposure to sunlight. Vitamin D is also available through foods, although the amounts present are somewhat unreliable. Food sources of vitamin D include fish (especially fattier fish such as salmon, tuna, sardines, and herring), fish oil supplements, egg yolks, and of course vitamin D-fortified foods.

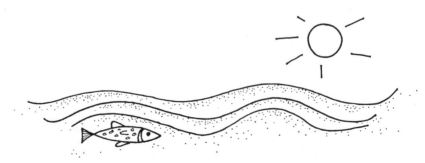

Synthetic vitamin D has been added to foods with the best intention, to prevent rickets in children. However, when calcium is artificially encouraged by added vitamin D, the calcium sometimes deposits in the wrong places, such as the soft tissues.[6] More natural sources of the vitamin are preferable.

Most of us manage to maintain adequate vitamin D in the body by spending at least 15 minutes outside every day. If you live in a northern climate or have dark skin, this may not be enough. If you're concerned about this nutrient, you may want to include fish, fish oil supplements, small amounts of dairy items, or eggs in your diet.

Iron

Q: *Can I get sufficient iron from a diet that contains little or no meat?*

A: Yes. Many plant foods are rich in iron. Beans, pumpkin seeds, almonds, dried fruits, greens, millet, quinoa, soybeans, and molasses are just a few. Dulse, a sea vegetable, has 11 milligrams of iron per quarter cup. Nonheme iron (from nonflesh sources) is absorbed more efficiently with the help of vitamin C. Foods rich in vitamin C include citrus fruits, berries, dark greens, broccoli, winter squash, sweet potatoes, tomatoes, potatoes, and peppers. Vitamin B6 and folic acid also aid iron absorption. These nutrients are abundant in unrefined foods. Cooking in cast-iron cookware also increases the iron content of food.

Q: *Don't I need to supplement my baby's diet with iron after six months of age?*

A: My first response is, "How come Nature screwed up? Why would babies be created with an automatic deficiency at six months of age? One that only a humanmade supplement could aid?" I never blindly accepted the idea that I needed to supplement my baby's diet with iron. Ferrous sulphate, the most common iron supplement, is poorly absorbed and can cause indigestion and constipation. I looked into the matter and this is what I found:

Your baby was born with a good store of iron that came from the mother during pregnancy. This is one reason why hematocrit levels are monitored in pregnant women. Part of a baby's iron supply comes through the umbilical cord shortly after birth, so it is important that the cord not be clamped or cut for at least five to ten minutes after birth. Premature cutting of the cord is unnecessary and diminishes a baby's iron stores.

---

6   Annemarie Colbin, *Food and Healing* (New York: Ballantine Books, 1986), 152-157. Colbin cites the studies of D.C. Anderson and others in the *British Medical Journal* (1968), Dr. Helen B. Taussig in the *Annals of Internal Medicine* (1966), and W.H. Taylor in *Clinical Science* (1972) to back her statement.

Breast milk contains a small amount of absorbable iron to meet your baby's needs. Babies can absorb up to 50 percent of the iron in breast milk, but only 4 percent of that in fortified formula. Vitamin C in breast milk increases the absorption of iron. Lactoferrin and transferrin, two specialized proteins in mother's milk, regulate the iron supply to your baby. As long as the mother was not anemic during pregnancy, your breastfed baby should have adequate iron for the first year of life.

Around six months, when solid foods are introduced, your baby begins to get iron from sources other than breast milk, formula, or stores accumulated in utero. With the transition into a simple, whole foods diet, your baby needs no supplements. Why start your baby on a refined grain cereal that has had most of its vitamins, minerals, protein, and fiber removed and some iron added back in? Serve your baby whole-grain cereals and freshly prepared fruits and vegetables, giving naturally occurring iron in the proportions their body needs. For extra iron, add sea vegetables to your baby's diet and use cast-iron cookware.

Fat

Q: *How should I monitor my family's fat intake?*

A: The best approach is to consider the whole diet, rather than focusing only on fat. Every few years the media "discover" one food or nutrient that is supposedly the culprit of all health evils. Salt got a bad rap for many years, then cholesterol. Fat is the bad guy of the 1990s. The response from food manufacturers has been to flood the market with thousands of new products that contain none of the bad guy, such as "no-salt this" and "fat-free that." I appreciate the manufacturers' responsiveness to the health-conscious consumer. However, health problems can rarely be linked to a single cause. Many diet and lifestyle habits enter into the whole health picture.

Focusing your diet around whole grains, beans, vegetables, and fruit creates meals naturally low in fat. Small amounts of high-quality fat are a necessary component of a healthy diet. By using organic nuts, seeds, poultry, dairy products, and fresh fish occasionally and in small amounts, you can keep fat at a high-quality minimum.

Approaching recipes and menu planning with common sense makes a huge difference. For instance, use a few teaspoons of oil to sauté vegetables instead of the half-cup called for in some recipes. If you choose a high-fat food, such as a nut sauce, as part of your meal, complete the menu with lower-fat dishes, such as whole grains and steamed vegetables. Serve raw or cooked fruit for desserts instead of baked goods. By applying these guidelines, you won't need expensive, artificially fat-reduced products, and you won't have to walk down the grocery aisle with a calculator.

Refined Sugar

Q: *Is it really unhealthy to eat refined sugar?*

A: There are varied opinions on the subject. In my own research I have found that eating large amounts of refined sugar may:

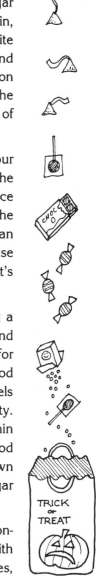

- **Deplete the body's vitamins and minerals.** Refined white sugar is not a *whole* food. It contains no vitamins, minerals, protein, fat, or fiber as do foods found in nature. Ingesting refined white sugar may disrupt your body's delicate balance of glucose and insulin. To recover from the imbalance, your body must call on its stores of vitamins, minerals, and other nutrients. Since the sugar provides no nutrients, your body goes into a state of depletion.

- **Cause cravings.** White sugar is refined to such a degree that your body doesn't even need to digest it. It can go directly into the bloodstream, similar to the action of a drug. You then produce insulin to compensate for the immediate rise in blood sugar. The insulin causes the sugar level in your blood to drop, leaving an excess of insulin circulating. You then crave more sugar to use up the insulin. This perpetuates a cycle. In lay terms, it's addictive.

- **Impair immune function.** Evidence indicates that ingesting a large quantity of refined white sugar (as well as honey and orange juice) impairs the function of your immune system for up to five hours. The sugar reduces the ability of white blood cells to destroy bacteria. In addition, the high glucose levels resulting from sugar intake can depress lymphocyte activity. This finding is based on evidence that blood glucose and vitamin C compete for membrane transport sites into the white blood cells; both require insulin.[7] No wonder children often come down with a sore throat or cold after a birthday party or holiday sugar fest.

- **Be linked with degenerative diseases.** The unprecedented consumption of refined sugar in this country has been linked with the rise in coronary heart disease, arteriosclerosis, diabetes, hypoglycemia, and obesity.

---

7   Michael Murray, N.D., and Joseph Pizzorno, N.D., *Encyclopedia of Natural Medicine* (Rocklin, CA: Prima Publishing, 1990) 63, 229, 459. Murray and Pizzorno cite studies published in the *American Journal of Clinical Nutrition* and other medical references.

- **Affect behavior.** Behavior problems, hyperactivity, learning difficulties, nervousness, depression, apprehension, and criminal behavior have been associated with eating refined sugar.[8] Recent studies, including one published in the *New England Journal of Medicine,*[9] claim that eating refined sugar has no adverse effect on children's behavior. This is not what I experience in my day-to-day life with children. I have yet to see a child fall in a heap, crying and begging for more black beans. I can see my child deteriorate physiologically and psychologically after a big dose of refined sugar. I have chosen not to keep sugar in my home. I buy and make snacks that are sweet-tasting without it. When Grace is offered sugar on holidays and birthdays, I don't make a big deal of it, but I encourage her to check in with how she feels after eating certain foods, not just sugar.

Q: *Why do I crave sweets?*

A: Besides the addictive nature of refined sugar, looking at the whole diet clarifies other reasons why people crave sweets.

There is a nutritional relationship between meat and sugar. Eating meat, which is all protein, signals a need in your body for carbohydrates. Meat is filling. Instead of desiring a fiber-rich, nutrient-dense whole food to satisfy the carbohydrate need, meat eaters crave the light, empty carbohydrates that can be found in white flour and sugar. Refined sugar gives you an immediate, quick-energy "high," while meat produces a slower, heavier feeling. It is difficult to eliminate one of these two foods from your diet without eliminating the other. If you're thinking of cutting back on sugar in your family's diet, it may also help to cut back your family's intake of animal protein.

According to some Eastern philosophies, as well as my experience, bingeing on salty foods is followed by a craving for sweets. Most junk-food favorites in our culture are based on this reciprocal craving. Sugary soft drinks are "required" with french fries, pizza, popcorn, and chips. Becoming aware of this seesaw effect is a starting place for managing the craving for salt or sugar.

Many students in my classes report that when they dutifully eat sparse, nonfat meals, they crave sweets later. In this case, the body, in its natural wisdom, is probably craving the fat and calories that usually accompany sugar in desserts. A balanced diet that includes all naturally occurring nutrients, including some fat, will be more satisfying and less likely to cause cravings.

---

8   Of the many books on the connection between sugar and behavior, I found these especially helpful: E.M. Abrahamson, M.D., and A.W. Pezet, *Body, Mind and Sugar* (New York: Pyramid Publications, 1951); John Yudkin, M.D., *Sweet & Dangerous* (New York: Bantam Books, 1972); William Dufty, *Sugar Blues* (New York: Warner Books, 1975). Refined sugar appears to be a mood-altering substance for many people.

9   M.L. Wolraich, et al., "Effects of Diets High in Sucrose or Aspartame on the Behavior and Cognitive Performance of Children," *New England Journal of Medicine,* Vol. 336, no. 5 (Feb. 3, 1994)

Q: *How would you suggest cutting back or eliminating refined white sugar in my family's diet?*

A: Begin by *adding* foods to the diet rather than deleting. Concentrate on eating more whole grains, fresh fruits, vegetables, and other nutritious foods for meals and snacks. Three whole foods meals daily leave little room for bingeing on sweets. Set small, realistic goals. Eating two cookies instead of a boxful is a good start.

Consider not only quality, but quantity. Simply replacing sugary items with goodies made from alternative sweeteners is not the whole answer. It's important to cut back on the amount of sweetened foods you take in to make room for more beneficial foods.

Read labels. Packaging can be confusing. A juice box label may read "10 percent real fruit juice," but it doesn't tell you that the other 90 percent is sugar and water. Sugar is used in products such as ketchup, mayonnaise, peanut butter, bread, and break-  fast cereal. You cannot avoid sugar without reading labels. Some products claim to be "sugar-free" or "low-sugar," but upon closer inspection you may discover they contain fructose or other chemical sweeteners — products whose long-term effects have not been determined. Many chemical sweeteners are forbidden for pregnant women for this reason. Manufacturers also deceive you by using pseudonyms for refined sugar such as "dextrose," "sucrose," "cane sugar," or "turbinado" on the label. We must be discerning shoppers to avoid pouring sugar into ourselves and our children.

Dietary Supplements

Q: *Should I give my family vitamin and mineral supplements?*

A: Vitamin and mineral pills can never replace good eating habits. Strive to obtain essential nutrients from fresh, simply prepared whole foods. Resort to supple- ments only when stress or imbalances demand them, and choose a qualified health-care practitioner to help you determine which supplements are suitable.

Vegetarian Diets

Q: *Do you have to be a strict vegetarian to be healthy?*

A: No. Vegetarian diets centered around refined grains, sugar, coffee, and dairy products are woefully out of balance. A strict vegetarian diet that includes sugar can magnify the detrimental effects of refined sugar. Read Annemarie Colbin's book *Food and Healing* for an excellent description of various "diets" and their relative healthfulness.

Not everyone feels comfortable on either a vegan (excluding all animal products) or vegetarian (some dairy and eggs allowed) diet. Some people function well and feel nourished on a vegetarian diet, while others, because of body type or a phase in development, prefer to include more animal protein. If you choose to eat animal products, seek out high-quality sources. Practices used to produce range-fed beef have proven to be more ecologically sound. Free-range, drug-free meat and poultry will become more available as consumers demand them.

Q: *What do you eat in your home?*

A: For breakfast, we usually eat a grain and a fruit; for dinner a grain, a bean or fish dish, and two vegetables, one raw and one cooked. Lunches evolve from dinner leftovers, and snacks are made from fruits, vegetables, and whole-grain products. This simple, economical approach to eating keeps all of us healthy and energetic. We also eat unhealthful things occasionally.

● ● ●

Finding the right balance of foods to feed yourself and your family is not a destination but rather an enlightening and unending process. Decide what dietary changes are most important to you, then give yourself plenty of time and space to incorporate them. Too many rules about dietary restrictions can be overwhelming and create tension. One of the biggest lessons we learn as parents is to be *flexible.* The dancer with the most flexibility maintains grace and balance with ease.

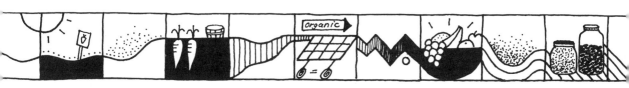

Making Changes

Beginning a new way of eating can be like entering a foreign country. Everything around us looks strange; we long for something familiar. We forget that it takes time and patience to make friends with strangers.

My first job in New York City was waiting tables. My friend Tom got me a job where he worked, at the Hungarian Rendezvous. Dressed in my black skirt and white blouse, I showed up the first day with a smile. My smile quickly faded and my demeanor turned to panic. Not only had I never waited tables before, but the menu was in Hungarian, the cook spoke only Hungarian, the dishwasher spoke only Spanish, and the waiters and waitresses had to mix the drinks as well as serve six-course meals. I almost cried when someone ordered a Rob Roy (who was that?).

I trudged home that first night in my little red, grease-stained apron and sobbed. I would never learn Hungarian. I simply wasn't strong enough to carry six heavy plates of duck dinners. I wanted to go back to Kansas.

But, with no other job prospects in sight, I slogged back the next night. And the next. The owners and staff were forgiving, and eventually I learned a great deal about Hungarian food, mixing drinks, and surviving in New York City.

When faced with a big transition, I often plant my feet in the dirt and emphatically list, to anyone who will listen, all the excuses why I cannot, should not, and will not change. I have learned that the more insistent I am about not changing, the bigger the rewards on the other side of the change.

To change something as basic as how we think about food, we need to listen to our resistance, grieve the perceived losses, and then take one step at a time into change.

Going Slowly

The first step in changing the way you eat is to become conscious of what goes in your mouth. Think about what you are buying at the store. Does this product deserve your hard-earned money? What's in it? Are you buying it out of habit or because the label looks attractive? Think about your food as you prepare it, as you eat it. Where did this food originate? Will it add to your vitality? For a while, observe what you eat without changing anything. You could write it down, but don't judge yourself during this process.

Take baby steps. Pick one thing to change, such as switching from white bread to whole-grain bread or learning to eat the fast-cooking grain quinoa. Make small changes over a period of weeks or months, and create the time and space needed to give your family deeply nourishing food a little at a time.

In order to modify old habits, you must feel an intrinsic desire to change. Many people change their diets for health reasons, often as the result of a live-or-die situation. But there are many reasons to change your food habits before a crisis occurs. In my classes, I have heard many stories of children who are influencing their parents to eat better. In one class, I had three pairs of mothers and daughters; all three daughters instigated their enrollment. It is inspiring to see family members align with each other about food and health.

Sometimes people tell me they can't change their family's food because one family member simply won't have it. If you're in this situation, talk to the person who objects. Let them know that your motivation comes from love. Perhaps the reluctant family member will agree to one small change — for instance, making one vegetarian meal a week, or having a fresh green salad every evening, or using brown rice instead of white rice once in a while. Go slowly, slowly. Make changing what you eat a gentle, healing process. There is no rush. Lasting changes take thought and patience.

Shopping and Storing Whole Foods

Most major cities have many fine natural foods grocery stores where you can purchase whole foods and whole food products. A surprising number of national supermarket chains now carry grains and beans in bulk, tofu and tempeh, alternative sweeteners, organic produce, and whole-grain products. Ask your local grocer to stock items you wish to buy regularly. This is how change begins.

Buying foods in bulk whenever possible reduces waste from unnecessary packaging. When buying packaged products, support manufacturers that use recyclable packaging.

Unprocessed foods tend to be more fragile than manufactured foods because they still contain life. Pay attention to the manufacturer's storage recommendations on the label. Always check the expiration date on perishable products before purchasing them.

For information on shopping and storing a specific ingredient, see the "Glossary of Ingredients" in the Appendix. Here are some guidelines on staples.

Whole Grains and Whole-Grain Flours

Whole grains, such as brown rice, buckwheat, oats, quinoa, and millet, can be stored in airtight containers at room temperature. Unground whole grains will keep this way for six to nine months. Whole-grain pastas stored in airtight containers will keep for over a year.

The essential oils in grains are released when grains are ground into flour, making them more susceptible to spoilage. Whole-grain flours, including whole wheat, barley, brown rice, buckwheat, and spelt flour, can be stored in airtight containers for up to two months at room temperature, six months in the refrigerator, and up to a year in the freezer.

Vegetables and Fruits

Vegetables and fruits should be purchased frequently and used within a few days to ensure freshness. Fresh produce is best, and frozen produce is a distant second. Use your senses when shopping for produce. Fresh fruit should have a fragrant smell, and fresh vegetables should look perky, with rich color.

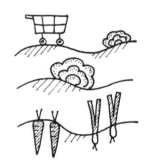

Store ripe fruits and vegetables separately in the refrigerator. Cut the leaves from root vegetables, since the flow of sap continues to the leaves at the expense of the root. Most fresh produce benefits from storage in plastic bags. You can wash, dry, and reuse your plastic bags to avoid waste.

Legumes

Shop at stores that have a rapid turnover of dried beans and peas, since older beans are less flavorful and take longer to cook. Dried legumes can be stored for a year on the shelf in airtight containers. Soybean products such as tamari, miso, tofu, and tempeh are versatile and easy to use. These soy products are individually described in the "Glossary of Ingredients."

Sea Vegetables

You can purchase sea vegetables in packages or occasionally in bulk. Sea vegetables, which are dried, should be stored in sealed containers in a cool, dark place. Properly stored, they will keep indefinitely.

Fish and Poultry

Buy fish and poultry as fresh as possible. Store it in the refrigerator and use it within 24 hours.

Look for fish that has firm flesh, a high sheen, and no offensive odors. If you are concerned about pollutants in fish, be aware that toxins tend to accumulate in fatty tissues, so choosing less fatty fish is safer. Pregnant women may want to avoid salmon, bluefish, swordfish, and lake whitefish, which tend to house more contaminants. Offshore species such as cod, haddock, flounder, ocean perch, Pacific halibut, and albacore tuna are usually harvested from less polluted waters.

Look for organically raised poultry to feed your family. Factory-produced poultry is notorious for being laden with antibiotics, hormones, and other toxins.

Nuts and Seeds

The best way to buy and store nuts and seeds is in the shell, for flavor as well as for freshness. Because of their oil content, nuts and seeds are subject to rancidity. Store shelled nuts and seeds in airtight containers in the refrigerator for up to three months or in the freezer for 12 months.

Dairy

Some consumers prefer to buy raw milk products because homogenization and pasteurization alter nutrient composition and digestibility. When buying raw milk products or other dairy products, buy from organic dairies.

Other Kitchen Staples

Eggs:

I recommend using fertile eggs from free-ranging hens in baked goods. If you wish to avoid eggs, substitute flaxseed and water. Grind 2 Tablespoons of flaxseed, add 6 Tablespoons boiling water, let mixture set 15 minutes, then whisk with a fork. This replaces two eggs in any recipe for baked goods and works equally well.

Herbs:

The leaves of certain temperate-climate plants can be used fresh or dried to add wonderful, distinctive flavors to whole foods. Some herbs have medicinal effects and are not appropriate for pregnant or nursing moms. For instance, sage can reduce the flow of breast milk. Store herbs in closed containers away from heat and light. Dried herbs keep their flavor for about six months.[10]

Oils:

Fats and oils should be used sparingly. Extra-virgin olive oil and unrefined sesame oil are the highest quality oils, the least processed and least likely to go rancid. Look for "cold-pressed" on the label of oils, which indicates the oil has been extracted by mechanical means rather than using heat and solvents. For baked goods, you may prefer using a tasteless oil such as cold-pressed safflower or canola oil, although unsalted butter makes a lighter, more digestible baked product. For infrequent light frying, cold-pressed canola or sunflower oil can hold a high temperature. Store oils in glass containers in the refrigerator and use within six months.

Natural condiments:

A variety of natural flavoring agents from different cultures can be found in most well-stocked natural foods stores. They include miso, mirin, umeboshi plums, and balsamic vinegar. For specifics on condiments mentioned in this book, check the "Glossary of Ingredients."

Sea salt:

Plain sea salt is preferable to commercial table salt, which contains unwanted additives used in processing.

---

10   Refer to Susun S. Weed, *Wise Woman Herbal for the Childbearing Year* (Woodstock, NY: Ash Tree Publishing, 1986) for more information.

Spices:

Spices are the whole or ground buds, fruits, flowers, barks, or seeds, usually of tropical-zoned plants. In traditional Indian cooking, spices are sautéed in butter or ghee to enhance their flavor before being added to a dish. To maintain optimum potency, spices should be stored in closed containers away from heat and light and used within six months.

Sweeteners:

A variety of naturally processed sweeteners can be used in dessert recipes. They include pure maple syrup, rice syrup, barley malt, and concentrated fruit sweetener. Most syruplike sweeteners should be refrigerated after opening; however, check the label for manufacturer's recommendations. Date sugar, Sucanat, Fruitsource, and other granulated, naturally processed sweeteners can be stored on the shelf. Dried fruit stored in an airtight container will keep about one year on the shelf.

Water:

Filtered tap water or bottled spring water is preferred. The Environmental Protection Agency (EPA) reports more than 700 potentially hazardous chemicals found in U.S. drinking water as a result of groundwater pollution. Most water filters remove up to 73 percent of known pollutants.

Buying Organic Products

Buying organic products is a form of voting. Your purchase says that you support the growers and manufacturers who produce food without using synthetic fertilizers, fungicides, or pesticides that pollute your body and your world. Buying organic produce, especially locally grown produce, also helps keep you in tune with the seasons. The vitamin and mineral content of organic produce is often higher than that of nonorganic produce. Soils rich in organic material and nutrients are needed to create healthy, insect-resistant plants.

The term "certified organic" means that a product has been certified by an independent party. The independent organization (for example, the Organic Growers and Buyers Association (OGBA), a nonprofit group) inspects the farm, interviews the grower, takes soil samples, and certifies that the product is grown according to standards it has set. A symbol on the front label identifies the organization that has certified an organic product. Unless that symbol appears on the front label or you know the farmer, it is difficult to know if a product is really organic. When in doubt, check with the produce manager or the buyer at your supermarket.

You might be surprised at the variety of organic products available, including jam, frozen vegetables, breakfast cereals, ketchup, pickles and pickle relish, tomato sauce, fruit juices, and soy beverages. Currently, organic products are more expensive than nonorganic ones because production costs are higher. As the demand increases for organic food, the prices will come down.

Make a special effort to use organic products when preparing food for pregnant or nursing moms, infants, and children. Toxins found in the mother's food can cross the placenta to the growing fetus or wind up in breast milk. What may be tolerated by a mature adult may prove harsh to the immature system of a fetus or infant. Current regulatory practices designed to control pesticides in foods do not safely protect infants and children, according to recent reports from the National Research Council.

Your decision to buy organic foods helps keep your family and your planet healthier.

Creating a Helpful Kitchen

It is important to make your kitchen as attractive and efficient as possible so you'll enjoy working and spending time there. Long-term investments in good cookware and equipment can be made as money permits. Taking time to rearrange what you already have so that it is easier to work with is a good first step. Here are some guidelines and suggestions.

- **Set up a large working area for chopping, sorting, and rolling.** A large piece of butcher block can be useful. The work area should be counter height or lower, to suit your height.

- **Keep tools and staples that you use often within easy reach.** Grids, pegboards, lazy Susans, colorful hooks, baskets, and pottery crocks can make things handy and the work area attractive.

- **Build a set of good-quality pots, pans, and baking dishes in a variety of sizes.** Stainless steel, porcelain enamel, glass, stoneware, and Corning Ware are good materials for cooking. Cast-iron equipment is excellent; it contributes to the iron content of food and it lasts a lifetime or two. I find a stainless steel pressure cooker helpful for turning whole foods into quick meals.

- **Invest in useful tools.** Sharp, sturdy knives for chopping and peeling are essential. Measuring cups and spoons, various sizes of wooden spoons, a metal and a rubber spatula, a grater, and a hard brush for scrubbing vegetables are also important.

- **A blender or food processor is helpful, and essential for preparing baby food.** You can use a small electric grinder (the size sold for grinding coffee beans) to grind small quantities of grains and nuts. Keep these utensils clean so residual oils from grains or nuts aren't left on the blades. A portable baby-food grinder is handy for traveling or eating out with your infant.

- **Store dry staples in airtight glass jars.** Jars can be arranged attractively and cleaned easily, and you can see what you have. A cheerfully painted bookshelf works well if you're short on pantry space. Jars are especially handy if you buy bulk items. Store nuts, seeds, and flours in the refrigerator or freezer to retard oxidation. Sea vegetables, herbs, and spices need to be kept away from light and heat.

- **Recycle disposable waste.** Check out the recycling programs in your area. Using large pails or bins to sort glass, metal, and newspapers makes recycling more efficient. What do you do with food scraps? Is there a resource for information on composting in your area?

    We have a worm bin in our yard. The worms turn our food scraps into high-nitrogen compost for our vegetable garden.[11] My daughter, Grace's, friends always want to peek into the bin and see the worms doing their job. Recycling is another aspect of conscious eating.

---

11   Mary Applehof, *Worms Eat My Garbage* (Kalamazoo, MI: Flower Press, 1982) explains the method.

- **Help yourself and the planet by using ecologically sound cleaning products.** Look for products that don't contain petroleum, ammonia, chlorine, phosphates, or lye. Toxic chemicals pollute our groundwater, and they're unsafe to use where food is prepared. Choose products that biodegrade in a natural environment within 24 hours.

- **Install a countertop or under-the-sink water filter in your kitchen.** Or you can use a refillable 5-gallon jug and purchase prefiltered water.

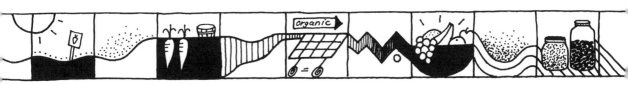

Feeding the Whole Foods Baby

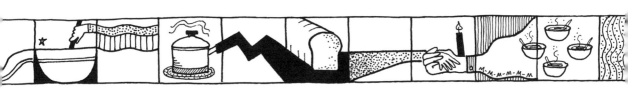

When I was a brand new mother, I had a two-week-old infant who liked to curl her fists up in tight balls and scream for several hours straight every evening. Her condition was delegated to the catchall term "colic." I worried about my breast milk being okay. I worried about her tiny digestive system. I was exhausted. I felt lost.

I chose to stay with Grace during her long tirades. I held her, walked with her, bounced her, and hung in there with her. When I could get past my own frustration, I would think about how difficult her transition must have been . . . from spirit to water baby in my womb to infant out in the world. It must be so hard to suddenly find your soul in a helpless, tiny body — a body that requires ingesting food and eliminating waste and wearing clothes and seeing lights and hearing noise. My heart went out to this tiny child who seemed to be quite angry about making this transition. Often silent tears would slide down my cheek, not only for her discomfort, but for mine.

We search for a sense of belonging and being loved all our lives. Giving food is one of our primary means of expressing love. Nothing can duplicate the reassurance that is conveyed when the food given to your baby is accompanied by the face, hands, voice, breast, or chest of a loving parent.

Start with the Best, the Breast

There is no better food you can give your newborn child than breast milk. Every year a new study appears discovering some nutrient or immunological factor found in breast milk that cannot be duplicated in the laboratory. Breast milk is designed by nature to help our species thrive. We have only begun to discover the myriad ways in which breast milk nourishes and protects both mother and child.

The first substance that comes from a mother's breast after birth is a thick liquid called colostrum. Colostrum does just what is needed immediately after birth: It helps the baby pass meconium, a substance in the baby's bowels that needs to come out before ordinary digestion can begin. Without the colostrum's laxative effect, a substance called bilirubin, found in the meconium, may be reabsorbed, resulting in jaundice. Colostrum contains half of the immunological properties the newborn needs, ensuring immediate protection. Colostrum decreases as mother's milk matures in the 10 to 14 days following birth.

Breast milk is the only food your baby needs for the first six months of life. No extra water, juice, tea, or anything else is necessary. Giving your baby a bottle of anything during the first few weeks of breastfeeding can cause nipple confusion. The breast and bottle require different sucking styles. Going from one to the other can result in frustration for both mother and baby. In our society, where the need for variety verges on obsessive, it is hard to believe that babies can thrive on the simplicity of breast milk alone. When well-meaning relatives and friends encourage you to feed the baby something else, thank them for their advice. They may be unaware of the bonuses Mother Nature includes in breast milk:

Bonuses for Your Baby

- Colostrum, the first substance from the mother's breast, helps your baby pass meconium, reduces the chance of jaundice, and supplies your baby with immunological properties.

- Breast milk contains antibodies to illnesses the mother has had, protecting your baby against infections and reducing the risk of allergies.

- Your baby can easily absorb the iron in breast milk, thanks to the presence of specialized proteins and vitamin C.

- Sucking at the breast enhances good hand/eye coordination and promotes proper jaw and teeth alignment.

Bonuses for Mother

- After birth, immediate breastfeeding helps contract the uterus and reduce the risk of hemorrhaging.

- The hormone prolactin, which appears in the mother as a result of breastfeeding, is a relaxant. This hormone is thought to help new moms feel "motherly."

- Breastfeeding aids in natural weight loss by using up an extra 500 calories a day.

- Studies show that women who breastfeed for at least 25 months during their lifetimes reduce their risk of breast cancer (which strikes one out of nine women in this country).

Bonuses for the Family

- Breastfeeding gives mother and baby a deep sense of security and love, and encourages physical closeness.

- Breastfeeding saves time and money. Formula feeding is expensive!

- Outings with baby are easier using naturally hygienic breast milk: no bottles, no sterilizing, no heating things up, no formula, no fuss.

In researching breastfeeding, I was awed by one discovery. A biological communication is established between mother and baby during nursing: The milk responds to the needs of the baby. Formula is static, but breast milk is not. It is a living, constantly changing food.

For example, the milk produced for a premature baby is different from the milk that comes in for a full-term infant. Breast milk even changes within a single feeding. The milk that comes out of the breast at the beginning of the feeding is more watery and satisfies thirst quickly. Toward the end of the feeding, the milk (called the hind milk) becomes richer in fat. Both are vital for your baby.

In addition, the interaction between the baby's mouth and the mother's nipple signals the mother's body to increase certain nutrients in the milk if needed, or to restrict substances that appear dangerous. No humanmade substance can duplicate the sensitive response of human breast milk. It's truly a miracle of nature.

Cultural influences have led women to sometimes see breastfeeding as a hardship. Even when women choose to nurse, their husbands, relatives, and friends may pressure them into early weaning because they are socially uncomfortable seeing the child and the mother's breast together. Social conditioning from advertisements by formula manufacturers and guidance by health-care practitioners unfamiliar with the advantages of breastfeeding perpetuate this message. To raise children strengthened by breastfeeding requires courage to ignore such outdated social stigmas.

If you are pregnant, contact your local La Leche League before your child's birth for additional support. This international organization has a network of meetings, counselors, and literature that promote and support breastfeeding. The Childbirth Education Association (CEA) provides breastfeeding classes and early mothering support classes. You may not be able to breastfeed simply by doing what you've seen women in your family do before. We are isolated, no longer privy to the shared wisdom

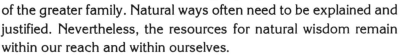 of the greater family. Natural ways often need to be explained and justified. Nevertheless, the resources for natural wisdom remain within our reach and within ourselves.

In instances where breastfeeding may not be possible, such as adoption, formula is the preferred second choice. No single brand of formula appears to be any better than another. Most commercial formulas contain sugar, salt, and cheap fats such as beef tallow or coconut oil, which are susceptible to rancidity.[12] Some creative nutritionists, naturopaths, and other health-care practitioners have attempted to invent better formulas, usually by combining soy milk or goat milk and high-quality vitamin and mineral supplements. You might explore your community for a reasonable alternative that you and your health-care practitioner can agree upon.

Parents have an instinctual need to nourish their children. The premise of this book is based on that drive. I encourage you to make whatever changes you require, in your lifestyle or in your head, in order to experience the power of breastfeeding in your family. It is a part of womanhood we need to reclaim and pass on to the next generation.

Foods for Breastfeeding Moms

Sometimes women who have been careful about their eating habits during pregnancy may forget, during nursing, that their bodies are still the source of nutrition for their child. Continuing good eating habits is important during breastfeeding, though sometimes harder to remember with a wee one in tow. The substances taken in by the nursing mother have a strong effect on the milk she produces.

For instance, the alcohol from a single drink consumed by a nursing mother appears in the breast milk in the same concentration as in the mother's blood within 30 minutes. Nicotine ingested by smoking cigarettes passes into the breast milk as well. Foods eaten by mom sometimes disagree with the breastfed child, especially high-dosage vitamins, supplements high in iron, artificial sweeteners, caffeine, heavily spiced foods, and

12   Gabrielle Palmer, *The Politics of Breastfeeding* (London: Pandora Press, 1988) 42-48

occasionally dairy products. Colicky or fussy babies may improve if the nursing mother's diet is changed. Consult with your health-care practitioner or lactation counselor.

Many women feel rushed to get rid of weight gained during pregnancy. The nursing period is not an appropriate time to diet. Dieting can compromise the mother's stamina and her milk supply. Environmental contaminants stored in the mother's body fat can be released into the milk if she loses more than four pounds a month. Overindulgence in caffeine found in coffee, diet soft drinks, or over-the-counter drugs can result in an overstimulated baby. Breastfeeding as long as is comfortable, regular nutritious meals, and exercise are the most important factors in finding your way back into your old jeans.

A common misconception in the United States is that nursing moms need to drink milk in order to produce milk. Not true. Cows do not drink milk in order to make milk, they eat grass. Acknowledging the wisdom of women in all parts of the world and throughout several centuries can give us helpful clues today.

The postnatal diets of tribal women throughout the world reveal a consistency of custom. Tribal diets focus on bland grain/vegetable soups, soft-cooked grains and

vegetables, greens, and fish soups. Women drink large quantities of warm water and tea to encourage the flow of milk. Fats, sweets, cold liquids, and, in some cases, meat are specifically avoided.[13]

At one time, African women used a grain called "linga-linga" when nursing. The same grain used in Peru was called "quinoa." This grain has an especially high mineral content. Quinoa has been rediscovered and is now grown and sold in this country. I use this delicious grain in several recipes throughout the book. Another grain purported to aid in producing a good milk supply is sweet brown rice, a cousin of brown rice that has a higher fat content. This grain is often eaten in the form of mochi or amasake. Foods that are known to produce rich breast milk, then and now, include whole grains, vegetables (especially dark green and orange ones), legumes, fish, and warm herbal teas — whole foods prepared in simple satisfying ways.

High-quality breast milk doesn't require you to eat perfectly balanced, home-cooked meals each and every day. Nature allows plenty of leeway. Do your best to eat well and sensibly throughout the day; drink plenty of liquids; sleep when you can; and love yourself and your baby. Then your milk will be blessed food.

---

13   Judith Goldsmith, *Childbirth Wisdom* (Brookline, MA: East West Books, 1990)

The New Eater

When to Start Your Baby on Solid Foods

There is no hurry. Look at your baby, not the calendar. Your baby will let you know when it's time to start. Around six or seven months old, your baby will give visible signs of readiness for solid foods. Here's what to watch for.

- **Can your baby sit up unattended?** Sitting upright is necessary for swallowing thicker substances.

- **Is your baby able to pick up small objects?** This indicates that your baby could put a small bit of food in their mouth.

- **Does your baby show an interest in what you're eating?** Mimicking your chewing, watching food go into your mouth, and grabbing for your food are signs of interest.

- **If you offer a little taste of food, can your baby swallow it, or is it pushed back out with the tongue?** There is some practice involved here; the tongue-thrusting reflex is a physiological protective device that begins to diminish around six months of age.

- **Has your baby begun teething?** Some cultures regard the appearance of teeth as a sign of readiness for solid food.

Your baby's digestive enzymes are not fully developed for several years; however, at six months of age they are developed enough for experimental feedings. Starting solids too early can result in allergies brought on by exposing the immature digestive system to foods it can't handle. And don't be fooled into thinking your baby will sleep through the night if you start giving solid foods. This is a myth in our "hurry up" society. Trust your observations. Wait until your infant is physically prepared for solids before introducing them.

How to Start Your Baby on Solids

Again, there is no hurry. The initial step is to introduce new tastes and textures. Your baby is getting all the nutrition needed from breast milk or formula. The transition to solid food as the primary source of nutrition should be long and slow. Once you feel your baby may be ready to experiment with solids, here's how to start.

- **Use one simple, whole food.** A soft fruit or a cooked sweet vegetable is a good choice.

- **Puree the food in a blender or processor, or mash it with a fork.**

- **Mix the food with a little breast milk or formula.** This will give your baby a familiar taste.

- **Begin with only a teaspoon of food.**

- **Choose a quiet time of day different from your regular nursing or bottle time.**

- **Talk to your baby about the food and the eating procedure.** Later the baby will respond to cues such as "Open your mouth!" or "Bananas, Henry?"

- **Taste a little of the food yourself.** You can model eating for your baby (home-made baby food can be appreciated here).

- **Offer the food from your finger or a spoon, or allow your baby to grab** (messier for you, fascinating for your baby).

- **Stay with one feeding a day of one simple food.** Wait about five days before introducing another new food. With each new food, be aware of allergic reactions such as rashes around the mouth or anus, diarrhea, skin reactions, lethargy, or unusual fussiness. Eliminate, for the time being, any food that causes a reaction and try it again when your baby is six months to 1 year older. Common allergens and other potentially disruptive foods that should be avoided are listed on pages 105 and 106.

- **After a few weeks of one small meal a day, you can increase to two small meals a day.** If your baby doesn't seem to enjoy eating solid foods, stop the feedings for a few weeks.

New Eater Foods

Whether your baby's first solid food should be a cereal, a fruit, or a vegetable is up to you. If your child is labeled underweight, a health-care practitioner or a relative may encourage you to start with cereals, but babies digest fruits and vegetables more easily and quickly than whole grains. Also be sure the underweight label is a fair assessment.[14]

Stay with simple fruits, vegetables, and whole grains for the first few months of solids. Your baby will let you know which are favorites. My daughter hated tried-and-true mashed avocado and mashed banana, but adored sweet potatoes and applesauce. Each child is unique. Remember to rotate the grains used for cereal to reduce the chance of allergies. Rotation provides your baby with a wider variety of nutrients since each grain is unique. Many ideas for beginners' foods are given in the recipe section, "Homemade Baby Foods" (page 89). Also, most of the recipes in this book include suggestions for ways to adapt each dish to make a meal for your new or experienced eater.

The Experienced Eater

Babies who have been eating simple cereals, vegetables, and fruits for about three months are ready for more food choices. Ground nuts and seeds, the smaller beans (lentils and peas), and other food combinations can be added to your baby's diet. Hold off on larger beans, fish, and animal foods until your baby has some side incisors and molars (usually after they are walking). As your baby begins to take less breast or bottle milk, these new foods fill in the nutritional spaces. Occasional small quantities of sea vegetables can provide additional vitamins and minerals for the experienced eater.

The proper time to introduce dairy products (made from cow's milk) is highly disputed. Many practitioners feel dairy is such a common allergen that all dairy products should be avoided until a child is at least 2 years of age. This can be difficult if you have chosen to wean your child from formula or breast milk before age 2. Others feel that, although cow's milk should be avoided, cultured dairy products such as yogurt (plain, no sugar) or cheese are okay after nine months. I advocate waiting to introduce dairy

---

14 Current growth charts are owned and distributed by Ross Laboratories, one of the largest formula manufacturers. The charts reflect the growth rates of mostly formula-fed babies, who tend to be larger than breastfed babies.

as long as possible. I have seen fewer problems associated with respiratory illnesses, ear infections, and digestive disorders in dairy-free babies. The key is to be aware of your baby's reaction when you introduce dairy. If you use dairy foods, don't overemphasize them so they don't crowd out other important foods.

With the addition of a few new foods to the experienced eater's diet, moms, dads, and other caretakers will have no problem finding items from their wholesome meals to offer baby. My child became less interested in pureed foods at around 11 months old and wanted food she could pick up and feed herself. This is where the list of finger foods on page 104 can come in handy.

Your baby deserves food that is delicious as well as nutritious. I often do a taste test with my students when I teach baby-food classes. Freshly made brown-rice cereal wins hands down over powdered commercial baby cereal mixed with water. Making baby food does not need to be a laborious task. Food for your baby can easily evolve from wholesome foods the rest of the family is eating. This simple method is economical, ecological, highly nutritious, and supportive of sound health for everyone.

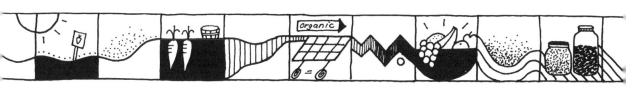

Attracting Children
to Healthy Eating

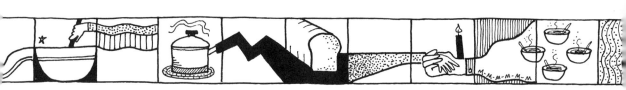

When I pick my daughter up from school, she usually wants to stay and play until all the other children are gone, so I often watch the children in her class.

One year, there was a mischievous elflike boy named Jonathan in her class. He would run and hide when the teachers wanted him to come in. He would dart outside without putting his shoes on. Once, I saw him sit down in the mud. He delighted in testing boundaries.

I formed opinions about him. I thought of him as a "handful." One time I thought the school probably needed an extra teacher just for Jonathan.

I was invited to school to make lunch with the children one Friday. I brought pinto beans, whole-wheat tortillas, brown rice, avocados, salsa, cheese, and lettuce and proceeded to make the fixings for a burrito lunch. The kitchen is near the classroom and the children were welcome to help. Some would stop by and assist for 10 or 15 minutes and then drift off to play.

One child stayed by my side all morning — Jonathan. He mashed beans, peeled avocados, and squeezed lemons. He followed instructions and was not only helpful, but gleeful, about making guacamole. I was humbled. This little elf reminded me about "respect," a word that means "to look again."

Children are remarkably malleable. As soon as we label them, thinking that we can predict their behavior in some way, they surprise us by doing the opposite. Children invite us to experience the world with awe. They remind us that we do not know what will happen next. Don't presume that Fred will never eat lima beans or that Judy will always want her apple peeled. Stay open to the little bits of magic lurking in every corner. Maybe you'll discover an elf in your kitchen.

Parents as Role Models

What are *your* eating habits? Children model themselves after their parents. The tiniest baby notices every move you make, every forkful that goes into your mouth. A well-intentioned friend I once knew carefully prepared homemade, whole-grain baby cereals and organic purees for her baby while she and her husband dined on pork ribs and doughnuts. As soon as the child could walk and grab, the baby wanted what mommy and daddy were eating. As trite as it may sound, parents' primary job in the food and nutrition department is to set a good example. This gravitation toward the parents' eating habits will wax and wane. Children hit many rebellious stages of rejecting whatever their parents do, but the underlying patterns they were shown about food remain.

Here are four suggestions to help you become a model of healthful eating habits for your children.

- **Become aware of how you feel about food.**
  What are some of your favorite foods? What kinds of feelings would surface if you could never have them again? What are some foods you hate? Do you know why you hate them? Many hated foods have their roots in our childhoods. How closely have you modeled your parents' eating habits? Are vegetables something you're supposed to eat, or do you really like them? Is sugar something you deserve if you've been good, had a bad day, or finished your plate?

  These unspoken attitudes are clearly transmitted to children. We may not be able to change our feelings about food just because we become parents, but we can become aware of how we think, feel, and act about various food choices. Take stock. Figure out which attitudes you may be unconsciously acting out, and decide whether they are beneficial to pass on to your children.

- **Set boundaries about food choices and mealtimes.**
  Many child-rearing books encourage parents to set gentle but firm boundaries with children to help them feel safe and protected. This concept applies to eating as well. Be sure to set boundaries that you can follow, too. It's not fair to have a no-sugar policy and then stay up late for some adults-only Godiva chocolates. Helpful boundaries that offer ways to instill nutritious eating habits in your children with minimum stress to you are outlined in "Setting Boundaries" on page 57.

- **Take time to educate.**
  As soon as your child can talk, you can begin to communicate information about nutrition. Offer specific reasons for each food choice rather than saying, "You can't have this. It's bad for you." You can describe to young children how they act or look when they've eaten foods with poor nutrition (whiny, grumpy, tired, "speedy").

Take your children shopping with you. Talk to them about what you're buying and why, such as why you choose organic produce. As your children get older, let them play detective in the store: Present them with a challenge, such as finding a jar of tomato sauce that's organic or a loaf of bread without sweeteners. Encourage your child to help you cook by slowing down and allowing for the longer preparation time necessary to include a willing participant. Check the section called "Involving Your Children in the Kitchen" on page 60 for ideas. As children get older, talk to them about how more nutritious foods can help them attain some of their desires (clearer skin, faster times on the 100-yard dash, better concentration). They may not accept everything you tell them, but occasionally they will see and feel results, and that can be powerful!

- **Let go.**
  Learning to bend the rules, being flexible, and letting go are perhaps the most important lessons of parenting. Relaxing at birthday parties and other social gatherings where junk foods are offered is easier if you know the food served at home is nutritionally sound. A woman in one of my classes proudly announced that she bakes no-sugar, whole-wheat birthday cakes for her child to take to parties, instead of allowing the child to share the cake being served. Rules that cause a child to feel uncomfortable in social situations are unnecessary and can be just as unhealthy as sugary cake. Watch out for setting up too many "forbidden fruits." Highly restricted foods may become irresistible and take on more power than they warrant.

We need to respect and think about our children's food choices. Children have a lot to teach us about instincts. Have you ever offered food to your child all day only to be repeatedly refused, then realized later they were coming down with a cold? The child's intuition not to eat at that time was right on the nose. My child, Grace, used to regularly come home from birthday parties and ask for several sheets of nori to eat. How did she know that one of the consequences of too much sugar is that it creates a mineral debt in the body and that seaweed contains more minerals than any other food? Many children intuitively select what their bodies need.

Children can teach us about simplicity, too. You may notice that young children tend to dislike casseroles or salad dishes containing many different ingredients. They'd rather have a plain food. A child's preferences can set a good example for parents to follow.

I have a little sign on my refrigerator that says, "Be a model, not a critic." It would be so much easier to glibly express platitudes and warnings to our children as we merrily indulge in our addictions and whims. Our children need to see us respect, be grateful for, and eat nourishing food with the knowledge that whole foods make us healthier on many levels.

Setting Boundaries

All children need and want boundaries. When we set boundaries, we are saying we care about them. When they're infants, we keep our children close to our bodies. With each year we give them a little more space to roam and a few more choices to make, even as we continue to provide a circle of boundaries to protect them. This concept also applies to food. An infant is given the simple security of breast or bottle. Preschoolers may be able to clearly tell you if they would prefer an apple or a rice cake. A 10-year-old can help plan the dinner menu. Keep the choices simple and limited for the younger ones while allowing older children more input. The following suggestions apply to children between the ages of 3 and 10.

- **Provide excellent choices.**
  Stock your cupboards and your refrigerator with fresh, healthful, whole food products. When all of the food in your home is food you feel good about serving your children, you can eliminate many problems around eating. It won't matter what your child chooses or asks for. You can't expect to keep junk foods and sugary items around the house and not be badgered, especially if your child sees you eating those items. If it's not there, it's harder to fight about.

  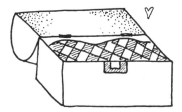

  If you pack a lunchbox for your child, make sure the choices inside are good ones. When there are candies and soft drinks and such in the lunchbox, children often eat or drink the sweets and skip the rest; however, if each item is substantial and nutritious, you don't need to worry about what your child eats or doesn't eat.

- **Honor mealtimes.**
  Share at least one common meal with your whole family each day. A family meal is not only a time for nourishment, but an opportunity for children to experience some social education. Emphasize social patterns with ritual: lighting candles, saying a verse, setting the table a special way, serving food a certain way. Consider keeping a regular time for the evening meal.[15]

---

15   For additional suggestions about mealtimes and families, see Shea Darian, *Seven Times the Sun* (San Diego: LuraMedia, 1994), chapter 2.

- **What's served is served.**

  Don't make the mistake of preparing a separate meal for your child. Let each person receive some portion of each dish that has been prepared. If your child refuses to eat one of the foods, encourage them to sample one or two bites, then say no more. This exposure to many foods will expand your child's repertoire. A child sometimes refuses a food because of appearance, then appreciates it when tasted.

  Children who refuse to eat anything on the plate should be asked to excuse themselves and told that no other food will be served until breakfast or until 8 o'clock that night or whatever time seems reasonable according to your child's age. If they come whining for food later, consider offering the leftover dinner. One way to avoid the "untouched meal" syndrome is to make sure that each meal has a sure winner: a simple side dish you know your child will like (see "Keep it simple" below).

  Incorporate a "no-critics-at-the-table" rule. Teach your children that it is inappropriate for any participant to offer harsh and cruel reviews such as, "I hate everything!" or "It looks like poop!" Remind such reviewers that their words are unkind and ask them to excuse themselves from the dinner table. Suggest alternative ways for expressing dislike of the menu. Let them know they will be welcome at dinner the next night, where they can practice being more considerate. I find that children who help prepare the food for a meal are less critical at the dinner table.

- **Keep it simple.**

  Children usually like simple food and sometimes refuse foods that have several ingredients. Let your child learn to appreciate simple foods by regularly offering them. There is nothing wrong with plain carrots, plain baked squash, plain noodles, or plain brown rice. Sometimes it takes an elaborate salad to please me, whereas my 5-year-old is happy with plain sliced cucumbers or lettuce without dressing. When planning meals, include something simple that you're certain your child will like, even if it's just a side dish of sliced bread or carrot sticks or applesauce.

- **Don't bribe, reward, or punish with food.**

  Offering or withholding sweets or any other "forbidden" food in exchange for good behavior is not a good idea. It sets up hard-to-reverse psychological attachments to food. Food is something you eat in order to get energy to play and to grow.

Avoid tension and save money by not serving desserts with weekly dinners. If you serve home-baked goodies occasionally as snacks, mealtimes won't become a constant negotiation about dessert. Save desserts for special occasions or weekend meals.

- **Listen to your child.**
  Children have good instincts. If they are being offered excellent foods, they will eat exactly what their bodies need. That may mean only fruit for several days (especially when it's warm outside); then they may request something heartier, like fish. Children create a balanced diet over many days rather than within one day. Watch. Often they hit all the food groups over a week or two. To eliminate worry about sufficient nutrients, offer excellent choices from a variety of whole foods steadily and consistently.

  But children's wonderful intuition can go awry. Refined sugar and highly salted foods can become addictive, and excessive amounts of either can mar your child's judgment. A diet high in animal protein can cause cravings for sugar. See "Frequently Asked Questions" on pages 22-32 for more information on this topic.

- **Be firmer during stressful times.**
  When your child is ill or has an infection, remove foods known to be stressful to the system. Enforce your greater knowledge and forbid sweets, dairy products, animal proteins, and fried foods. Bodies  recover from illness much quicker when they are given simple foods, such as soups and grains. Explain what you're doing in a way your child will understand.

  Holidays can be stressful, too. Most holidays seem to center around sugar. Provide some reasonable rules to curb the heavy intake of sugary foods at these times. When my child is given a bag of candy at a birthday party, we usually let her choose one piece a day to eat. This works, and she sometimes loses interest after a few days. If your child is over age 5, let them help create the rules.

When setting boundaries, remember to respect your child's individuality. Children who are sensitive to certain foods may benefit from firmer boundaries. Others may show so little interest in food that you may not need to set many limits. Some children are natural vegetarians, while others want or need some animal protein. Listen to your child's requests and guide them toward the healthier, whole foods way of fulfilling them. Young children appreciate the boundaries about food we set for them. It helps them feel guided, protected, and safe.

Involving Your Children in the Kitchen

Children need to feel a sense of belonging. It is one of their primary drives. In the days of farms and big families, children were a natural part of daily activities. Every child was needed to do chores in order for food to get to the table. Today, children often lose the opportunity to be needed, to contribute to the daily work routine of house and family. Meals are often prepared for the children, not by the children.

Even children who have just begun walking can help out in the kitchen. They can learn many things about food, cooking, nutrition, math, science, and recycling by helping prepare food. Kitchen participation helps teach self-reliance and the importance of contributing to the functioning of the household.

Most 3-to-6-year-olds can handle the tasks listed below. Match the task to your child's skill level. If the task seems too difficult at first, let it go and try again in several months. Remember to use simple, short sentences to describe how the work is done, and do the task slowly as you show and tell your child how it is done. Be patient, and pretty soon you'll have an ace kitchen helper.

Helping Your Helper

- Clear out a low cupboard for your child. Keep pots and pans there so your toddler can play near you, copying you.

- For your preschooler, use the space to store unbreakable dishes that they can serve with or use for imaginary house-play. Older children may enjoy having their own kitchen tools or snacks on a reachable shelf.

- Keep a small pitcher of water or diluted juice on a low shelf in the refrigerator that your child can reach and pour.

- Get a sturdy stool or small chair that your child can move in order to reach the counter and sink.

Things Your Child Can Do to Help with Meals

Preparing

- Help with menu selection (this provides a lesson on listening to the body's clues and balancing meals)

- Carry groceries into house

- Unload grocery bags and put things away

- Retrieve items from the refrigerator

- Pick herbs, fruits, or vegetables from the garden

- Wash fruits and vegetables

- Stir wet or dry ingredients

- Sift flour

- Knead dough

- Peel carrots, cucumbers, potatoes

- Grate carrots, cheese

- Grind grains or nuts in a grinder or processor

- Crack nuts

- Cut vegetables or fruit (your child should be at least 4 or 5 years old)

- Measure and pour liquid ingredients

- Measure and add dry ingredients

- Turn blenders and food processors on and off

- Use mixer, with supervision

- Roll out dough with rolling pin

- Form cookies with hands

- Cut out cookies with cutters

- Put muffin cups in muffin tins

- Oil pans and cookie sheets

- Tell you when something is boiling

- Tell you when the timer goes off

- Spin the salad spinner

- Tear lettuce or greens into small pieces

- Toss a salad

- Put spreads on breads, crackers, rice cakes, or tortillas

- Pour pancake batter with cup

- Flip pancakes

Serving

- Set the table with mats, silverware, cups or glasses, and napkins

- Put candles on table and blow candles out

- Pick flowers and put them in a vase of water

- Make place mats out of construction paper with crayons or pens

- Roll napkins into napkin rings

- Make place cards for guests

- Call the family to dinner

Cleaning

- Carry dishes from table to sink

- Wash dishes

- Dry dishes

- Load dishes in dishwasher

- Unload dishes from dishwasher

- Sweep the floor (a child-size broom is helpful)

- Wipe table, place mats, or floor with a sponge

- Put recyclable items in bins

- Take food scraps to worm bin or compost pile

- Sort clean silverware into compartments

Beauty Is in the Eye of the Beholder

Presentation of food is important for young children. Your child may refuse a sandwich unless it's cut a certain way or has the bread crusts cut off. You may be able to delight a child into eating something new by putting a face on it or cutting it into a heart shape. Dust off your imagination and expand on the following ideas for creative food preparation for youngsters.

Decorate Food

Here are some starter suggestions. I'm sure you'll think of more.

- Stock a variety of cookie cutters and use them to cut sandwiches and pancakes. Find cutters in the shapes of your child's favorite animals. Asian markets sometimes have small, strong cutters for making vegetables into beautiful shapes. These can be fun for turning zucchini or carrot slices into flowers.

- Serving brown rice, potatoes, or other foods with a large ice cream scoop makes miniature mountains on your child's plate.

- Make food friendlier by using raisins, small pieces of vegetables, small crackers, or whatever you can dream up to put a face on the food. Bowls of soup, mashed potatoes, or plates of rice suddenly become funny personalities for your child to devour. Apple slices make sweeping smiles; olives make 3-D eyeballs.

    I once cut a sheet of nori into paper dolls for my 3-year-old. Decorating food brings humor and light to your child's day — and yours.

Use Delightful Dinnerware and Playful Packaging

- You might buy a special plate, cup, or even silverware for your child. This can be as extravagant as a complete Winnie-the-Pooh set or simply "Katie's yellow plate." Having personal dinnerware can enhance your child's enjoyment of meals. Children also derive security from being able to count on the same bowl or spoon every day. Serving red zinger tea in a special cup or plopping a crazy straw into a fruit shake can make all the difference.

- Lunchbox packaging can have charm, too. Your child may love having lunch packed in a recyclable paper bag with a big colorful monster drawn on the outside. Another child may prefer a basket with a lid and ribbons tied on the handle. Asian markets sell interesting merchandise designed for packing food to go. Sometimes you can find beautiful container boxes in pretty colors that have little compartments inside.

- Fun surprises hidden inside a lunchbox need not be sweets. How about a marble, a seashell, an envelope with a note or stickers inside, or a little pad of paper and a tiny pencil? There are many ways to convey a loving message.

Tell a Story

- Can you turn a plate of spaghetti into a pail of hay for a pretend lamb in your kitchen?

- Can a bowl of yellow split pea soup become a bowl of melted gold for your pirate?

Pretend play is important to young folks. Why not use it to everyone's advantage in the nutrition department? Make up a wild story about what you're serving that makes it impossible not to devour (or at least taste).

Moms and dads won't feel like decorating and storytelling every day, three times a day. Don't create any superparent expectations to be at your imaginative peak every day. These ideas are meant to uncover fun for you and your child, not to produce guilt.

"My Child Won't Eat Vegetables"

One of the most common worries expressed in my cooking classes is that kids won't eat vegetables. With children who eat their fair share of whole grains, fruits, and beans, you can relax some; these foods contain a wide variety of vitamins and minerals. However, parents are right to be concerned if their children subsist mainly on sugar and white-flour products and milk. Vegetables are rich in vitamins not found in refined foods or animal products.

Remember that some children's favorite foods *are* vegetables, such as corn, sweet potatoes, carrots, and winter squash. One excellent way to improve your child's interest in vegetables is to let them help you plant and harvest a small vegetable garden.

Don't make a big fuss if your child refuses vegetables. Instead, eat them yourself and regularly offer them to your child. Remembering that beauty is in the eye of the beholder, here are some alternative forms of vegetables that may appeal to your child.

- **Juices**
  My students report great success in getting children to drink various vegetable juices. Carrot juice is a favorite, especially mixed with a little apple juice. But remember, juice is not a whole food; the fiber is gone and the sugars become highly concentrated. Dilute all vegetable and fruit juices, one-half juice, one-half water.

- **Dippers**

  You can use raw vegetables as dippers for your child's favorite dip. Bean dips, guacamole, and tofu dips can be scooped up on a carrot stick, celery stick, or a slice of zucchini. To make vegetables easier to chew and digest, boil or steam them for two to three minutes. Remove and immediately plunge them into ice water to stop the cooking process. Drain and chill in refrigerator and serve with dip. This process enhances the flavors of cauliflower, carrots, and broccoli.

- **Soups**

  Children who refuse a serving of vegetables will often eat the same vegetable in a soup. If vegetables in their whole form are a turnoff, puree the soup (see Rosemary Red Soup on page 151 or Golden Mushroom-Basil Soup on page 155).

- **Muffins**

  You can add vegetables to muffins and other baked goods (as in Sweet Squash Corn Muffins on page 215 or Halloween Cookies on page 233). Zucchini, corn, squash, carrots, and sweet potatoes taste great in a muffin mix.

- **Sandwich spreads**

  When you're pureeing beans or tofu or avocado into a tasty sandwich spread, add vegetables. Parsley, red pepper, or scallions work well to enhance flavor and nutritive value. Sometimes I add corn, grated zucchini, or chopped green peppers to burritos. Amidst the beans, salsa, tortillas, and other ingredients, they are hardly noticed.

- **Salads**

  Sometimes just the sight of combined ingredients turns kids off to salads. Experiment by offering a single raw vegetable or different vegetables in separate piles, not mixed together. Try different shapes and sizes. Grated beets or radishes, finely sliced cabbage, zucchini, summer squash, daikon (white radish), or even plain lettuce bites can be fun to pick up with small fingers.

Beyond Cupcakes

Marking the day of our birth reminds us that we are growing and changing. But the reason for birthdays often becomes lost in a frenzy of "who gets the cupcake with the pink icing?" If you're nutritionally conscious, your mind probably boggles at the number of times a year children are lured into a sugar fest. Not only are there the major holidays and your child's birthday, but friends and each child in your child's class have birthdays. That's a lot of cupcakes.

Model some new ways of celebrating children's birthdays. Instead of sugary treats, you could take some of the following enriching and fun items to school or parties. Remember, an activity that all the children can participate in is most successful.

Collect old hats at thrift stores and garage sales, and bring a hat for each child. Let each child pick one and decorate or put their name on it. The birthday child can have a special hat to which everyone adds an individual "touch."

Perhaps your family has a special food tradition that your child enjoys — say, a dish from the history of your family. You could prepare the dish for the group. The mothers of Japanese children in my child's preschool prepared beautiful nori rolls for everyone.

A tea party might be appropriate, especially if your ancestors were English as were those in my husband's maternal family. Bring an old tea set or give the class a secondhand one. Set out tablecloths, scones, a variety of interesting herb teas, and serve tea.

How about creating a birthday cape? Supply sequins, buttons, embroidery thread, fabric paint, etc., and let each child add something. The class can keep it, and other children can wear it on their birthdays.

Videotape each child for a few minutes, perhaps responding to a question like, "What advice do you have for Eli on turning 6?" Then arrange to play the tape for the group.

Buy a tree, shrub, or flowers for the schoolyard. Let the birthday child pick it out. With the school's permission, the class can plant it and have a long-remembered lesson in planting, growing, and patience.

Present the class with a cassette tape of favorite classical, jazz, or children's music. Bring in some scarves or streamers or balloons and encourage a dance!

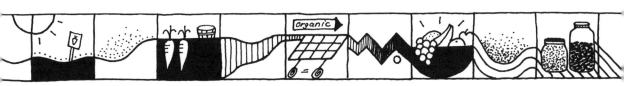

Balancing Family Life

A teacher of mine once told me that some of the most brilliant minds in history belonged to people who were known to spend hours sitting and staring out the window. I have always remembered this and regularly schedule "down time" for myself. This is time when I'm not responsible for the needs of others, and I can sit and do nothing and let my mind roam — a challenging goal for most of us.

One rare morning as I was rocking in our rocker and staring at the yard, I remembered an idea I'd had ages ago: an all-women's clothing swap. I sent out some invitations for a Sunday afternoon in September. My daughter, Grace, colored them with crayons. I asked my women friends to bring nice, in-style clothes that they no longer wore — clothes they might want to give to their sisters.

That Sunday, my husband, Michael, hung a rake and a hoe handle across the living room to make a dress rack. I laid out a blanket on the floor for folded items, made jam-filled cookies for the children, and set out some homemade black bean dip and chips for the adults.

The women arrived with boxes, bags, and armloads of clothing. While the children played in the yard, we looked, tried on clothes, giggled, and talked. There was much debate over who would end up with the strapless, red-flowered dress that Joy brought. I think we all tried it on. I love vivid colors and snatched Holly's much-too-bright-for-her, yellow cotton skirt. Susan was delighted to claim Nina's too-short-in-the-arms, lavender down-filled coat. The children came in after play and went for the chips and black bean dip. The women seemed to prefer the jam-filled cookies. Everyone went home with new treasures to wear and a satisfied feeling. I took the leftover clothing to the Sacred Heart shelter the next day.

This event exemplifies many of the values I hold regarding food. I believe in slowing down enough to respect and enjoy eating. I feel that simplifying my needs for food and other material goods helps me and my planet. I strive to use what is readily available or leftover rather than always shopping for the new and different. I continually seek to build a community of friends who share or support these values.

When I have the space in my life to plan and carry out a women's clothing swap, I feel healthy. I know that time spent staring out the window is as beneficial to myself and the people around me as making a home-cooked meal. I encourage you to stare out the window, too. Maybe not every day, but once in a while. It's important to create spaces so we can find our brilliance.

Fixing Fast Meals for Busy Families

This section may be the most closely read part of this book. I am a parent and a wife, and I have two freelance careers outside the home. I know how important it is to be able to throw together a quick, nutritious meal.

Below is a list of time-saving tips on planning and preparation. Following that is a list of menu ideas using the quicker recipes in this book. Don't forget to light a candle and enjoy the fast meal slowly.

Time-Saving Tips

- **Keep your kitchen well-stocked with whole grains, whole-grain noodles, flours, beans, oils, herbs, spices, and other condiments.** Staples such as these need only be purchased monthly, and weekly shopping trips can center around fresh produce and other perishables.

- **Choose one day or evening a week to do some cooking.** Make a couple of kinds of beans, a large pot of rice, a soup, and maybe some fresh bread or muffins. This could set you up for a week of fast meals.

- **Cook when you cook.** Sometimes when I'm cooking dinner on Tuesday, I'll also put on some millet and a pot of kidney beans for another day. The extra grains and beans require little preparation time, just cooking time. With precooked grains or beans, you can put a meal together in about 20 minutes.

- **Make double recipes.** For instance, make more black beans than you need and freeze the rest. As long as you remember to defrost, you've got two quick black bean tostada meals ready for the coming weeks.

- **Cook while you shower.** It usually takes 40 or more minutes to shower, get dressed, get your children dressed, and pack lunchboxes. Put on a pot of rice, beans, soup, or other slow-cooking food before you start your routine. Turn it off before you leave the house (set a timer so you don't forget) and place the cooked food in the fridge. The food will be waiting when you come home, ready to be turned into a quick meal.

- **Wash greens ahead of time and store them in plastic bags in the refrigerator.** This cuts time off salad making.

- **Learn a new recipe.** One of the main reasons people don't change to healthier dietary habits is that they want to make dinner without studying a cookbook and making an extra trip to the grocery store. Pick one new recipe that you think your family will like, and make it several times within a two-to-three-month period. When you've got it down so that you only need to glance at the recipe book, start learning another new recipe. With time you'll have a new set of "regulars" in your meal-planning pattern.

- **Get familiar with some of the new convenience products.** Many companies now can organic beans, freeze tofu lasagna, and package vegetarian sandwich spreads. Check out your local natural foods store. These items may cost more than homemade and may not be quite as fresh, but when you're in a pinch, nutritious convenience foods are better for your body than most takeout items from a fast-food joint.

Time-Saving Menus

Below is a list of menus using recipes in this book. These meals can be made in 35 to 45 minutes. I have also included simple, familiar dishes such as steamed broccoli to round out a meal. (Recipes for those are not in the book.) When I'm planning a meal, I usually combine one whole grain, one cooked vegetable, one raw vegetable, and a bean dish or some fish. I downplay raw vegetables in winter (they're cooling to the body) and include more salads and raw foods in summer.

I have chosen four breakfast menus and 16 lunch or dinner menus and grouped them according to season. Remember: If you already have cooked grains or beans on hand, almost any recipe in this book can be considered a fast meal.

Spring

- *Sweet Sunday Brunch:*
  Goldie's Whole-Grain Pancakes (page 116)
     with homemade applesauce (page 91, Fruit Sauce)
  Tempeh Bacon (page 119)

- *Celebrate Spring Cleaning:*
  Nina's Famous Spring Beet Soup (page 158)
  Mustard Green Salad with Tofu-Dill Dressing (page 196)
  Gingered Lentil Sandwich Spread (page 136)
  whole-grain bread

- *Healthy Southern Comfort:*
  Arame and Black-Eyed Peas with Cilantro (page 170)
  Summer Corn Bread (page 214)
  Creamy Cole Slaw (page 198)

- *Spring into Greens:*
  Cream of Asparagus Soup with Dill (page 149)
  Tempeh Club Sandwiches (page 134)
  Sesame Greens (page 191)

- *Friday Night at Home:*
  Tofu Vegetable Scramble (page 117)
  Abby's Healthy Home Fries (page 118)
  Watercress Salad (page 197) with Sweet Poppyseed Dressing (page 200)

Summer

- *Saturday Morning Camp-out:*
  Orange Hazelnut Muesli (page 111) with fresh strawberries
  Hot Mocha Milk (page 256)

- *Respite from Yardwork:*
  Asian Noodle Salad with Toasted Sesame Dressing (page 131)
  White Beans and Fresh Herbs Soup (page 152)
  cooked and chilled beets

- *Invite a Friend to Lunch:*
  Quick Quinoa Salad (page 132)
  steamed and chilled string beans
  Tofu-Chive Spread (page 138) on whole-grain crackers

- *Picnic with the Kids:*
  Sloppeh Joes (page 181) on whole-wheat buns
  Lemon Basil Potato Salad (page 127)
  steamed fresh peas

- *Backporch Supper:*
  Hiziki Pâté (page 184) on whole-grain crackers
  fresh corn on the cob
  Spinach Salad with Balsamic Vinaigrette (page 201)

Autumn

- *Back to School Bustle:*
  5-Grain Morning Cereal (page 109) with banana slices
  peppermint tea

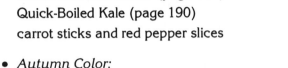

- *Indian Summer Evening:*
  Indian Rice and Lentils (page 162)
  Quick-Boiled Kale (page 190)
  carrot sticks and red pepper slices

- *Autumn Color:*
  Mixed-Vegetable Stir-Fry with Nutty Ginger Drizzle (page 168)
        served over Quinoa (page 82)
  sliced cucumbers with Sesame Vinaigrette (page 124)

- *Hearty Harvest Meal:*
  Peasant Kasha and Potatoes (page 164) with
        Creamy Ginger-Garlic Dressing (page 193)
  Basic Baked Winter Squash (page 206)
  steamed bok choy

- *Stroganoff by the Fire:*
  Tempeh and Red Pepper Stroganoff (page 178)
  Udon noodles (page 85)
  Romaine Radicchio Salad with Lemon-Olive Oil Dressing (page 194)

Winter

- *Baby, It's Cold Outside Breakfast:*
  Warming Miso Soup with Gingerroot (page 115)
  Applesauce Muffins (page 216)

- *Cozy Winter Supper:*
  Golden Mushroom-Basil Soup (page 155)
  Sweet Squash Corn Muffins (page 215)
  Susan's Succulent Supper Salad (page 199)

- *Good Eating before the Meeting:*
  Szechuan Tempeh (page 180) served over Quinoa (page 82)
  steamed broccoli

- *Company's Coming:*
  Japanese Marinated Fish Steak (page 187)
  Potato Gratin (page 204)
  Dark Greens Salad (page 193) with Sweet Poppyseed Dressing (page 200)

- *Rib-Sticking Meal:*
  Curried Lentils and Cauliflower (page 175) served over brown basmati rice
  Cooked Cabbage Salad with Sweet Sesame Dressing (page 195)

Recycling Food Using Leftovers

Plan to have leftover food. Make more than you need. There are many ways to transform leftover whole foods into new forms, new textures, and new tastes. Adding a fresh ingredient to leftovers gives the food new life. Here are some ways to keep rotating food using the recipes in this book.

If you have leftover,	*transform it into:*
Brown rice	Whole-Grain Baby Cereal (page 94)
	Confetti Rice Salad (page 124)
	Dilled Brown Rice and Kidney Beans (page 125)
	Rice Balls Rolled in Sesame Salt (page 133)
	filling for Savory Sandwiches to Go (page 142)
	filling for Grain and Bean Roll-Ups (page 142)
	Rice Bread (page 212)
	Nut Burgers (page 177)
Millet	Whole-Grain Baby Cereal (page 94)
	Millet Croquettes (page 166)
	Mom's Marvelous Veggie Loaf (page 169)
	Orange Millet Raisin Bread (page 213)
	Gracie's Yellow Birthday Cake (page 247)
	Dark Sweet Carob Cupcakes (page 250)
Quinoa	Quick Quinoa Salad (page 132)
	Red Bean and Quinoa Chili (page 163)
	Quinoa Garlic Herb Bread (page 212)

Kidney, Pinto, or Black Beans	finger food for baby
	Dilled Brown Rice and Kidney Beans (page 125)
	Santa Fe Black Bean Salad (page 126)
	filling for Savory Sandwiches to Go (page 142)
	filling for Grain and Bean Roll-Ups (page 142)
	Dark Beans and Sensuous Spices Soup (page 153)
	Mom's Marvelous Veggie Loaf (page 169)
	Mexican Bean and Corn Casserole (page 174)
	Three Sisters Stew (page 172)
	Black Bean Tostadas (page 176)
	garnish for salad
	Bean Apple Rye Bread (page 213)
Baked Winter Squash or Sweet Potato	baby food
	breakfast food
	add to pancakes, breads, cakes, muffins, breakfast cereal
	Pumpkin Muffins (page 217)
	Sweet Squash Corn Muffins (page 215)
	Squash Soup (Winter Squash Variations, page 208)
	Halloween Cookies (page 233)
	Yummy Yam Frosting (page 252)
Quick-Boiled Greens	Cynthia's Hearty Vegetable-Miso Soup (page 148)
	add to Creamy Broccoli Soup (page 156)
	Tofu Kale Supper Pie (page 182)
	Sesame Greens (page 191)
	Cashew-Curry Greens (page 191)
	Dark Greens Salad (page 193)
	use in sandwiches instead of lettuce
Tofu (freshen leftover tofu by boiling in salted water for 30 seconds)	Tofu Mash (page 102)
	Tofu Cubes (page 102)
	Tofu-Chive Spread (page 138)
	Cynthia's Hearty Vegetable-Miso Soup (page 148)
	Hiziki Pâté (page 184)
	Mad Dog Rice Salad (page 130)
	Creamy Ginger-Garlic Dressing (page 193)
	Tofu-Dill Dressing (page 196)
	Tofu Cheesecake (page 244)
	Banana Cream Frosting (page 252)

Leftover food beyond its prime can be fed to the worms in a worm bin.[16] Have you ever seen one? They're great. The worms turn food scraps into rich compost for your vegetable garden, which gives you nutritious produce. Round and round it goes.

Building Community with Whole Foods

Though our lifestyles tend to keep us isolated from one another, we are always striving to be connected and involved. We create churches, schools, babysitting co-ops, support groups, and community gardens in an effort to support each other and share common beliefs.

Here are some ways to create community through food. When the foods chosen are simple, whole foods — those found in nature — we help to create a well-nourished community.

- **Host potlucks on holidays.** Create a core group of families that come together to share meals on holidays or to mark season changes.

- **Update and reestablish the custom of bringing food to families during times of stress.** These include the birth of a child, a death in the family, or illness of a parent of young children. Life brings many occasions, happy and sad, when meal preparation can be a burden.

  The custom needs some updating. Rather than a cooked ham and German chocolate cake, we can give a pot of vegetarian chili, brown-rice salad, or homemade corn bread. Some women in my community would occasionally take turns bringing food to friends who had just had babies. Nina brought food to the new mom on Wednesday. Nancy brought something by on Friday. We might help for two weeks or more this way. The mother was always very grateful.

- **Trade meals with a close friend.** When cooking dinner, make a double recipe of everything and give half of it to a friend's family. Your friend can reciprocate the next week. The regular family cook gets one night off a week!

- **Prepare a wholesome snack with your child's school class.** Ideas include baking bread or muffins, making homemade applesauce, roasting nuts, or simply cutting up fruit and vegetables. Bring plenty of utensils so anyone who wants to can help. This could become something you do regularly with your child's class.

16   Mary Appelhof, *Worms Eat My Garbage* (Kalamazoo, MI: Flower Press, 1982) explains the method.

- **Give wholesome food items as gifts.** This is a way to save money and encourage health. For example:

  - A gift certificate for a gourmet whole foods dinner for four that you will prepare

  - Homemade condiments such as curry paste, sesame salt, tamari-roasted nuts, granola, ghee, home-grown herbs

  - A breakfast basket with Goldie's Whole-Grain Pancake Mix (page 116) and a bottle of Grade A, organic maple syrup

  - A container of homemade soup and a loaf of homemade bread

  - Cookies or sweets made from alternative sweeteners

  - A basket of fresh fruit or vegetables (from your garden?)

- **Organize a food-buying club.** Several families can order large amounts of commonly used natural foods directly from distributors. You'll save big bucks and support each other in healthy eating habits.

- **Support efforts that encourage mothers in your community to nurse their infants at work and in public places.**

- **Boycott candy sales for fund-raising and suggest healthier alternatives.** Set up a "whole-grain, fruit-sweetened" section in bake sales you're involved in.

- **Encourage holding hands and saying a blessing before meals.** This is a good ritual whether the crowd is large or small. Lighting a candle is nice, too. Being grateful for our food increases our awareness of our planet and the living entities we share it with.

• • •

Gathering around food not only builds community, it gives us an opportunity to learn. Becoming conscious about the food we eat brings light to many problems we face in our world. Pollution, violence, overconsumption, and wastefulness are also food issues that apply to each individual inhabiting the planet. Significant changes begin with the individual. Then, like ripples of water, the changes move out and encompass our families, our communities, and our world. Respecting and honoring Mother Earth begins with respecting and honoring ourselves, our children, our neighbors, and even the food on our plates.

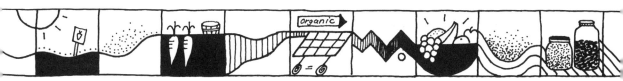

Part II

DOWN-TO-EARTH RECIPES

The recipes in this section are designed to fit a wide variety of ages, tastes, and nutritional needs. The recipes include hints for simple adaptations so you need not cook twice for babies or "picky" eaters. Everyone can benefit from sharing a meal of simple, home-cooked food.

Food is altered in some way by everything it comes into contact with. The energy from our hands as we knead bread and the song we hum as we stir soup become a part of the food we're making. Our bodies respond differently to meals prepared by someone who loves us. A little time spent cooking food is valuable to the well-being of everyone in your home.

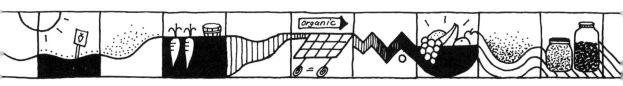

Grain and Bean Basics

Whole Grains

If you're unfamiliar with any of the following grains, see the "Glossary of Ingredients" in the Appendix. For tips on shopping and storage, see "Shopping and Storing Whole Foods," page 35.

Washing

Millet, quinoa, and rice need to be washed prior to cooking to remove chaff, dust, or other debris. Bulgur, couscous, kasha, rolled oats, and polenta do not require rinsing. The best way to wash grains is to place them in a pan with a generous amount of water. Swirl the grains in the water with your hand. As you touch the grain, remember your gratefulness to the Earth for providing this food. Pour off the water through a fine strainer. REPEAT this process until the water you pour off is clear of debris.

Cooking

Don't stir cooking grains. Whole grains create their own steam holes so they cook thoroughly. Stirring them disturbs the steam holes. Whole grains that have been ground and cereals are another matter. They can be stirred occasionally.

A pinch of salt brings out the sweetness in grains; however, it may be omitted.

Bulgur

Bulgur is a good grain for salads or for use as a base with vegetables or beans on top.

1 cup water
Pinch of sea salt
1 cup bulgur

Bring water and salt to a boil in a small pan. Add bulgur. Cover pan and remove from heat. Let stand 10 minutes. Fluff grain with a fork before serving. Add a few drops of oil to the cooked bulgur to keep it loose.

Preparation time: 15 minutes

1 cup water
Pinch of sea salt
1 cup couscous

Bring water and salt to a boil. Add couscous. Cover pan and remove from heat. Let stand 5-10 minutes. Fluff grain with a fork before serving. Stir in a few drops of oil to keep the couscous from clumping.

Preparation time: 15 minutes

Couscous

Couscous is a great grain for salads and stuffings, and an excellent base for vegetables or beans.

1 cup millet
2 - 3 cups water
Pinch of sea salt

Wash millet and drain. REPEAT the rinsing 2 or 3 times. Place millet in a pan and dry-toast it for a nuttier flavor (this is optional). Heat the washed grain in a pot or skillet, stirring constantly until it is toasted dry and gives off a nutty aroma. Add water to toasted millet, 2 cups for a fluffy grain, 3 cups for a creamier grain. Bring water, millet, and salt to a boil; lower heat, cover, and simmer 30-40 minutes, until all the water is absorbed.

Preparation time: 45-50 minutes

Millet

Millet works well for a dinner grain or a breakfast porridge. It can even be used to make a cake. See Dark Sweet Carob Cupcakes, page 250.

2 cups water
Pinch of sea salt
1 cup kasha

Bring water and salt to a boil. Add kasha. Cover pan, reduce heat, and let simmer 15-20 minutes.

Preparation time: 25 minutes

Kasha

Kasha has a hearty, robust flavor.

Oats

Rolled or steel-cut oats
are commonly used
for a breakfast porridge.

1 cup rolled or steel-cut oats
Pinch of sea salt
3 cups water
1/4 cup raisins (optional)
1/2 teaspoon cinnamon (optional)

Place oats in a pot with salt and water; bring to a boil. Reduce heat, cover, and let simmer on low for 20 minutes. Add raisins and cinnamon during the last 10 minutes of cooking if desired.

Preparation time: 25 minutes

Polenta

Polenta is often used
to make tortillas, breads,
and muffins.

2 cups water
Pinch of sea salt
1 cup polenta
1 teaspoon extra-virgin olive oil or butter

Bring water and salt to a boil. Add polenta and oil. Lower heat, stirring constantly. When your stirring spoon can stand on its own (10-15 minutes), lower heat and let simmer, covered, for 25-30 minutes. Spread polenta into an 8-by-8-inch dish. Let cool and slice.

Preparation time: 45 minutes

Quinoa

(keen-wah)

Quinoa cooks quickly and
has a delicious nutty flavor.

1 cup quinoa
Pinch of sea salt
2 cups water

Rinse quinoa well with warm water and drain. Quinoa has a natural coating called saponin that detracts insects and birds. Rinsing with warm water removes saponin, which can create a bitter taste. Place rinsed quinoa, salt, and water in a pot; bring to a boil. Reduce heat to low, cover, and let simmer 15-20 minutes, until all the water is absorbed. Fluff with a fork before serving.

Preparation time: 20-25 minutes

Boiling method:
1 cup brown rice
Pinch of sea salt
1 3/4 - 2 cups water

Rinse and drain rice. Place rice in a pot with salt and water; bring to a boil. Turn heat to low. If you have a gas stove, a "flame-tamer" or "heat diffuser" is handy for keeping a low, even heat. Cover the pan and let the rice simmer for 45-50 minutes or until all the water is absorbed. Don't stir the rice while it is cooking.

Preparation time: 55 minutes

Pressure-cook method:
1 cup brown rice
Pinch of sea salt
1 1/2 cups water

Pressure-cooking makes a chewier rice, which many people find satisfying.

Rinse and drain rice. Place rice, salt, and water in pressure cooker. Close cooker. Place on medium heat and bring up to pressure; you will hear a gentle, steady, hissing sound. Lower heat and time for 35-40 minutes. Remove from heat and allow pressure to come down naturally or by running cold water over the top.

Preparation time: 45 minutes
Servings: 1 cup whole grain yields 2 1/2 - 3 cups
*   cooked grains or 4 servings*

Rice can be used to make salads, breads, burgers, and many other dishes. Long-grain, short-grain, and basmati brown rice can all be prepared by either of these methods.

Whole-Grain Noodles and Pastas

Selecting

Many cooks count on pastas and noodles for quick dinners, but not all noodles are created equal. The usual refined, white-flour noodles have at least two drawbacks: They offer little nutritional value because the grain's nutrient-packed inner germ and fiber-rich outer bran have been removed, and we tend to overeat the fiberless product in an attempt to feel full. Many whole-grain noodles and pastas are on the market; here are some examples and directions on preparation.

Amaranth: Flour is ground out of tiny amaranth seeds to make a variety of pastas including spaghetti.

Artichoke: Artichoke noodles are usually made from a blend of refined or whole-wheat flour and Jerusalem artichoke flour, which is ground from the roots of the Jerusalem artichoke. Look for artichoke noodles that are made with whole-wheat flour. Artichoke noodles come in the standard shapes — angel hair, shells, elbows, and fettuccine.

Brown rice: Many types of pastas and noodles are made from nutritious brown-rice flour. One trade name for a variety of brown-rice pastas is Pastariso. Udon, a popular Japanese noodle, and a favorite of mine, is made from a combination of brown-rice flour and either whole-wheat or refined flour.

Buckwheat: Soba, another traditional Japanese noodle, is made from hearty buckwheat flour. Soba can be made from 100 percent buckwheat flour (which has a strong taste) or a combination of wheat and buckwheat flour.

Corn: A wide variety of noodles and pastas are made from corn flour, including elbows, shells, and spaghetti.

Quinoa: This recently rediscovered, very nutritious grain is used to make a wide gamut of pastas and noodles including flats, elbows, and pagodas.

Sesame rice: Sesame-rice noodles are usually made from 80 percent whole-wheat flour and 10 percent each rice flour and sesame flour, creating a nutty-tasting noodle.

Soy: Soy noodles contain mostly whole-wheat flour with about 10-20 percent soy flour added. This makes for a high-protein pasta.

Spelt: Another recently revived ancient grain, spelt proves to be excellent for making noodles and pasta.

Vegetable: Vegetable pastas are made from a combination of whole or refined wheat and vegetable flours. Shop for the whole-wheat variety. Spinach is the most common; beet, carrot, and tomato paste are also used. Vegetable pastas come in a variety of popular shapes.

Whole wheat: Spaghetti, lasagna, fettuccine, alphabets, and elbows made from hearty whole wheat can be found. Brands vary; find one that cooks up light, not tough.

Basic Noodles and Pasta

6 - 8 quarts water
Pinch of sea salt
Drop of extra-virgin olive oil
8 ounces of any whole-grain noodles or pasta

To prepare whole-grain noodles, choose a pot large enough to give the noodles plenty of room to dance; a 6- or 8-quart pot works well. Bring water to a boil. Add a pinch of salt and a drop of oil; drop the noodles in slowly. To prevent sticking, stir the noodles gently with a wooden spoon for the first few minutes.

Follow package directions for cooking time. Udon noodles take about 7-8 minutes, while whole-wheat noodles can take as long as 12-15 minutes to cook. Whole-grain noodles generally take a bit longer than white noodles. Test noodles for doneness by eating one. You are aiming for a tender, yet firm noodle that is a bit chewy. Put cooked noodles in a colander and rinse well. Let them drain well as excess moisture can lead to mushiness. Toss with a little oil if not serving right away to prevent stickiness.

Servings: 8 ounces of noodles usually serves 4 people

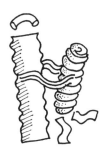

Whole grain pasta with a favorite sauce or dressing makes a quick and healthy meal. Give Karen's Sesame Noodles (page 122) or Asian Noodle Salad (page 131) a whirl on your dinner plate.

Beans

Selecting

Buy beans at a store that has a rapid turnover of dried beans and use them within a few months. Sort through beans bought in bulk and pick out any stones or bits before soaking.

Soaking

The smaller beans, such as peas and lentils, do not require soaking. Bigger beans benefit from being soaked. Soaking reduces cooking time and aids digestibility. Use one of the following methods:

Slow-soak method:
Place 2 cups dried beans in a pot with 4 cups water. Let beans soak for 8 hours.

Quick-soak method:
Place 2 cups dried beans in a pot with 4 cups water; bring to a boil. Turn heat off and let beans soak for 2 hours.

Basic Small Beans

(no soaking)

Azuki beans
Black-eyed peas
Green or brown lentils
Green or yellow split peas
Mung beans
Red lentils

2 cups small dried beans
4 - 5 cups water
2-to-3-inch strip of kombu, soaked in water 5 minutes
1/2 teaspoon sea salt

Rinse and drain beans. Place beans, water, and kombu in a 3- or 4-quart pot; bring to a boil. Reduce heat, cover, and simmer. Most of the smaller beans take 45-50 minutes to cook, except azuki beans, which take an hour, and red lentils, which cook in 20-25 minutes. Don't salt the beans until the end of cooking time.

Preparation time: 30-50 minutes
Servings: 2 cups dried beans make about
6 cups cooked beans

Boiling method:

2 cups dried beans, soaked

6 cups fresh water

3-inch piece of kombu, soaked 5 minutes in cold water

1 teaspoon sea salt

Drain off soaking water. Put soaked beans, fresh water, and kombu in a pot; bring to a boil. Let simmer, covered, until beans are quite tender (55-60 minutes). A bean is well-cooked if you can easily mash it on the roof of your mouth with your tongue. Add water during cooking if needed. Salt beans at the end of cooking time. Salting them earlier will produce tough beans.

Preparation time: 60 minutes

Pressure-cook method:

2 cups dried beans, soaked

4 cups fresh water

3-inch piece of kombu, soaked 5 minutes in cold water

1 teaspoon sea salt

Drain off soaking water. Put soaked beans, fresh water, and kombu in pressure cooker. Attach lid. Bring up to pressure on medium heat. You should hear a soft hissing sound. Lower heat and let beans cook 40-45 minutes. Remove from heat and allow pressure to come down naturally, or run cold water over the top of the cooker. Add salt after cooking.

Preparation time: 45-50 minutes

Slow-cook method:

Using an electric slow cooker allows you to sleep or work while your beans cook. Follow the basic instructions for boiled or pressure-cooked beans for soaking and preparing beans, then follow the directions that apply to your slow cooker. This typically requires 8 hours on high heat. A thick folded towel on top of the lid helps conserve heat.

Preparation time: About 8 hours
Servings: 2 cups dried beans make about
6 cups cooked beans

Basic Big Beans

(soaking required)

Black beans
Cannellini beans
Chick-peas (garbanzos)
Christmas limas
Great northern beans
Kidney beans
Lima beans
Navy beans
Pinto beans
Swedish brown beans

Pressure-cooking is my favorite way to cook beans. It gives the beans a creamy texture and a deep flavor not possible with boiling. And the cooking time is reduced.

Reducing Gas

Raffinose sugars in beans are responsible for producing digestive gases. Here are some tips on reducing these sugars in beans.

- Soak beans overnight and replace the soaking water with fresh water for cooking.

- Cook beans with a piece of kombu seaweed. Kombu contains glutamic acid which acts as a natural bean tenderizer. The kombu also adds vitamins and minerals, especially trace minerals, to any dish it is cooked with.

- Adding 2 Tablespoons of the herb winter savory or 4 Tablespoons of the Mexican herb epazote to beans as they cook reduces the effects of raffinose sugars.

- Let beans cook slowly for a long period of time so they are very tender. Can you easily mash the bean on the roof of your mouth?

- Don't add baking soda to soaking water. It destroys nutrients and affects the food's flavor and texture.

- Eat more beans. You can expect a digestive adjustment when beans are new to the diet. Eat small amounts frequently and allow the body to get used to digesting them.

- Improve your overall digestion. Chew foods slowly and thoroughly. Avoid washing foods down with liquids. Eat fewer kinds of foods at the same meal (good-bye smorgasbord). Drink plenty of water between meals.

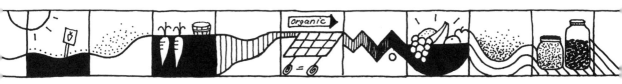

Homemade Baby Foods

Safety in Serving and Storing Homemade Baby Foods

- Before using any equipment to prepare baby food, wash it with hot water and soap.

- Never serve your baby food hot off the stove. Room temperature or slightly warm is fine. You have a hungry baby, but cereal's too hot? Stir it with an ice cube for quick cooling.

- Microwaving sometimes heats food unevenly. This can create "hot spots" in the food or bottle that can burn your baby's mouth. Use caution if microwaving or avoid it.

- If you've made a large batch of food, remove a small portion to a separate dish to serve your baby.

- Discard leftover food that has had spoon-to-mouth contact.

- Store leftovers that have not had spoon-to-mouth contact in the refrigerator and use within two or three days.

- Freeze extra pureed food in ice-cube trays. Frozen cubes can then be stored in the freezer in plastic bags. For a quick meal, place a cube or two of frozen food in a small dish and heat in a covered pan of boiling water. Use frozen baby food within four weeks.

- Store ground grains for cereals in sterile jars in the refrigerator or freezer (canning jars or jelly jars work fine).

- Label all stored foods.

New Eater Recipes

The following recipes are for the baby who is just starting to eat solid foods:

- **Summer Fruit Puree**

- **Fruit Sauce**

- **Sweet Vegetable Puree**

- **Green Vegetable Puree**

- **Whole-Grain Baby Cereal**

- **New Eater Combinations**

Choose one: (Select very ripe fruit.)
Apricot
Avocado
Banana
Melon
Nectarine
Papaya
Peach
Persimmon
Watermelon

Pit, peel, and discard any seeds. Either mash the fruit with a fork, run it through a baby-food grinder, or give it a quick whir in a blender. Stir in a little water or breast milk if the mixture seems too thick. Do not freeze this dish as the fruit may turn brown.

Preparation time: 2-3 minutes
Servings: Depends on size and type of fruit

Summer Fruit Puree

No cooking!
Most of the fruits best for pureeing are in season in the summer, though many can be purchased year-round. They are fruits you would probably keep around for the whole family.

Choose one:
Apple
Blueberry (remember a bib!)
Cherry
Pear
Plum

Use 1 cup water per 1/4 cup cut-up fruit. Peel and slice apples, pears, or plums. Remove pits and stems from cherries. Place cut-up fruit and water in a pot; bring to a boil. Reduce heat and simmer until fruit is tender and water has cooked off (about 15 minutes). Puree in a blender.

For children and adults: Keep skin on fruit if it is organic. Season fruit sauce with cinnamon and nutmeg. Serve fruit sauce on pancakes, whole-grain cereals, with granola, or by itself.

Preparation time: 20 minutes
Servings: 1 cup fruit yields about 1 cup fruit sauce

Fruit Sauce

By cooking and pureeing the firmer fruits, you can create wonderful fruit sauces that everyone in your family can enjoy. In addition to the old favorite, applesauce, experiment with newer versions such as pear sauce or plum sauce.

Sweet Vegetable Puree

Choose one:
Acorn squash
Baking potatoes
Buttercup squash
Butternut squash
Carrots
Delicata squash
New potatoes
Parsnips
Rutabaga
Sweet potato

Scrub vegetables with a vegetable brush and water.

Baking method:
Preheat oven to 400 degrees F. Cut squashes in half lengthwise and scoop out seeds. Potatoes and yams can be left whole; cut carrots into large chunks. Place vegetables in a baking dish, squash halves face down, and bake for 1 hour or until tender when pierced with a fork. Scoop meat of the vegetable out with a spoon and place in a baby-food grinder or blender with a little water, breast milk, or formula; blend until smooth.

Steaming method:
Cut the scrubbed vegetables into large slices or chunks. Scoop seeds out of squashes. Put steamer basket and water to bottom of basket in a large pot. Add vegetable peelings to steaming water for extra flavor and nutrients if desired. Bring water to a boil. Place vegetable chunks in steamer basket and cover with a lid. Lower heat and steam for about 25 minutes, until vegetable is tender when pierced with a fork. Scoop meat of the vegetable out with a spoon if not peeled beforehand. Complete puree as in baking method.

For children and adults: Pureed sweet vegetables are great. Season with a little cinnamon and nutmeg.

Preparation time: 65 minutes for baking,
  30 minutes for steaming
Servings: Depends on size and number of vegetables used

I used sweet potato for my daughter, Gracie's, first solid food, and it is a favorite food of hers to this day.

Choose one:
Fresh or frozen peas
Green beans or string beans
Zucchini
Avocado (optional)

Wash vegetables. If using zucchini, cut it into slices. Break off the ends of string beans. Put steamer basket and water to bottom of basket in a pot. Bring water to a boil. Place vegetables in steamer basket and cover pot with a lid. Lower heat and steam vegetables until tender (3-5 minutes). Put vegetables and a little of the steaming water in a blender; blend until smooth. If your baby likes avocado, toss a slice or two in the blender with the steamed vegetable to produce a creamy consistency.

Preparation time: 7 minutes
Servings: Depends on amount of vegetables used

Green Vegetable Puree

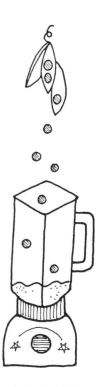

Compare the color of baby food made from fresh green vegetables to commercial baby food in a jar and you'll know why homemade is best.

Whole-Grain Baby Cereal

Choose one:
1 cup brown rice
1 cup hulled barley (not pearled)
1 cup millet
1 cup sweet brown rice
1 cup whole oats
1 cup whole spelt

To toast grain:

Toast grains for better digestibility and flavor. Place grains in a fine strainer; rinse and drain. Toast grains in one of two ways:

Oven toasting:
Preheat oven to 350 degrees F. Spread grains on a cookie sheet and toast in oven until they give off a nutty aroma (12-15 minutes).

Skillet toasting:
Place washed grains in a large skillet on burner and toast on medium heat, stirring constantly, until grains give off nutty aroma (about 5-8 minutes).

Let toasted grains cool and store in sealed container. You can toast a big batch of several different grains at one time and store them in separate jars. This will keep your baby and everyone in your family full of wholesome cereal for many moons.

To grind grain:

For optimum nutrition, grind the grains in a small electric grinder or food processor just prior to using. Once a grain is ground it begins to lose nutritional value within 24 to 48 hours. Store the whole toasted grains in labeled, sealed containers and grind the amount you need before cooking.

To cook ground grains into cereal:

Baby-size portion of cereal:[17]
Mix together 2-3 Tablespoons ground cereal and 1/2 - 3/4 cups water in a small pot; bring to a boil. Reduce heat to low and simmer, covered for 5 minutes.

Family-size portion of cereal:
Use 1/3 cup ground cereal and 1 cup water per person. Combine cereal and water in a pot; bring to a boil. Reduce heat to low and simmer, covered, for 10-12 minutes. Using a flame-tamer or heat deflector while simmering helps prevent scorching or sticking.

For children and adults: Top plain cooked cereal with a little maple syrup, apple butter, date sugar, fruit sauce, or dried fruit puree. Fresh fruit and a sprinkle of granola make another nice topping.

Preparation time: 8-15 minutes for toasting,
    5-12 minutes for cooking cereal
Servings: 1 cup toasted grains cook into 8 baby-size
    portions or 4 child- or adult-size portions of cereal

Grains are the staple food of people everywhere. Making your own baby cereal is nutritious, economical, and quite delicious. In fact, I don't like calling this food "baby cereal" because this cereal is for everyone.

17   Whole-grain baby cereal can also be made by taking an already cooked whole grain and pureeing it in a blender with a little water.

New Eater Combinations

Once you have a repertoire of single foods that work for your baby, you can combine them into dynamic duos. The variations are endless. Find some partners that dance together well for you and your baby. Here are a few to start you thinking:

Apple and blueberry sauce
Apple and fig sauce
Baked apple and rutabaga puree
Banana and prune puree
Buttercup squash and parsnip puree
Delicata squash and sweet brown-rice cereal
Dried apricot puree and brown-rice cereal
Green-bean puree and millet cereal
Green-pea and brown-rice puree
Mashed sweet potatoes and pear sauce
Nectarine puree and barley cereal
Peach puree and oat cereal
Plum puree and millet cereal
Potato and carrot puree
Sweet brown-rice and oat cereal
Zucchini and avocado puree

Experienced Eater Recipes

The following recipes are for the baby who has been eating solids for three to four months:

- **Nut Milks**

- **Combination Cereals**

- **Winter Fruit Puree**

- **Split Pea Delight**

- **Red Lentils and Butternut Squash**

- **Tofu Cubes**

- **Tofu Mash**

- **Big Bean Puree**

Almond Sesame Milk

1/4 cup almonds
1/4 cup sesame seeds
2 cups water
1 Tablespoon barley malt or brown-rice syrup

Almond Cashew Milk

1/4 cup almonds
1/4 cup cashews
2 cups water
3 pitted dates

Nut Butter Milk

2 Tablespoons almond, sesame, or peanut butter
2 cups water
1 Tablespoon brown-rice syrup

For each recipe, place all items in a blender and blend until smooth. For milks using whole nuts or seeds (Almond Sesame Milk and Almond Cashew Milk), pour the contents of the blender through a fine strainer lined with cheesecloth to remove nut pulp. Pick up the ends of the cheesecloth and squeeze pulp to get all the milk. Nut milk can be kept in the refrigerator for a couple of days, although it may separate and need to be reblended.

For children and adults: You can toss some fresh fruit in a blender with some nut milk and make a nutty fruit shake.

Preparation time: 3-5 minutes
Servings: 2 cups

Nut milks, a nutritious and versatile group of foods, taste good on cereals or fruit desserts. You can also use them to replace cow's milk in a recipe.

Combination Cereals

Sweet Rice-Sesame Cereal

1 cup brown rice

1 cup sweet brown rice

1/2 cup whole oats

1/2 cup sesame seeds

Almond Millet Cereal

1 cup millet

1 cup brown rice

1 cup almonds

Barley Oat-Pumpkin Seed Cereal

1 cup hulled barley

1 cup whole oats

1/2 cup sweet brown rice

1/2 cup pumpkin seeds

Super Iron-Fortified Cereal

Dulse, millet, amaranth, and quinoa are all rich in iron, especially dulse.

1 1/2 cup millet

1 cup amaranth or quinoa

1/2 cup sunflower seeds

3 Tablespoons dulse flakes

To toast grain:

Place all grains, nuts, and seeds in a fine strainer; rinse and drain. Dulse does not need to be toasted, but can be added when cooking cereal. Toast grains, nuts, and seeds in one of two ways:

Oven toasting:
Preheat oven to 350 degrees F. Spread grains on a cookie sheet and toast in oven until they give off a nutty aroma (12-15 minutes).

Skillet toasting:
Place washed grains in a large skillet on burner and toast on medium heat, stirring constantly, until grains give off a nutty aroma (5-8 minutes).

Let toasted grains cool and store in sealed container. You can toast a big batch of several different grains at one time and store them in separate jars.

To grind grain:

For the best nutrition, grind grains just prior to using in a small electric grinder or food processor. Once a grain is ground it begins to lose nutritional value within 24 to 48 hours. Store the whole toasted grains in labeled, sealed containers and grind the amount you need before cooking.

To cook ground grains into cereal:

Baby-size portion of cereal:
Mix together 2-3 Tablespoons ground cereal and 1/2 - 3/4 cups water in a small pot; bring to a boil. Reduce heat to low and simmer, covered, for 5 minutes.

Family-size portion of cereal:
Use 1/3 cup ground cereal and 1 cup water per person. Combine cereal and water in a pot; bring to a boil. Reduce heat to low and simmer, covered, for 10-12 minutes. Using a flame-tamer or heat deflector used while simmering helps prevent scorching or sticking.

For children and adults: Top plain cooked cereal with a little maple syrup, apple butter, date sugar, fruit sauce, or dried fruit puree. Fresh fruit and a sprinkle of granola make another nice topping.

Preparation time: 25-30 minutes
Servings: Makes 3 cups dry cereal, which yields
*   9 adult servings or 12-15 baby-size portions*

With the addition of a few ground nuts and seeds, you can create many delicious combination cereals.

Winter Fruit Puree

Choose one:
1/4 cup dried apples
1/4 cup dried apricots
1/4 cup dried peaches
1/4 cup dried pears
1/4 cup figs
1/4 cup prunes

Noncooking method:
Soak dried fruit overnight in 1 cup water. Remove fruit from soaking water and reserve water. Cut fruit into smaller pieces and puree in a blender or food processor, adding some soaking water if necessary to get a smooth consistency.

Cooking method:
Place 1 cup water per 1/4 cup dried fruit in a small pan; bring to a boil. Reduce heat and simmer about 20 minutes or until liquid has been absorbed. Blend in a blender until smooth. Add a little additional water if necessary.

For children and adults: Use as a topping for cereal, pancakes, crackers, breads, or muffins. Purees of dried fruits also make wonderful alternative sweeteners in recipes. Use extra dried fruit puree to sweeten breads, cakes, cookies, and other goodies. See "Adapting Recipes that Contain Sugar," page 228.

Preparation time: 5 minutes for noncooking method,
   25 minutes for cooking method
Servings: Makes 1/3 cup

Cold weather yields less fresh fruit, and we naturally turn to dried fruits. The sweetness is more concentrated in dried fruits, so serve it in small amounts.

1/4 cup dried green split peas
1/2 carrot, sliced
1 1/4 cups water
1/4 sheet toasted nori

Wash peas and scrub carrot. Put peas, carrot, and water in a small pan; bring to a boil. Reduce heat and simmer, covered, for 20-30 minutes. Puree in a blender with nori.

For children and adults: Quadruple the recipe, remove a portion to puree for your baby, and then add sautéed garlic, onions, and celery to the remainder for family lunch or dinner.

Preparation time: 30-35 minutes
Servings: Makes a little over a cup or 4-5 baby servings

Split Pea Delight

Split peas have a mild, sweet flavor that babies like. Introduce the mineral-rich sea vegetable nori with this simple recipe.

1/4 cup dried red lentils
1/2 cup butternut squash,
    peeled and cut into small chunks
1 1/2 cups water
1 Tablespoon chopped parsley

Wash and drain lentils. Put lentils, squash, and water in a small pan; bring to a boil. Reduce heat and simmer, covered, for 25-30 minutes. Puree in a blender with parsley.

For children and adults: Quadruple the recipe, remove a portion to puree for your baby, and then add sautéed garlic, onions, and curry powder to the remainder.

Preparation time: 35 minutes
Servings: Makes 1 1/2 cups or 6 baby servings

Red Lentils and Butternut Squash

This is a sweet, golden-orange entrée for your baby. Any type of winter squash works in this recipe; sweet potato also suffices.

Tofu Cubes

Children of all ages like to munch on these bouncy little cubes, which little hands can easily pick up. Boiling the cubes changes the texture and helps the cube retain its shape.

1/2 pound tofu

Fill a medium-size pan with water and bring to a boil. Cut tofu into 1/2-inch cubes. Drop into boiling water. When cubes rise to the surface (about a minute), remove them with a strainer and let cool.

For children and adults: Add tofu cubes to salads or stir-frys.

Preparation time: 5 minutes
Servings: Makes 32-40 cubes

Tofu Mash

This quick and easy mixture makes a wonderful base for creating a tasty sandwich spread.

1/4 pound tofu
1 teaspoon tahini

Mash tofu in a small bowl with a fork. Add tahini and mash again, mixing thoroughly.

For children and adults: Double the recipe, remove part for your baby, then add sliced scallion and 1/2 teaspoon tamari to the remainder. Blend together and use as a sandwich spread.

Preparation time: 3 minutes
Servings: Makes 1/3 cup

Big Bean Puree

2 cups dried big beans (select from the list on page 87)
Fresh water
3-inch piece of kombu, soaked 5 minutes in cold water

Sort through beans and pick out any stones. Soak dried beans overnight in 4 cups water, or bring beans to a boil in 4 cups water and soak for 2 hours. Drain off soaking water and put soaked beans, fresh water, and kombu in a pot. Cook beans by boiling, pressure-cooking, or slow-cooking according to directions on page 87. Be sure that beans for baby are very tender. Do not add any salt.

Puree a small amount of plain, cooked beans in a blender to serve your baby. Some babies can handle beans that have simply been mashed with a fork. For variety, puree or mash beans with cooked carrot, squash, sweet potato, or cooked grains.

For children and adults: Add spices and salt after removing part for your baby.

Preparation time: 60 minutes for boiling,
    45 minutes for pressure-cooking
Servings: 2 cups dried beans make about
    6 cups cooked beans

Add protein to the experienced eater's diet by serving small amounts of well-cooked beans. Use the ample leftovers to create soups, stews, burritos, chili, or other hearty dishes for the whole family.

Ideas for Finger Foods

Around the time babies start walking, they become interested in picking up food with their own hands and feeding themselves. Use your judgment about what your baby can handle. Stay within earshot when experimenting with finger foods. These snacks are generally okay for babies 1 year old and up:

- Chopped vegetables steamed until soft (carrots, peas, zucchini, etc.)
- Cooked whole grains
- Crispy Cakes (a commercial rice cracker that melts in the mouth)
- Dried fruit (soak it in water to make it softer)
- Nori (tear into small pieces; it melts in the mouth)
- Oatios, brown-rice crispies, whole-grain flakes, or other high-quality dry cereals
- Pieces of baked or boiled potato (white or sweet)
- Pieces of baked or steamed squash
- Pieces of ripe peach, nectarine, banana, plum, or melon
- Pieces of steamed apple or pear
- Tofu (cooked in cubes or mashed with a fork)
- Well-cooked beans
- Whole-grain bread, whole-wheat pita
- Whole-grain noodles or pasta

Foods Babies Often Choke On

When trying any new snack, be sure your baby is within eyesight and earshot so you can quickly help if a problem develops. Children should sit when eating; choking most often occurs when they are walking or running. To prevent accidents, never give the following foods to babies under 1 year old:

- Apple chunks or slices
- Dry cereal
- Grapes
- Hard candy
- Hard cookies
- Hot dogs (even tofu dogs)
- Meat chunks
- Peanut butter or other nut butter sandwiches
- Popcorn
- Potato chips
- Raw carrot sticks or slices
- Rice cakes
- Whole-corn kernels
- Whole nuts and seeds
- Whole or unseeded berries

"Not-So-Good" Food for Babies

Caffeine. Caffeine is a stimulant, not a food. Soft drinks and cocoa not only contain sugar; they have as much caffeine as coffee. Caffeine can cause elevated blood sugar and stimulate the heart and lungs. This kind of stimulation can be detrimental for babies.

Chemical Additives. Avoid aspartame, saccharin, other artificial sweeteners, BHT, artificial flavors and colors, MSG, nitrates, and other additives. The effect of chemical additives on adults is not entirely known. There certainly can be no benefit to introducing these chemicals into your baby's immature system. Read labels.

Chocolate. Chocolate products almost always contain sugar and caffeine. Chocolate can also be a severe allergen. It is inappropriate for children under 2 years old and should be used sparingly thereafter.

Common Allergens. Wheat, citrus, cow's milk products, corn, and egg whites are common allergens. Many health-care practitioners advise omitting these foods from your baby's diet. Hold off for the first year and then experiment. It is always best to rotate common food allergens, serving them once every three to five days.

Cow's Milk. Cow's milk is not appropriate for babies under 1 year old. It can cause bleeding of the intestines, resulting in iron-deficiency anemia.

Raw Honey. Uncooked honey sometimes contains botulism toxins in amounts that are detrimental to infants. Barley malt, brown-rice syrup, or fruit concentrate can be substituted for honey.

Salt. Heavily salted foods can stress your baby's immature kidneys and interfere with your baby's natural appetite. Sufficient salt (sodium) is readily available in many foods in their natural state.

Sugar. A prime source of empty calories, sugar has almost no nutritive value. Eating large amounts of sugary foods can displace more nutritional foods, resulting in vitamin and mineral deficiencies. Refined sugar consumption has been linked with tooth decay, heart disease, arteriosclerosis, diabetes, obesity, learning difficulties, and behavior problems. Why let your baby develop a taste for it?

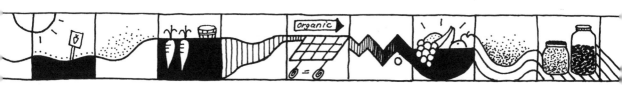

Bustling Breakfasts

Ancient Grain Raisin Cereal

Toasted cereal mix:

1 cup hulled barley
1 cup millet
1/2 cup sesame seeds
1 cup whole oats
1 cup polenta
1 cup amaranth

Place barley, millet, sesame seeds, and oats in fine strainer; rinse with water and drain. Toast barley, millet, sesame seeds, and oats with polenta and amaranth in one of two ways:

Oven toasting:
Preheat oven to 350 degrees F. Spread grains on cookie sheet and toast in oven until they give off a nutty aroma (12-15 minutes).

Skillet toasting:
Place washed grains in large skillet on burner and toast on medium heat, stirring constantly, until grains give off nutty aroma (5-8 minutes). Let toasted grains cool. Store in a sealed container.

To cook cereal:

1 cup toasted cereal mix
1/3 cup raisins
3 cups water
Pinch of sea salt

Grind toasted cereal mix in a small electric grinder or food processor. Combine ground cereal, raisins, water, and salt in a small pan. Stir constantly as you bring to a boil. Turn heat to low, cover, and let simmer 10-15 minutes. Stir frequently to prevent sticking.

For experienced eaters: Omit salt when cooking cereal.

Preparation time: 15-20 minutes for toasting,
*   15 minutes for cooking cereal*
Servings: Makes 5 1/2 cups dry cereal mix;
*   1 cup dry mix makes 4 servings cooked cereal*

These grains meld to make a creamy cereal with an earthy flavor. I like the recipe because it doesn't use wheat, a grain many of us tend to overuse.

5-Grain Morning Cereal

Toasted cereal mix:

1 cup wheat berries

1 cup millet

1 cup spelt

1 cup brown rice

1 cup quinoa

Place all grains in a fine strainer; rinse and drain. Toast grains in one of two ways:

Oven toasting:
Preheat oven to 350 degrees F. Spread grains on cookie sheet and toast in oven until they give off a nutty aroma (12-15 minutes).

Skillet toasting:
Place washed grains in large skillet on burner and toast on medium heat, stirring constantly, until grains give off nutty aroma (5-8 minutes). Let toasted grains cool and store in sealed container.

To cook cereal:

1 cup toasted cereal mix

3 cups water

Pinch of sea salt

Grind toasted cereal mix in a small electric grinder. Combine ground cereal, water, and salt in a small pan. Stir constantly and bring to a boil. Turn heat to low, cover, and simmer 10-15 minutes. Stir occasionally to prevent sticking.

For experienced eaters: Omit salt when cooking cereal.

Preparation time: 15 minutes for toasting,
*   15-20 minutes for cooking cereal*
Servings: Makes 5 cups dry cereal mix;
*   1 cup dry mix makes 4 servings cooked cereal*

I keep a canister of these five grains mixed together. In the morning, I grind a cup of the grains and cook the freshly ground grains into this nutritious cereal.

Steel-Cut Oats with Dates and Cinnamon

Steel-cut oats have a heartier flavor than rolled oats and can be "dressed up" in any number of ways.

1 cup steel-cut oats
3 cups water
4 pitted dates, cut into small pieces
1/2 teaspoon cinnamon
1/8 teaspoon sea salt

Place all ingredients in medium-size pan and stir briefly; bring to a boil. Reduce heat to low, cover, and simmer for 15 minutes.

For new or experienced eaters: Omit dates, cinnamon, and salt; briefly puree cooked cereal before serving.

Preparation time: 20 minutes
Servings: Makes 4-6 servings

Peaches 'n' Millet

One summer morning, we added ripe peaches to millet and the combination became a favorite. When the season for fresh fruit unfolds, try apricots, pears, or plums. Yummy!

3/4 cup millet
1 peach, sliced (or other seasonal fruit)
2 cups water
Pinch of sea salt

Topping:
Unsweetened apple butter

Place millet in fine strainer; rinse and drain. Combine millet, fruit, water, and salt in a 2-quart saucepan; bring to a boil. Cover and simmer on low for 20-25 minutes (until all water is absorbed). Serve in bowls with dollops of apple butter on top.

For new or experienced eaters: Omit salt; puree and serve.

Preparation time: 30 minutes
Servings: Makes 4 servings

Variation: Orange 'n' Millet with Currants
Substitute 1 cup orange juice for 1 cup water and use 1/4 cup currants instead of peach.

Orange Hazelnut Muesli

2 cups rolled oats or rolled barley (or some of both)
1/3 cup hazelnuts, chopped
1/3 cup raisins
1/2 teaspoon cinnamon
2 cups boiling water
Juice of 2 oranges

Optional toppings:
Dollop of plain yogurt
Grated apple
Sliced pears

Place grain, nuts, raisins, and cinnamon in mixing bowl. Pour boiling water over mixture and stir. Juice oranges; add juice to mixture and stir again. Cover bowl with plate or cloth and allow moisture to soften grains overnight. Serve topped with apple, pear, and/or yogurt.

For children: Some may prefer a plainer muesli. Omit nuts and raisins, and let those who wish add them as toppings in the morning.

*Preparation time: 10 minutes
    (excluding overnight soaking)
Servings: Makes 4 servings*

Muesli is handy for camping trips and hurried breakfasts. Preparing rolled oats this way gives them a slightly different texture you'll enjoy.

Nut and Seed Granola

3 cups rolled oats
1/2 cup sesame seeds
1/2 cup sunflower seeds
1/2 cup pumpkin seeds
1/2 cup almonds, chopped
1 cup whole-wheat pastry flour
1/2 teaspoon cinnamon
Pinch of sea salt

1/3 cup cold-pressed vegetable oil
1/3 cup brown-rice syrup or maple syrup
1/4 cup apple or orange juice
1 teaspoon vanilla extract
1/4 teaspoon almond extract

Preheat oven to 300 degrees F. In a large mixing bowl, combine oats, seeds, almonds, flour, cinnamon, and salt; mix well.

In a separate bowl, combine oil, syrup, juice, and extracts. Slowly pour wet ingredients over dry ingredients, using a spatula to fold and evenly coat the dry mixture with the wet. Spread on a cookie sheet or in a shallow pan and bake. Turn granola every 15 or 20 minutes so it toasts evenly. Bake until granola is dry and golden (45-60 minutes). Store in airtight jar.

Preparation time: 70 minutes
Servings: Makes 8 cups

To keep granola within the limits of a "low-fat" diet, use it as a topping on hot cereal, fresh fruit, or puddings. Homemade granola makes a quick snack for children on the move.

2 teaspoons unrefined sesame oil or ghee
1 small onion, chopped
1 clove garlic, minced
Pinch of sea salt
1 cup kasha
2 cups boiling water
1/4 cup chopped parsley

Optional toppings:
Tahini
Tamari or shoyu

Heat oil in a 2-quart pan or 10-inch skillet. Add onion, garlic, and salt; sauté until onion is soft. Add kasha to onion mixture and stir well. Add boiling water, reduce heat to low, cover, and allow to set for 15 minutes. Remove lid, add parsley, and fluff before serving. Top each serving with a small bit of tahini and/or tamari if desired.

Preparation time: 20 minutes
Servings: Makes 4-6 servings

Kasha for Breakfast

The versatile kasha (roasted buckwheat) need not be reserved for dinner. I've eaten at a Ukrainian restaurant on New York's Lower East Side that serves kasha and eggs to large breakfast crowds.

Jam-Filled Mochi

The pounded sweet brown-rice product called mochi makes a warm, chewy, quick-to-fix breakfast treat. Mochi comes in several flavors and plain, but cinnamon-raisin mochi is the breakfast favorite at our home.

1 block mochi
All-fruit jam or preserves (your favorite flavor)

Preheat oven to 400 degrees F. Break mochi into squares. The block is usually scored so that it can be broken easily into 2-by-2-inch squares. Place squares on cookie sheet and put in oven. Bake until mochi puffs up (10-12 minutes). Remove from oven. Open each square and slip a teaspoon or 2 of jam inside. Serve immediately.

Preparation time: 15 minutes
Servings: Makes 6 mochi squares

Sprouted Essene Bread[18] and Fresh Fruit

One of my favorite warm-weather breakfasts is a thick slice of Essene bread warmed in the oven and served with a bowl of fresh fruit.

4 1-inch slices of Essene bread
4 - 6 cups fresh, seasonal fruit
    (blueberries, strawberries, peaches, etc.)

Heat oven to 300 degrees F. Place bread slices on cookie sheet and warm in oven for 5-10 minutes. Serve warm bread with bowl of fruit.

For experienced eaters: Serve as is.

Preparation time: 12-15 minutes
Servings: Makes 4 servings

---

18   The Essenes were a Jewish monastic brotherhood in biblical times who prepared a sweet, moist, flourless bread by slow-cooking sprouted wheat. For more information about this now commercially made bread, see the "Glossary of Ingredients."

4-inch piece of wakame
6 cups water
1 Tablespoon grated gingerroot
1/4 pound firm tofu, cut into cubes
4 Tablespoons light or white miso

Garnish:
2 scallions, thinly sliced

Place wakame in small bowl of water and soak for 5 minutes. Put 6 cups water in 3-quart pot and bring to a simmer. Remove wakame from water and chop into small pieces, removing the spine. Add chopped wakame to soup. Simmer 10 minutes, adding gingerroot and tofu cubes in the last minute or 2 of cooking time. Pour a bit of broth into each serving bowl and dissolve 1 Tablespoon miso into each bowl. Fill bowl with soup and stir gently. Garnish each bowl with scallions.

Preparation time: 15 minutes
Servings: Makes 4 servings

Warming Miso Soup with Gingerroot

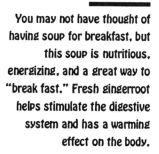

You may not have thought of having soup for breakfast, but this soup is nutritious, energizing, and a great way to "break fast." Fresh gingerroot helps stimulate the digestive system and has a warming effect on the body.

Goldie's Whole-Grain Pancake Mix

This basic pancake mix comes from Goldie Caughlan, nutrition educator at Puget Consumers' Co-op in Seattle. The beauty of this mix is that it works equally well for waffles, a Sunday tradition at our house.

Pancake mix:
1 1/2 cups buckwheat flour
1 1/2 cups barley flour
1 1/2 cups whole-wheat pastry flour
1/2 cup cornmeal
1/2 cup nutritional yeast (optional)
1/2 cup dry powdered buttermilk or powdered soy milk
2 Tablespoons + 1 teaspoon baking powder

Combine all ingredients and store in an airtight container.

To make pancakes or waffles:
2 cups pancake mix
2 1/2 cups water

Use whisk to mix ingredients well. Cook on hot, lightly oiled griddle.

For children: Fill a squeeze bottle with batter and squeeze out letters or shapes on the griddle to delight your child.

Preparation time: 20 minutes
Servings: Makes 6 cups dry mix;
2 cups dry mix yields 10 pancakes

Blueberry Sauce

This topping tastes great on pancakes, waffles, or hot cereal, and also makes a beautiful finishing touch for the Tofu Cheesecake (page 244) or Gracie's Yellow Birthday Cake (page 247).

2 Tablespoons kuzu[19]
1 cup fruit juice (apple or berry)
1 cup blueberries (fresh or frozen)
2 Tablespoons concentrated fruit sweetener
1 teaspoon freshly squeezed lemon juice

Dissolve kuzu in fruit juice. Put in small pan with berries and sweetener. Use medium heat and bring mixture to a simmer, stirring constantly. Cook for about 3 minutes, until mixture turns clear and purple. Remove from heat, add lemon juice, stir, and serve immediately.

Preparation time: 10 minutes
Servings: Makes 2 cups

---

19   Kuzu is a natural thickening agent that comes from the dried root of the kuzu plant.

2 - 3 teaspoons extra-virgin olive oil

1/2 medium onion, chopped

2 cloves garlic, minced

1 scallion, finely chopped

1/2 red pepper, chopped

1/2 cup finely chopped red cabbage

1 teaspoon cumin

1/2 teaspoon coriander

1 pound firm tofu

2 teaspoons turmeric

1 Tablespoon tamari or shoyu

2 Tablespoons chopped parsley

Tofu Vegetable Scramble

Place oil in a 10-inch skillet on medium heat. Add onion, garlic, and scallion; sauté for several minutes. Add red pepper, cabbage, cumin, and coriander; continue to sauté until vegetables are soft. Crumble tofu into skillet with vegetables and stir. Sprinkle turmeric over top and mix well. Add tamari and parsley; stir again. Serve warm.

For experienced eaters: Use extra tofu and make Tofu Mash or Tofu Cubes (page 102).

Preparation time: 15-20 minutes
Servings: Makes 6 servings

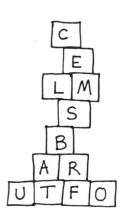

This colorful dish goes well served with Abby's Healthy Home Fries (page 118) and whole-grain toast for a big Sunday breakfast. Any vegetable can be substituted for the ones listed; however, this combination is scrumptious.

Abby's Healthy Home Fries

4 - 6 small red potatoes
1/4 teaspoon paprika
1/4 teaspoon sea salt
Freshly ground pepper
1 - 2 teaspoons butter, melted (optional)

Preheat oven to 350 degrees F. Scrub potatoes and slice into 1/4-inch rounds. Place on a lightly oiled baking sheet. Sprinkle with paprika, salt, and pepper. Bake 30 minutes. Lightly brush potato slices with melted butter during last 5 minutes of baking if desired.

For new or experienced eaters: Reserve some plain baked or boiled potato. Blend or mash with breast milk or water.

Preparation time: 25-30 minutes
Servings: Makes 4 servings

Variation: Light Home Fries

Scrub potatoes and cut into bite-size chunks. Bring a large pot of water to a boil, add potatoes, and simmer until tender (10-15 minutes). Pour off hot water and add fresh, cold water to stop cooking. Place 1 Tablespoon butter or oil in a 10-inch skillet on medium heat. Drain potatoes and place in preheated skillet. Add salt, paprika, and pepper. Turn potatoes several times and let them brown for 5 minutes.

Just about everybody loves fried spuds. My friend Margaret shared this healthy version of fries that is a favorite of her daughter, Abby.

2 - 4 Tablespoons cold-pressed canola oil
1 8-ounce package tempeh, cut into 1/4-inch strips
1/2 teaspoon oregano
1/2 teaspoon thyme
1/2 teaspoon basil
1 Tablespoon tamari or shoyu

Tempeh Bacon

Heat 10-inch skillet, add 1-2 Tablespoons oil, and then half of the tempeh strips. Let them quick-fry, about 30 seconds on each side. Sprinkle half of the herbs over tempeh as it fries. Remove tempeh and place on a paper towel. REPEAT process with the remaining oil, tempeh, and herbs. When finished, sprinkle fried tempeh with tamari and serve.

Preparation time: 7-10 minutes
Servings: Makes 4-6 servings

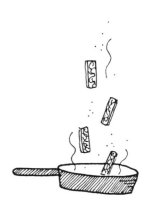

This crispy treat usually accompanies pancakes, but also makes a wonderful sandwich. Toast some whole-grain bread, spread on catsup or mustard, add a few pickles, lettuce, and tomato, and chow down.

Commercial Breakfast Cereals

Quite a variety of organic, whole-grain, fruit-sweetened cereals are available in supermarkets today. Many resemble the sugary, refined cereals of the 1950s. To find products that match your criteria for a wholesome breakfast, read the lists of ingredients on cereal boxes. Ask your grocer to stock cereals you wish to buy regularly.

If you'd like an alternative for cow's milk to use with cereal, most natural foods stores and some traditional grocery stores carry several. Soy milks, amasake, White Almond Beverage, and Rice Dream beverage can be found on the shelf in aseptic packages to be refrigerated after opening. Goat's milk is usually kept with dairy products in the refrigerated section. Nut Milks can be made at home (page 97). Here are some choices:

- Amasake, a creamy drink made from sweet brown rice

- Goat's milk

- Nut Milks (page 97)

- Rice Dream, a nondairy beverage made from brown rice and water

- Soy milk or soy beverage. Edensoy and WestSoy are popular commercial names; soy milks come plain, flavored, "lite" (low-fat), and "plus" or "extra" (with added nutrients).

- White Almond Beverage, a nondairy beverage made from water, almonds, and brown-rice syrup

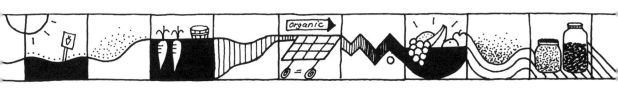

Lively Lunchboxes

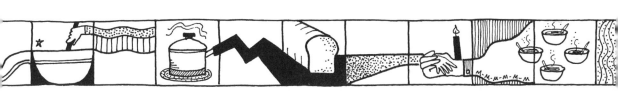

Karen's Sesame Noodles

8 ounces dry whole-grain noodles[20]

Sauce:
3 Tablespoons tahini
1 Tablespoon almond or peanut butter
1 teaspoon maple syrup
2 Tablespoons brown-rice vinegar
2 Tablespoons tamari or shoyu
1 teaspoon toasted sesame oil
1 1/2 teaspoons coriander
1 Tablespoon water, or to desired consistency

Cook noodles in plenty of boiling water according to directions on package. While noodles cook, put ingredients for sauce in small bowl and blend until creamy. Rinse and drain cooked noodles. Pour sauce over noodles and toss gently.

For experienced eaters: Omit sauce. Cut some of the plain noodles into bite-size pieces.

Preparation time: 15 minutes
Servings: Makes 4 servings

My daughter's godmother, Karen Brown, always made these for our potlucks in New York, and they were the first entrée to disappear.

20   Udon or soba noodles work well in this dish. Since 100 percent buckwheat soba is too strong for this dish, look for soba that is a blend of buckwheat and wheat.

4 ounces dry whole-grain noodles

Lunchbox Noodles

Dressing:
1 Tablespoon toasted sesame oil
1/2 teaspoon hot pepper oil
1 Tablespoon brown-rice vinegar
1 Tablespoon tamari or shoyu

Optional garnish:
1 - 2 Tablespoons parmesan cheese

Cook noodles according to package directions or follow general directions for whole-grain noodles on page 85. While noodles are cooking, whisk together oils, vinegar, and tamari in small bowl. Rinse and drain noodles. Pour dressing over cooked noodles and toss. Garnish with parmesan cheese if desired.

For children: You may want to omit the hot pepper oil.

Preparation time: 15 minutes
Servings: Makes 2 servings

Dress up any noodles for a tasty lunchbox treat. Try this simple dressing (omitting parmesan) on leftover brown rice.

Confetti Rice Salad with Sesame Vinaigrette

Salad:

4 cups cooked brown rice[21]

1 cup red pepper, chopped

1 carrot, grated or chopped

2 Tablespoons fresh chives or 1 scallion, finely chopped

1 cup chopped red cabbage

1 cup chopped parsley

1/3 cup sunflower seeds

Vinaigrette:

6 Tablespoons unrefined sesame oil

4 Tablespoons brown-rice vinegar

2 teaspoons toasted sesame oil

1 teaspoon tamari

Toss brown rice with chopped vegetables and sunflower seeds until evenly mixed. Pour vinaigrette ingredients in a bottle or jar; shake vigorously. Drizzle dressing on rice and vegetables; toss gently.

For new or experienced eaters: Reserve some cooked brown rice. Blend in a blender with a few Tablespoons of water for a fine cereal. Or steam an extra carrot and puree it with a little water and parsley.
For children: Reserve some cooked rice and cut-up vegetables; serve separately, omitting the vinaigrette.

Preparation time: 10 minutes
Servings: Makes 8 servings

This whole-grain salad looks beautiful. Brightly colored vegetables lend eye appeal, and sesame vinaigrette integrates the fresh flavors.

21   If rice is freshly cooked, allow to cool before assembling the salad.

Dilled Brown Rice and Kidney Beans

Salad:

2 cups cooked brown rice

1 1/2 cups cooked kidney beans

1/3 cup red onion, chopped

Dressing:

3 Tablespoons extra-virgin olive oil

3 Tablespoons brown-rice vinegar

1 Tablespoon umeboshi plum vinegar

2 Tablespoons fresh dill (or 2 teaspoons dried)

Put rice, beans, and onion in a medium-size bowl.

Mix oil, vinegars, and dill with whisk, or shake in small jar. Pour dressing over rice and beans; toss gently. If possible, let set an hour or two as flavors mellow with time.

For new eaters: Reserve some cooked brown rice and blend with water or breast milk.
For experienced eaters: Reserve some plain cooked kidney beans and plain rice. Blend to desired consistency, adding water if necessary.

Preparation time: 10 minutes
Servings: Makes 4-6 servings

Dill and red onion give this grain-and-bean combination a genuine zip. This recipe is incentive for keeping already-cooked brown rice and beans on hand.

Santa Fe Black Bean Salad

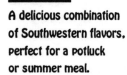

A delicious combination of Southwestern flavors, perfect for a potluck or summer meal.

Salad:
1 red pepper, roasted, peeled, and cut into small strips
2 cups cooked black beans
1/2 cup cooked corn
1/3 cup chopped cilantro

Dressing:
2 - 3 cloves garlic
1/2 teaspoon sea salt
2 Tablespoons extra-virgin olive oil
2 Tablespoons lime juice
1/4 teaspoon cayenne

To roast red peppers:

Gas stove method:
Place pepper directly on the low flame of a gas burner, letting skin char. Keep turning pepper until skin is charred on all sides. Let cool and remove black char under cool running water. Cut pepper open; remove seeds and stem.

Electric range method:
Place red pepper in shallow pan and put in oven under the broiler. Let skin char. Turn pepper every few minutes until skin is completely charred. Remove pepper from oven and place in brown paper bag. Close bag and let pepper sweat for 15-30 minutes. Remove pepper and peel off charred skin under cool running water. Cut pepper open; remove seeds and stem.

To make salad:

Combine strips of roasted red pepper, beans, corn, and cilantro in medium-size mixing bowl; set aside. Place garlic and salt on a cutting board; chop to a pastelike consistency. In a separate small bowl, mix together garlic paste, oil, lime juice, and cayenne. Pour dressing over beans and vegetables; toss gently.

For experienced eaters: Reserve some plain cooked black beans and corn; puree together.

Preparation time: 20 minutes
Servings: Makes 3 cups or 6 servings

Lemon Basil Potato Salad

Salad:

6 - 8 cups cubed red potatoes

Dressing:

3 - 4 cloves garlic

1/2 teaspoon sea salt

1 teaspoon lemon zest

3 - 4 Tablespoons extra-virgin olive oil

3 - 4 Tablespoons freshly squeezed lemon juice

1/3 cup tightly packed fresh basil leaves[22]

Wash, scrub, and cut potatoes. Place potatoes in large pot of boiling water. Cook 10-12 minutes or until tender. While potatoes are cooking, place garlic, salt, and lemon zest on cutting board. Chop together to a pastelike consistency. Combine paste with oil and lemon juice; set aside. Place basil on board and chop fine. Drain potatoes and let cool. Place potatoes in a serving bowl. Add dressing and basil; toss gently. Serve immediately or chill to serve later.

For new or experienced eaters: Reserve some boiled potato; mash with water or breast milk.

Preparation time: 20 minutes
Servings: Makes 6 servings

Fresh basil makes an impressive contribution to the flavor of soups, vegetables, noodles, beans, and fish. You can grow basil in your yard or your kitchen window.

22   When fresh basil is unavailable, substitute 2 or 3 Tablespoons pesto.

Aunt Cathy's Crunchy Ramen Cole Slaw

Salad:

3 cups shredded green cabbage

3 scallions, finely sliced

3 - 4 Tablespoons toasted sunflower seeds[23]

1/2 cup grated carrot

1/2 package (single serving) brown-rice ramen

Dressing:

4 Tablespoons extra-virgin olive oil

3 Tablespoons balsamic vinegar

Sea salt

Freshly ground pepper

Combine cabbage, scallions, sunflower seeds, and carrot in large mixing bowl. Break block of ramen noodles in half. Using a rolling pin, roll over uncooked noodles to break into small pieces; add to salad. Toss salad with oil and vinegar; add salt and pepper to taste.

For experienced eaters: Cook unused half of ramen noodles according to package directions. Cut into small pieces and serve plain.

Preparation time: 10-15 minutes
Servings: Makes 6 servings

Ramen is a small block of curly noodles that can be prepared in just minutes. This cole slaw uses the noodles dry to create a wonderful texture and taste.

23 Toast seeds quickly by placing in dry skillet on medium heat. Stir or shake constantly until seeds begin to emit a nutty aroma (5 minutes).

Salad:

1 cup whole-wheat bulgur

1 cup boiling water

1/3 cup finely chopped parsley

2 scallions, finely chopped

1/2 cup cucumber, chopped into small pieces

1/2 cup tomato, chopped into small bites

1/4 cup chopped mint

Dressing:

1/4 cup freshly squeezed lemon juice

3 Tablespoons extra-virgin olive oil

1 Tablespoon tamari or shoyu

Tabouli

Place bulgur in a mixing bowl. Pour boiling water over bulgur; cover and let stand 15 minutes. Fluff grain with fork. While grain is cooling to room temperature, chop vegetables. Add parsley, scallions, cucumber, tomato, and mint to cooled bulgur; toss together.

Blend lemon juice, oil, and tamari with whisk. Pour over bulgur and vegetables; toss again. Serve immediately or store in refrigerator in covered container.

For experienced eaters: Reserve a little plain bulgur and serve as a finger food with chopped cucumber and mint on the side. *For children:* Keeping chopped vegetables separate from grain and serving small piles of each may work for those who refuse salads or combinations of foods.

Preparation time: 30 minutes
Servings: Makes 4 servings

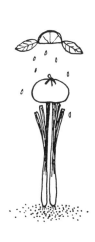

Traditional Tabouli salad makes good lunchbox fare or a quick summer meal, and packs well for a picnic or potluck. Serve Tabouli with Hummus (page 137) and a fresh green salad.

Variation: Quinoa Tabouli

Substitute 2 1/2 - 3 cups cooked quinoa for the cooked bulgur, and use 1/4 cup freshly squeezed lime juice instead of lemon juice.

Mad Dog Rice Salad

Salad:

3 cups cooked brown rice[24]

1 cup fresh or frozen green peas

1 cup fresh or frozen baby lima beans

2 teaspoons extra-virgin olive oil

1 onion, chopped

1/2 pound tofu, cut into cubes

1 carrot, cut into small pieces

1 stalk celery, chopped

Dressing:

2 Tablespoons extra-virgin olive oil

Juice of 1/2 lemon

1 teaspoon tamari or shoyu

1 teaspoon toasted sesame oil

1 1/2 teaspoons balsamic vinegar

Mix ingredients for dressing in small bowl or jar; pour over rice. Toss thoroughly and set aside. Bring water to a boil in small pan and cook peas and limas; drain and set aside. Put oil in skillet and sauté onion until soft but not limp.

Prepare tofu. To impart better texture to tofu, drop cubes in saucepan of boiling water until they rise to the top, then drain. Add peas, limas, onion, tofu, carrot, and celery to dressed rice; toss thoroughly. Serve immediately or cover and refrigerate. Return to room temperature before serving.

For new eaters: Cook extra peas or baby limas; puree in a blender.
For children: Serve individual portions of peas, brown rice, or tofu cubes.

Preparation time: 65-75 minutes
Servings: Makes 6 cups

Novelist Jack Kelly invented this salad while researching Depression-era outlaws. It is a nutritionally complete meal in itself.

---

24   Salad works best if freshly cooked rice is used. Warm rice absorbs the dressing better, creating a more flavorful dish. If using leftover rice, be sure it is at room temperature before dressing.

Asian Noodle Salad with Toasted Sesame Dressing

Salad:

1 8-ounce package soba noodles[25]

1/4 cup chopped cilantro

1/4 cup toasted sesame seeds

Dressing:

2 Tablespoons toasted sesame oil

3 Tablespoons tamari or shoyu

3 Tablespoons balsamic vinegar

1 Tablespoon maple syrup

1 Tablespoon hot pepper oil

Optional additions:

Chives

Chopped red cabbage

Cubed tofu

Finely sliced radishes

Sliced scallions

Cook soba noodles according to package directions. Drain and rinse in colander.

Combine toasted sesame oil, tamari, vinegar, maple syrup, and hot pepper oil in small bowl; whisk together. Place drained noodles in a large bowl. Add dressing, cilantro, and sesame seeds; toss gently. Add optional chopped vegetables and toss again.

For experienced eaters: Reserve some plain noodles and cut up.
For children: Omit hot pepper oil in dressing. Some children may prefer plain noodles with cut-up vegetables on the side.

Preparation time: 20-25 minutes
Servings: Makes 4-6 servings

In my Whole Foods Salads classes, Asian Noodle Salad is always the favorite dish.

25   Since 100 percent buckwheat soba is too strong for this dish, find a soba that is part wheat and part buckwheat.

Quick Quinoa Salad

Salad:
1 2/3 cups dry quinoa
3 1/3 cups water
Pinch of sea salt
1 cup chopped carrots
3/4 cup minced parsley
1/3 cup sunflower seeds
4 cloves garlic, minced

Dressing:
1/3 cup freshly squeezed lemon juice
3 Tablespoons extra-virgin olive oil
3 Tablespoons tamari or shoyu

Optional garnishes:
Sliced black olives
Tomatoes cut in wedges

Rinse quinoa with warm water and drain through a fine strainer. Place quinoa in a 3-quart pan with water and salt; bring to a boil. Turn heat to low, cover, and simmer for 15 minutes. Allow quinoa to sit on very low heat, uncovered, for an extra 5 minutes so it dries out. This makes the grain fluffier for salads. Toss quinoa with fork and let cool.

Add carrots, parsley, seeds, and garlic to quinoa; mix thoroughly. Combine lemon juice, oil, and tamari. Pour over quinoa and toss well. Garnish with olives and tomatoes if desired.

For new eaters: Reserve some plain cooked quinoa. Puree quinoa with water or breast milk.

Preparation time: 35-45 minutes
Servings: Makes 6-8 servings

Quinoa has an excellent nutritional profile (10.5 grams of protein per cup). It is also rich in calcium and iron. I find myself getting very hungry for this salad.

2 cups pressure-cooked brown rice[26]

Sesame salt:
1 cup unhulled sesame seeds
1 teaspoon sea salt

Rice Balls Rolled in Sesame Salt

To make sesame salt:

Rinse sesame seeds and drain through a fine strainer. Put seeds in a skillet on medium heat. Toast seeds, stirring constantly until seeds begin to pop, change color slightly, and give off a toasty aroma. Put toasted seeds and salt in a suribachi (a serrated ceramic mortar) and grind with a pestle; or grind seeds and salt together in a blender or food processor. This condiment can be stored in a sealed container and used to flavor many foods (I like it on popcorn).

To make rice balls:

Spread about 1/3 cup of the sesame salt on a plate or shallow baking pan. Moisten hands with water and gather a small handful of cooked rice. Press your hands around the rice, packing it into a small ball about the size of a ping-pong ball. Roll the ball in the sesame salt, covering all sides. REPEAT until rice is used up or desired amount is obtained. Rice balls will keep for 5 days in a covered container in the refrigerator.

For adults: Make a tamari-ginger sauce for dipping. Add 1 teaspoon grated gingerroot to 1/4 cup tamari and 1/4 cup water.

Preparation time: 20 minutes
Servings: Makes 12-15 rice balls
*   and 1 cup sesame salt*

I did a cooking project on brown rice with elementary-school children. To my surprise, they literally licked the bowls when we prepared this simple snack.

---

26   Follow directions for pressure-cooking rice on page 83. Boiled rice will not hold together to form balls. Allow rice to cool to room temperature before making rice balls.

Tempeh Club Sandwiches

1 8-ounce package of tempeh

Marinade:[27]
3 cloves garlic, sliced
4 - 5 slices (1/8-inch thick) of fresh gingerroot
1 cup water
1 Tablespoon brown-rice vinegar
1 Tablespoon mirin
1/4 cup tamari or shoyu

Sandwich:
1 Tablespoon cold-pressed canola oil
8 slices of whole-wheat bread

Optional garnishes:
Avocado slices
Catsup
Lettuce
Mayonnaise
Mustard
Pickle slices
Sprouts
Tomato slices

To marinate tempeh:
Slow method:
Slice the tempeh block in half. Cut each half through the middle to make 4 pieces of tempeh, each slightly smaller than a slice of bread. Put tempeh and all marinade ingredients in a sealed storage container. Refrigerate for 2-4 days.

Quick method:
Flavors will be weaker than in slow marinade method. Put sliced tempeh and all marinade ingredients in a large pan; bring to a boil. Turn heat off and let tempeh marinate for 10 minutes.

---

27   This marinade also works well for marinating or poaching fish filets.

To make sandwiches:

Heat oil in a skillet over medium heat. Remove tempeh pieces from marinade and brown in the skillet for a minute or so on each side. Place on bread with your favorite garnishes.

Preparation time: 5 minutes for marinade;
  tempeh marinates in 2-4 days;
  5 minutes for sandwiches
Servings: Makes 4 sandwiches or
  2 "monster" sandwiches

Variation: Tempeh Reuben Sandwich

Put mustard on bread slices; add a layer of marinated tempeh and a layer of sauerkraut for each sandwich.

I especially like this hearty and tasty sandwich with pickles on it. With a simple vegetable soup, it's an easy-to-prepare meal.

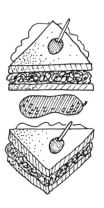

Gingered Lentil Sandwich Spread

2 cups cooked lentils
2 Tablespoons extra-virgin olive oil
1 Tablespoon grated gingerroot
1 Tablespoon whole-grain mustard
3 mushrooms, sliced
2 scallions, sliced
1/2 teaspoon sea salt
1/4 cup water

Put cooked lentils and all other ingredients in a food processor or blender; blend until smooth. If using a blender, blend 1/4 of the mixture, then add the rest a little at a time. Will keep in the refrigerator for several days.

For experienced eaters: Reserve some plain cooked lentils and puree with a little water. Add cooked brown rice or baked sweet potato to puree for a tasty combination.

Preparation time: 10 minutes
Servings: Makes 2 cups

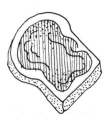

Gingered lentil sandwich spread tastes scrumptious on whole-wheat toast with lettuce, tomato, and mayonnaise, or wrapped snugly in a whole-wheat chapati. Works well as a party spread for crackers, too.

Hummus

2 cups cooked chick-peas
5 Tablespoons tahini
1/2 teaspoon sea salt
1/3 cup freshly squeezed lemon juice
    (juice of 1 1/2 - 2 lemons)
2 - 3 cloves garlic
3 Tablespoons extra-virgin olive oil
1/4 cup cooking liquid from beans
    or water to desired consistency

Optional garnishes:
Chopped parsley
Paprika

Place cooked chick-peas in food processor or blender with tahini, salt, lemon juice, garlic, and olive oil; blend until smooth. Add cooking liquid from beans or a little water to get desired consistency. Garnish with chopped parsley or paprika if desired. Stores well refrigerated for at least a week.

For experienced eaters: Reserve some plain cooked chick-peas and mash. Some may enjoy picking up and eating chick-peas; be sure the peas are well-cooked.
For children: Hummus may be too spicy; reduce lemon juice and garlic by half.

Preparation time: 10 minutes
Servings: Makes 2 3/4 - 3 cups

Hummus is a traditional Middle Eastern dish excellent for vegetarian sandwiches. The combination of chick-peas and sesame seeds creates a high-protein spread.

Tofu-Chive Spread

1/2 pound firm tofu
2 Tablespoons tahini
2 Tablespoons brown-rice vinegar
1 Tablespoon umeboshi plum paste
2 - 3 Tablespoons chopped fresh chives or scallions

Use fork to break up tofu in a bowl. Gently mix in all other ingredients and mash with a fork.

For experienced eaters: Reserve some tofu and mash with a teaspoon of tahini.

Preparation time: 5 minutes
Servings: Makes 1 cup of spread

Variation: Tofu-Chive Dip
Place all ingredients with a few Tablespoons of water in a blender; blend until smooth. Prepare raw or steamed vegetables for dipping.

Try this tasty spread of Nancy Rankin's with a leaf of red cabbage and a slice of fresh tomato on whole-grain bread. It's also great served on whole-grain crackers with your favorite soup.

3/4 cup almonds
3/4 cup cashews
1/4 cup sunflower seeds
1/4 cup pumpkin seeds
2 Tablespoons tamari or shoyu
1/2 teaspoon cumin
1/2 teaspoon coriander
Pinch of cayenne (optional)

Tamari-Roasted Nuts

Preheat oven to 300 degrees F. Place nuts and seeds on cookie sheet. Toast in oven until they begin to turn golden and give off a nutty aroma (10-12 minutes). Mix tamari and spices together. Sprinkle over toasted nuts; stir and return to oven to dry out (2-3 minutes). For a more even coating, put tamari mix in a spray bottle and mist roasted nuts, then stir in spices, and dry. Store in a sealed jar.

For children: Omit cumin, coriander, and cayenne. Tamari-roast just one kind of nut instead of mixing several.

Preparation time: 15 minutes
Servings: Makes 2 cups

Tamari-roasted nuts
make a crunchy addition
to the lunchbox. Sprinkle a few
on salads or grains to liven up
the flavor and texture.
A jar of these nuts makes
a welcome gift as well.

Savory Sandwiches to Go

4 12-by-12-inch pieces of plastic wrap or waxed paper (wrapped in plastic this sandwich will keep for a week refrigerated; wrapped in waxed paper it should keep for 24 hours)

4 whole-wheat tortillas

2 cups filling (your choice of grain, bean, or vegetable combinations; see "Suggestions for Sandwich Filling," page 142)

Place one square of plastic wrap or waxed paper flat on your working space. Put the tortilla in the center of the square. Pack a 1/2-cup measure (or a large ice cream scoop) with filling. Put filling in a mound in the center of the tortilla (Figure 1).

Pull up the lower left and upper right corners of the tortilla and overlap (Figure 2). Use a light touch to avoid compressing the filling. Hold this configuration in place with your left hand by putting all your fingers on one side of the mound and your thumb on the other (Figure 3). This way you can wrap without smashing the filling.

Begin wrapping the sandwich with the right hand. Take the lower right corner of plastic wrap or waxed paper and pull it over the top of the sandwich, taking the tortilla with you (Figure 4). Take the lower left corner of wrap or paper and pull it up over the mound, removing your left hand as you do it (Figure 5). Take the upper left corner of plastic wrap or waxed paper and bring it over the top of the mound, taking the tortilla with it (Figure 6). With 3 sides wrapped you have a fairly firm package. For a final touch, roll the whole sandwich toward the upper right corner (Figure 7). This seals it. If using waxed paper, tack the end down with a piece of tape.

The people at Essential Foods (a Northwestern food company) were kind and patient enough to let me spend a morning on the assembly line and learn how to wrap their popular sandwiches.

The trick is to work quickly and wrap tightly. You will need to practice a few times. Once you have mastered the technique, you'll want to create and eat one of these handy sandwiches every day. Try one warmed or dipped in a little salsa or both. Accompanied by a fruit juice spritzer, these whole foods sandwiches may be the burger and cola of the 1990s!

Preparation time: 15 minutes
Servings: Makes 4 sandwiches

SAVORY SANDWICHES TO GO

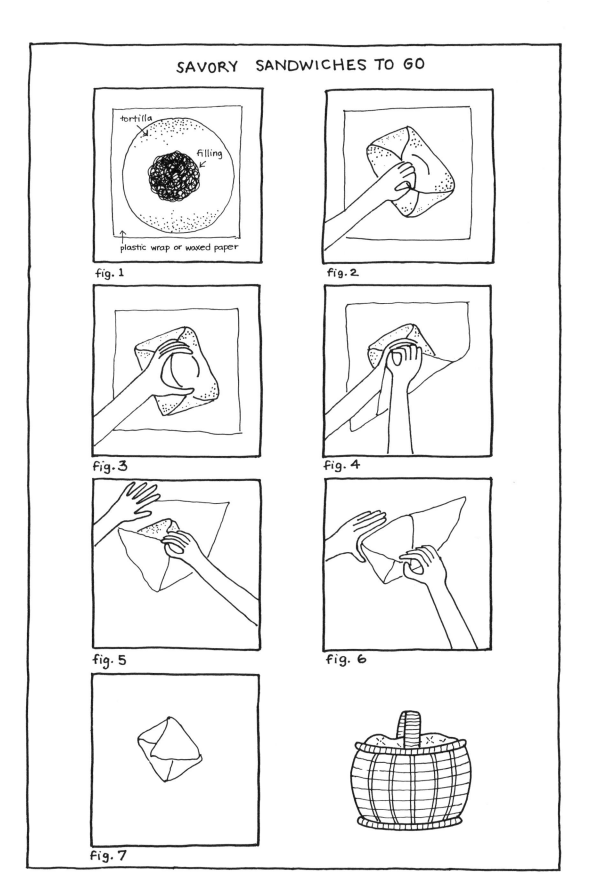

fig. 1

tortilla
filling
plastic wrap or waxed paper

fig. 2

fig. 3

fig. 4

fig. 5

fig. 6

fig. 7

Suggestions for Sandwich Filling

- black beans and brown rice with scallions and cilantro
- Confetti Rice Salad (page 124)
- Dilled Brown Rice and Kidney Beans (page 125)
- Gingered Lentil Sandwich Spread (page 136)
- Grilled Vegetables (page 200)
- Hiziki Pâté (page 184)
- Hummus (page 137) with sprouts and tomato
- Indian Rice and Lentils (page 162)
- Mad Dog Rice Salad (page 130)
- Mom's Marvelous Veggie Loaf (page 169)
- pinto beans with brown rice and grated cheese
- Quick Quinoa Salad (page 132)
- Santa Fe Black Bean Salad (page 126)
- Sassy Red Beans (page 171) with grains
- Tofu Vegetable Scramble (page 117)
- Sloppeh Joes (page 181)
- Tabouli (page 129) with cooked chick-peas
- Tofu-Chive Spread (page 138)

Grain and Bean Roll-Ups

Roll-ups are a simple variation on Savory Sandwiches to Go. Use the suggestions above for fillings or create your own. They are scrumptious topped with a drizzle of Lemon-Tahini Sauce, page 222.

4 whole-wheat tortillas or chapatis
2 cups filling (your choice of grain, bean, or vegetable combinations; see "Suggestions for Sandwich Filling," above)

Optional garnishes:
Avocado slices
Lettuce
Salsa
Sliced olives
Sprouts

Place tortilla flat on your working surface. Spread the filling in a fat line down the middle. Put whatever garnishes you want on top. Roll it up like a rug.

Preparation time: 5 minutes
Servings: Makes 4 roll-ups

1/2 cup tahini
1 Tablespoon light or white miso
Whole-grain bread
Fruit-sweetened raspberry jam

Put tahini and miso in small bowl; mix well, adding a little water if necessary. Spread miso-tahini on one piece of bread and raspberry jam on the other. Put slices together.

For children: Make a special sandwich with a heart-shaped cookie cutter.
For adults: Skip the jam and add finely chopped scallions to the miso-tahini mixture. Spread on bread or crackers.

Preparation time: 5-10 minutes
Servings: Makes 2/3 cup miso-tahini spread
*   or 4 - 5 sandwiches*

Miso-Tahini and Raspberry Jam Sandwich

Miso and tahini mixed together makes a wonderful spread with endless variations. For a superb whole meal, spread miso-tahini on bread; serve with a vegetable soup and salad.

1/3 cup unsweetened apple butter
1 teaspoon light or white miso
Whole-grain bread
1/4 cup almond butter

Put apple butter in a small bowl and stir miso into it. Spread bread with a light layer of almond butter on one side and apple-miso butter on the other. Put slices together.

Preparation time: 5 minutes
Servings: Makes 4 - 5 sandwiches

Apple-Miso Almond-Butter Sandwich

Try this sweet and nutty combo for a new twist on the usual peanut butter and jelly.

Packing a Wholesome Lunchbox

Choose one item that is a "growing food": whole grains, beans, or perhaps a hearty sandwich on whole-grain bread. Add one vegetable and one fruit for a well-rounded meal. You and your child may want to plan some favorite combinations on a copy of the chart below and post it for easy reference.

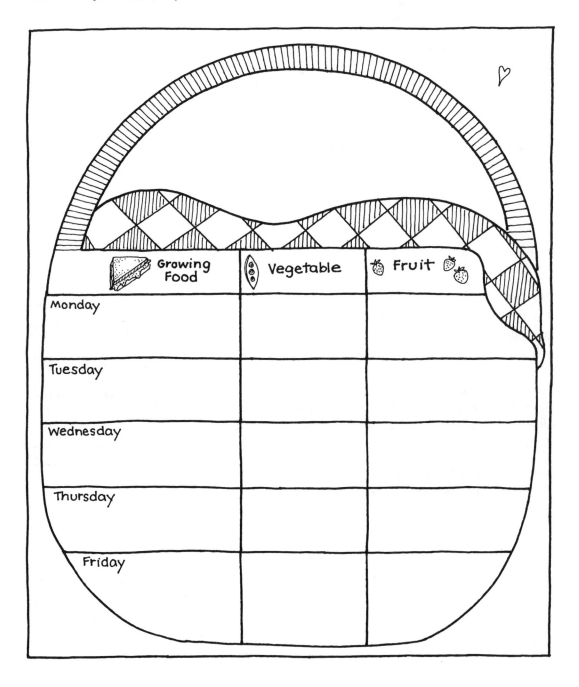

	Growing Food	Vegetable	Fruit
Monday			
Tuesday			
Wednesday			
Thursday			
Friday			

Sample Lunchboxes

To give you some lunchbox ideas, here are some of my family's favorite combinations:

Growing Food	Vegetable	Fruit
burrito (whole-wheat chapati, mashed pinto beans, grated cheese, and salsa)	carrot sticks	orange
tofu slices sautéed in butter and tamari, rice cake	nori cut into shapes	plums
Lunchbox Noodles (page 123), Tamari-Roasted Nuts (page 139)	mashed sweet potato	red grapes
Rice Balls Rolled in Sesame Salt (page 133)	blanched bok choy	kiwi slices, raisins
whole-wheat spaghetti with tomato sauce	corn	apple slices
Apple-Miso Almond-Butter Sandwich (page 143)	sugar snap peas	melon slices
Sweet Squash Corn Muffins (page 215), kidney beans	steamed green beans	nectarine slices
Cynthia's Hearty Vegetable-Miso Soup (page 148), whole-wheat pita bread	celery sticks	pear
Abby's Healthy Home Fries (page 118) with yogurt dip, Tempeh Bacon (page 119)	red pepper slices	dates
Asian Noodle Salad (page 131) or Karen's Sesame Noodles (page 122)	cucumber slices	strawberries
avocado, cucumber, and sprouts sandwich	Roasted Potatoes and Carrots (page 203)	pineapple

On days when you feel like adding something extra, add a fresh flower, a poem, a neat rock or crystal, a jingle bell, a cartoon, a finger puppet, or a note from you instead of candy. Rather than packing juice, tuck in a small container of fruity herbal tea or lemon water. For an earth-friendly lunchbox, use a bright-colored cloth napkin and silverware instead of wasteful paper and plastic.

Carrot Flowers

1 pound carrots (about 4 or 5)
1/4 cup apple or orange juice
1 cinnamon stick, optional

Wash carrots and trim off ends. Cut into 4-inch lengths. Using a sharp paring knife, make a lengthwise slit into each carrot, about 1/8 inch deep. Make another lengthwise slit at an angle to the first. Remove the V-shaped strip from the carrot. Cut out 4 more V-shaped strips at equal intervals around the carrot. REPEAT this process on each 4-inch length of carrot.

Now slice the carrot lengths into 1/4-inch rounds, creating flower-shaped slices. Bring juice and cinnamon stick to a boil in a 1-quart saucepan. Add carrot flowers and reduce heat to medium. Steam 15 minutes or until tender.

For experienced eaters: Serve as is.

Preparation time: 25 minutes
Servings: Makes 6 servings

My friend Theresa Lewis
sent me this recipe.
She made Carrot Flowers
for her son's preschool class,
and they were quite the rage.
Children appreciate the magic
of turning carrots into flowers.

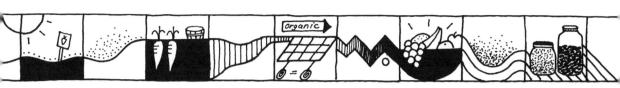

Soothing Soups

Cynthia's Hearty Vegetable-Miso Soup

5-inch piece of wakame
6 cups water
1 potato, diced
1 carrot, chopped
1 cup finely chopped greens
    (watercress, kale, collards, or bok choy)
1/4 - 1/2 pound firm tofu, cut into small cubes
4 Tablespoons light or white miso

Garnish:
2 scallions, thinly sliced

Place wakame in a small bowl of cold water and soak for 5 minutes. Put 6 cups water, potato, and carrot in a 3-quart pot; bring to a boil. Remove wakame from water and chop into small pieces, removing the spine. Add chopped wakame to soup. Lower heat, cover pot, and let soup simmer 15-20 minutes until vegetables are tender.

Near the end of cooking time, add chopped greens and tofu cubes; let them simmer 2-3 minutes. Ladle about 1/4 cup broth from the soup into each soup bowl. Dissolve 1 Tablespoon miso in each bowl of broth. Add more broth with plenty of vegetables to each bowl and stir gently. Garnish each bowl with scallions.

For new eaters: Remove some boiled potato or carrot from soup after it simmers; mash with fork. Your baby will benefit from the nutritious broth made by the seaweed.
For experienced eaters: Those who can chew soft food items can enjoy some pieces of cooked vegetables and tofu cubes from the soup.

Preparation time: 25 minutes
Servings: Makes 4 servings

This hearty soup is excellent when a family member is fatigued. Served with a bowl of brown rice and a salad, it is a regular meal in our home.

2 teaspoons extra-virgin olive oil or ghee
1 onion, chopped
1 bunch asparagus, washed and trimmed
5 cups stock or water
1/2 cup rolled oats
1/2 teaspoon sea salt
Freshly squeezed lemon juice

Garnish:
Fresh dill (or dried)

Heat oil in pot. Add onion and sauté until soft. Cut asparagus into small pieces. Add to onion and sauté a few more minutes. Add stock, oats, and salt; bring to a boil. Simmer 15 minutes. Transfer to a blender and puree. Reheat if necessary. Add lemon juice to taste and serve garnished with dill. This soup can also be served cold in warm weather.

Preparation time: 25 minutes
Servings: Makes 6 servings

Cream of Asparagus Soup with Dill

It is easy to make a creamy soup without the cream. Rolled oats add extra whole-grain nutrition and help make the creamy texture. Use this simple recipe to make a tasty soup out of any seasonal vegetable.

Dean Street Yellow Split Pea Soup

2 cups dried yellow split peas[28]
1 Tablespoon extra-virgin olive oil or ghee
1 large onion, chopped
3 carrots, sliced
2 stalks celery, chopped
6 cups water
1 Tablespoon fresh dill (or 3 teaspoons dried)
Sea salt and freshly ground pepper to taste

Clean and wash peas. Heat oil in a large pot; add onion and sauté until clear. Add peas, carrots, celery, and water; bring soup to a boil. Lower heat and simmer until peas are soft enough to fall apart (about 45 minutes). Leave the pot uncovered for several minutes if you want a thicker consistency. Stir in dill, salt, and pepper to taste before serving.

Preparation time: 60 minutes
Servings: Makes 6-8 servings as a main course

Variation: Curried Yellow Split Pea Soup

Add 1 Tablespoon curry powder or 1 Tablespoon Homemade Curry Paste (page 226) to the onion while sautéing. Omit dill.

My dear friend Judy Loebl, who lives in a big house on Dean Street, works as a physical therapist and is the mother of three. If Judy can find the time to make this soup, anyone can.

---

28   Soaking split peas for 2 hours prior to cooking creates a creamier soup.

3 medium carrots
1 beet (2 if small)
1 Tablespoon extra-virgin olive oil
1 large onion, diced
1 cup dried red lentils
6 cups water or stock
2 bay leaves
1 3-inch sprig of fresh rosemary
   (or 1 teaspoon dried)
1 Tablespoon chopped fresh oregano
   (or 1 teaspoon dried)
2 - 3 Tablespoons light or white miso

Rosemary Red Soup

Scrub and chop carrots and beet. Heat oil in a soup pot; add onion and sauté until soft. Add carrots and beet; sauté a few minutes more. Wash and drain lentils. Add lentils, water, bay leaves, rosemary, and oregano to sautéed onion; bring to a boil. Lower heat and simmer 40 minutes. Remove bay leaves and stems of fresh herbs. Puree soup in a blender with miso. Gently reheat before serving.

For new eaters: Steam a few extra carrot slices and puree with water.
For experienced eaters: Reserve some pureed soup before adding the miso and serve.
For children: Make a face in the bowl with crackers!

Preparation time: 50 minutes
Servings: Makes 6-8 servings

This gorgeous red soup has a deep, satisfying taste to match. Because of the combination of legumes and vegetables, all you need to add is some bread and salad to have a beautifully balanced meal.

Recycled Bean Soups

White Beans and Fresh Herbs Soup

2 teaspoons ghee or extra-virgin olive oil
1 onion, chopped
1 clove garlic, minced
1 carrot, chopped
1 rib celery, chopped
2 Tablespoons chopped parsley
1/4 cup chopped fresh basil leaves
1 1/2 cups cooked white beans
1 1/2 cups water or vegetarian soup stock
1 Tablespoon tamari or shoyu
    (if beans were not already salted)
1 teaspoon brown-rice vinegar

Heat oil in a 4-quart soup pot. Add onion and garlic; sauté until soft. Add carrot and celery; sauté a few more minutes. Next, add herbs, beans, and water; stir together. You can puree all of the soup in a blender for a smooth soup, or puree part of it for a chunkier cream soup. Return pureed part of soup to pot. Season with tamari and vinegar; reheat before serving.

For experienced eaters: Reserve some plain cooked beans and puree with a little water or soup stock. Serve with steamed carrot slices.

Preparation time: 10 minutes
Servings: Makes 4 servings

Dark Beans and Sensuous Spices Soup

2 teaspoons ghee or extra-virgin olive oil

1 onion, chopped

1 clove garlic, minced

1 teaspoon cumin

1 teaspoon oregano

1 teaspoon coriander

1 carrot, chopped

1 rib celery, chopped

1 1/2 cups cooked red or black beans

1 1/2 cups water or vegetarian soup stock

1/4 cup chopped cilantro

1 Tablespoon tamari or shoyu

1 teaspoon brown-rice vinegar

Another good use for leftover beans! These two soups make a quick meal served with Sweet Squash Corn Muffins (page 215) and Watercress Salad (page 197).

Heat ghee in a 4-quart soup pot. Add onion and garlic; sauté until soft. Add dry spices and sauté briefly. Add carrot and celery; sauté a few more minutes. Next, add beans and water; stir together. You can puree all of the soup in a blender for a smooth soup, or puree part of it for a chunkier cream soup. Return pureed part of soup to pot. Add cilantro, season with tamari and vinegar, and reheat before serving.

For experienced eaters: Reserve some plain cooked beans and puree with a little water or soup stock. Serve with steamed zucchini slices.

Preparation time: 10 minutes
Servings: Makes 4 servings

Indian Red Lentil Soup (Masoor Dal)

2 teaspoons ghee or butter
1 onion, chopped
1 - 2 Tablespoons minced garlic
1/2 teaspoon sea salt
1 teaspoon turmeric
1 teaspoon ground cumin
1/8 teaspoon cayenne
1 cup chopped tomatoes
1 cup dried red lentils
4 cups water

1/2 teaspoon ghee or butter
1 teaspoon cumin seeds
1 teaspoon mustard seeds
1/4 cup chopped cilantro

Heat ghee in a large pot. Sauté onion, garlic, and salt in ghee until soft. Add spices and stir for 2-3 minutes. Add tomatoes and cook until they break down. Wash and drain lentils. Add lentils and water to pot. Let simmer for 45 minutes, stirring often.

Heat ghee in a small skillet and fry seeds until they pop. Stir fried seeds and cilantro into finished soup.

Preparation time: 60 minutes
Servings: Makes 4 servings

A lovely Indian vegetarian restaurant in Seattle called Silence-Heart-Nest serves this very flavorful and satisfying soup called Masoor Dal. I have adapted it to family-size proportions.

1 teaspoon extra-virgin olive oil
4 cups chopped onions (2 large or 3 medium onions)
1/2 teaspoon sea salt
2 cups diced potatoes (2 medium potatoes)
1/2 cup chopped celery (2 ribs)
1 large carrot, diced
3 1/2 - 4 cups water
2 Tablespoons cashew butter
2 Tablespoons tamari or shoyu

2 teaspoons extra-virgin olive oil
3/4 pound mushrooms, sliced
1/2 cup fresh basil leaves
Sea salt and freshly ground pepper

Golden Mushroom-Basil Soup

Heat oil in a 3-quart pot. Add onions and salt. Cover the pot and simmer on low heat, stirring occasionally until onions cook down to a nice mush (15-20 minutes). Add potatoes, celery, carrot, and water to onion mush; cover and simmer until potatoes are soft (15-20 minutes). Put soup mixture in a blender with cashew butter and tamari; blend until smooth. Run the soup through a strainer to remove celery strings. Return soup to pot.

Heat oil in a small skillet. Add mushrooms and sauté until soft. Finely chop basil. Stir sautéed mushrooms and basil into finished soup. Add salt and pepper to taste and serve.

For new eaters: Remove some cooked potato or carrot from the soup and puree.
For experienced eaters: Omit salt, tamari, and mushrooms. Reserve a portion of soup for your baby; then add these ingredients to remainder of soup for others.

Preparation time: 45 minutes
Servings: Makes 6 servings

The following three creamy soups are versions of Jeff Basom's sensuous nondairy soups served at the Bastyr University cafeteria in Seattle. Jeff's inventive use of vegetables, plus a touch of cashew butter, creates a taste everyone loves.

Creamy Broccoli Soup

1 or 2 large stems of broccoli with flowerets
1 teaspoon extra-virgin olive oil
4 cups chopped onions (2 large or 3 medium onions)
1/2 teaspoon sea salt
1 teaspoon coriander
2 cups diced potatoes (2 medium potatoes)
1/2 cup chopped celery (2 ribs)
3 1/2 - 4 cups water
2 Tablespoons cashew butter
1/4 cup chopped cilantro or parsley
Sea salt and freshly ground pepper

Cut off the broccoli flowerets, cut into bite-size pieces, and reserve. Peel the broccoli stems and dice into small, bite-size pieces. Heat oil in a 3-quart pot. Add onions, salt, and coriander. Cover the pot and simmer on low heat, stirring occasionally, until onions cook down to a nice mush (15-20 minutes). Add broccoli stem pieces, potatoes, celery, and water to the onion mush; cover and simmer until potatoes are soft (15- 20 minutes). Put soup mixture in a blender with cashew butter and blend until smooth. Run the soup through a strainer to remove celery strings. Return soup to pot.

Bring a pan of water to a boil. Drop in the broccoli flowerets and let them cook about 30 seconds. Stir blanched flowerets and cilantro into finished soup. Add salt and pepper to taste and serve.

For new eaters: Remove some cooked potato from soup and puree it.
For experienced eaters: Reserve some blanched broccoli flowerets and puree with a few slices of ripe avocado.

Preparation time: 45 minutes
Servings: Makes 6 servings

A smooth way to enjoy the goodness of broccoli. Serve this soup with Tempeh Club Sandwiches (page 134). A simple feast for a hungry family.

1 teaspoon extra-virgin olive oil
4 cups chopped onions (2 large or 3 medium onions)
1/2 teaspoon sea salt
3 cups diced potatoes (2 medium potatoes)
1/2 cup chopped celery (2 ribs)
1 large carrot, diced
3 cups bite-size cauliflower pieces
3 1/2 - 4 cups water
2 Tablespoons cashew butter
2 Tablespoons tamari or shoyu
1/3 cup dried dulse
Sea salt and freshly ground pepper

Thick Potato Cauliflower and Dulse Soup

Heat oil in a 3-quart pot. Add onions and salt. Cover the pot and simmer on low heat, stirring occasionally until onions cook down to a nice mush (15-20 minutes). Add 2 cups potatoes, celery, carrot, 1 cup cauliflower pieces, and water to the onion mush; cover and simmer until potatoes and cauliflower are soft (15-20 minutes). Put soup mixture in a blender with cashew butter and tamari; blend until smooth. Run the soup through a strainer to remove celery strings. Return soup to pot.

Prepare remaining 1 cup potatoes and 2 cups cauliflower. Place the potatoes and cauliflower pieces in a pan of boiling water; cook until tender (10-12 minutes). Prepare dulse by washing in cold water and gently tearing into bite-size pieces. Drain the cooked potato and cauliflower. Stir cooked vegetables and dulse into finished soup. Season with salt and pepper and serve.

For new eaters: Steam some extra cauliflower pieces until very soft (20 minutes). Puree with a pinch of dulse and serve.
For experienced eaters: Omit salt, tamari, cauliflower pieces, and pepper. Reserve a portion of soup for your baby; then add these ingredients to remainder of soup for others.

Preparation time: 45 minutes
Servings: Makes 6 servings

Iron-rich dulse marries well with the simple flavors of potatoes and cauliflower.

Nina's Famous Spring Beet Soup

1 teaspoon extra-virgin olive oil

1 medium onion, cut into thin crescents

1 clove garlic, minced

1/8 teaspoon sea salt

3 - 4 cups water

1 bunch spring beets, cut into large matchsticks
   (save the beet greens)

1 carrot, cut into large matchsticks

1/4 head green cabbage, shredded

2 Tablespoons freshly squeezed lemon juice

1 Tablespoon tamari or shoyu

Garnish:
1 Tablespoon fresh dill (or 1 teaspoon dried)

Heat oil in soup pot. Add onion, garlic, and salt; sauté until soft. Add water, beets, carrot, and cabbage; bring to a boil. Lower heat and simmer, covered, for 10-15 minutes until vegetables are tender. Meanwhile, wash beet greens, remove tough stems, and cut greens into short, thin strips. Add beet greens, lemon juice, and tamari to soup; simmer another 3-5 minutes. Serve at once, garnished with dill.

For experienced eaters: Remove some cooked beet and carrot pieces from the soup; puree or serve whole as finger foods.

Preparation time: 30 minutes
Servings: Makes 4 servings

Do you ever get the urge to clean in the spring? Here is a delicious, cleansing soup for your body that my friend Nina invented. It's bursting with nutrients and flavor. The fresher the beets, the better.

1 1/2 cups dried navy beans, soaked
2 teaspoons extra-virgin olive oil
1 onion, chopped
2 chipotle chiles, soaked 10-15 minutes in cold water
4 cups water or vegetable stock
1 - 2 teaspoons sea salt
1 teaspoon brown-rice vinegar
Freshly ground pepper

Chipotle Navy Bean Soup

Drain soaking water off beans. Heat oil in soup pot or pressure cooker. Add onion and sauté until soft. Add drained beans, chiles, and water. Bring to a simmer, or close pressure cooker and bring up to pressure. Cook for 1 hour in soup pot or 45 minutes in pressure cooker, until beans are creamy. Remove chile pods. For added creaminess, puree part of the soup in a blender, then add back to the pot and stir in. Stir in salt, vinegar, and pepper and serve.

Preparation time: 65 minutes for boiling,
*   50 minutes for pressure-cooking*
Servings: Makes 6 servings

Chipotle chiles are smoked, dried jalapeño peppers that richly enhance humble beans. The smoky flavor is similar to that of beans cooked with ham. Lima beans or pinto beans work equally well.

Easy Vegetarian Soup Stock

1 carrot, cut into large chunks
1 rib of celery, cut into chunks
1 scallion or leek
Skin of 1 yellow onion
1 3-inch piece of kombu
1 bay leaf
1 teaspoon marjoram
1 teaspoon thyme
1 quart water

Put all ingredients in a large soup pot and bring to a boil. Lower heat and simmer 15-20 minutes. Let cool. Strain liquid into an empty quart jar (a rinsed-out juice bottle works well). Stores well in refrigerator while awaiting its debut in your next soup. Should last 3-4 days.

For experienced eaters: Use soup stock to puree food for extra nourishment.
For children: Make a gentle and nourishing broth by stirring a teaspoon of light miso into a cup of this stock.

Preparation time: 25 minutes
Servings: Makes 1 quart of soup stock

You probably don't often have time to make elaborate stocks for an elegant soup du jour. However, if you have some leftover vegetables, this soup stock is a good way to put them to use.

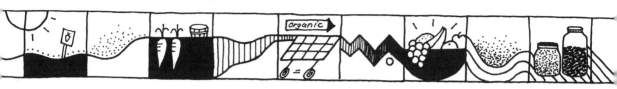

Substantial Suppers

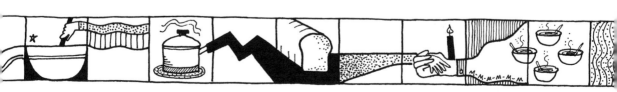

Indian Rice and Lentils (Mojadra)

1 cup short-grain brown rice
1 cup dried brown or green lentils
1 bay leaf
4 cups water

1 Tablespoon extra-virgin olive oil or ghee
2 large onions, sliced into thin rounds
2 cloves garlic, minced
1/2 teaspoon sea salt
1 1/2 teaspoons coriander
1 teaspoon cumin
1/8 teaspoon cayenne

Topping:
1/2 cup plain yogurt with 1 teaspoon fresh dill mixed in

Rinse and drain rice and lentils. Place in a 3-quart pot with bay leaf and water; bring to a boil. Lower heat and simmer 45 minutes.

Meanwhile, put oil in hot skillet. Add onions, garlic, and salt; sauté until onions begin to soften. Add spices and cook until onions are limp. When all water is absorbed from lentils and rice, remove from heat and take out bay leaf. Serve rice and lentils topped with spiced onions and a dab of yogurt with dill.

For experienced eaters: Puree some of the lentil-rice mixture before adding onions and spices.

Preparation time: 50 minutes
Servings: Makes 6 servings

Mojadra is an economical and flavorful dish. Use it as a standby for hurried days. Cook the rice and lentils in the morning; just 10 minutes evening preparation, and you have a fast homemade meal.

1 cup dried kidney beans, soaked
3 cups water
1 teaspoon cumin

2 teaspoons extra-virgin olive oil
1 medium onion, chopped
1/2 teaspoon sea salt
2 cloves garlic, minced
1 large green pepper, chopped
1 - 2 teaspoons cumin
1 teaspoon dried oregano
1/8 teaspoon cinnamon
1/8 teaspoon cayenne
2/3 cup quinoa, rinsed in warm water and drained
1 cup fresh or frozen corn
1 - 2 cups organic tomato sauce
1 cup water

Optional garnish:
A few Tablespoons grated cheese

Red Bean and Quinoa Chili

Drain soaking water off beans. Place beans in a large pot with water and cumin; bring to a boil. Then simmer over low heat, covered, until tender (50-60 minutes).

Heat oil in skillet on medium heat. Add onion, salt, garlic, pepper, and spices; sauté for several minutes. Add rinsed quinoa and stir in. Add onion and quinoa mixture to the cooked beans together with corn, tomato sauce, and water. Simmer together for 1/2 hour. Top each bowl with a sprinkle of grated cheese if desired.

For experienced eaters: Serve some of the plain cooked, mashed beans or puree some extra cooked corn with water.

Preparation time: 60 minutes for cooking beans,
   45 minutes for preparing chili
Servings: Makes 6-8 servings

I often serve this vegetarian chili to guests and they love it. By precooking the kidney beans, you can make a one-dish meal in 45 minutes.

Peasant Kasha and Potatoes

2 teaspoons toasted sesame oil

1 small onion, chopped

2 cloves garlic, minced

Pinch of sea salt

2 medium red potatoes or 1 large baking potato

3 - 4 mushrooms, sliced

1 cup kasha

2 cups boiling water

Freshly ground pepper

Heat oil in a 2-quart pot. Add onion, garlic, and salt; sauté until the onion is soft. Scrub potatoes well and cut into 1/2-inch cubes. Add potatoes and mushrooms to onion; sauté 1-2 minutes. Add kasha to mixture and stir. Pour in boiling water. Turn heat to low. Cover pot and simmer 15 minutes. Fluff up and serve garnished with pepper.

For experienced eaters: Omit onion, garlic, and salt.

Preparation time: 25-30 minutes
Servings: Makes 6 servings

Variation: Kasha Salad

Turn leftover kasha and potatoes into a salad for lunch. Add fresh chopped vegetables, such as parsley, cabbage, red pepper, and scallions, plus a Tablespoon of your favorite vinaigrette.

Whole grains and vegetables have been the chief foods of common people for centuries. Kasha and potatoes combine here for a rib-sticking meal.

Polenta Pizza

2 teaspoons extra-virgin olive oil

1 onion, chopped

1 - 2 cloves garlic, minced

1 Tablespoon chopped fresh oregano
   (or 1 teaspoon dried)

1 Tablespoon chopped fresh basil leaves
   (or 1 teaspoon dried)

1/2 medium zucchini

1/2 eggplant

1 patty-pan squash

1/2 green pepper

1 1/2 cups chunky tomato sauce

Polenta:

2 cups water

1 teaspoon sea salt

1 cup polenta

1 teaspoon butter

1 - 2 Tablespoons parmesan cheese

Optional garnish:

8 Tablespoons grated jack cheese

Preheat oven to 350 degrees F. Heat oil in a skillet. Sauté onion until soft. Add garlic and herbs; sauté a few minutes more. Cut zucchini, eggplant, squash, and pepper into 1/2-inch cubes. Put vegetables, onion mixture, and tomato sauce into a lightly oiled 8-by-8-inch pan. Cover and bake for 1 hour. While the vegetables bake, prepare the polenta. Bring water and salt to a boil. Add polenta and butter. Lower heat slightly and cook, stirring constantly, until polenta is thick enough to hold the spoon up on its own. Remove from heat. Spread polenta evenly into a 10-inch pie pan. Sprinkle parmesan on top and bake for 30 minutes. Remove both dishes from oven. Spoon tomato vegetable mixture on top of the baked polenta. Cut into slices and serve with grated cheese on top if desired.

For new eaters: Reserve some zucchini, steam, and puree it. *For children:* Some may prefer a slice of the plain baked polenta.

Preparation time: 60 minutes
Servings: Makes 8 slices

A new and healthful way
to enjoy pizza
without white flour
and mounds of fatty cheese.
Bake a double amount
of vegetables and
freeze half for another day.

Millet Croquettes with Shoyu-Scallion Gravy

1 cup millet
2 1/4 cups water
1/4 teaspoon sea salt

1 carrot
1 small onion or 1/2 large onion
1/3 cup chopped parsley
1/4 cup cold-pressed canola oil
1/4 cup whole-wheat pastry flour

Gravy:
1 - 2 Tablespoons kuzu
1 cup water
1 scallion, finely sliced
3 Tablespoons shoyu or tamari

Garnish:
Lemon wedges

To make millet:

Rinse and drain millet 2 or 3 times. Put millet, water, and salt in a pot; bring to a boil. Reduce heat to low, cover, and let simmer 25-30 minutes, until all water is absorbed. Remove from heat.

To make croquettes:

Chop carrot, onion, and parsley by hand or in a food processor. By hand, grate carrot and chop onion and parsley very finely. For food processor, roughly chop the vegetables and then place them in the processor. Pulse briefly until vegetables have reached a fine consistency.

Add chopped vegetables to cooked and cooled millet. Mix in well. Form mixture into patties with moist hands. If you have time, refrigerate the patties for an hour or more. Refrigeration helps hold patties together when they're cooked.

Heat oil in a large skillet. Lightly flour both sides of each patty. Fry in skillet, turning once. Both sides should have a crispy golden crust.

To make gravy:

Dissolve kuzu in water. Put in a small pan. Add sliced scallion. Bring mixture to a boil, stirring constantly. When mixture becomes clear and thick (5 minutes), turn heat off. Stir in shoyu. Serve immediately over croquettes, as gravy becomes jellylike if allowed to sit and cool.

Garnish each plate with a lemon wedge. A squeeze of lemon is tasty on the croquettes.

For new eaters: Reserve some cooked millet and puree with water or breast milk.
For experienced eaters: Reserve some cooked millet and puree with an extra carrot that has been sliced and steamed.
For children: Cook some extra millet and serve plain with a little maple syrup drizzled on top.

Preparation time: 45 minutes
  (excluding refrigeration time)
Servings: Makes 6-8 patties and 1 cup gravy

This has been my favorite way to eat millet for many years. If you cook the millet in the morning, you'll cut your dinner preparation time in half.

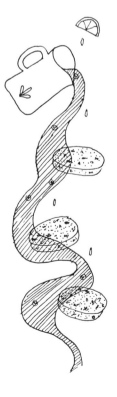

Mixed-Vegetable Stir-Fry with Nutty Ginger Drizzle

Stir-Fry:

1 - 2 teaspoons toasted sesame oil

1 large onion, chopped

1/4 teaspoon sea salt

2 cups broccoli flowerets

1 carrot, cut into thin slices

1 cup red cabbage strips

1/2 red pepper, cut into thin strips

1/4 cup arame, soaked in cold water for 5 minutes

Nutty Ginger Drizzle:

1/4 cup creamy almond butter or peanut butter

2 teaspoons maple syrup

2 Tablespoons tamari or shoyu

1 Tablespoon brown-rice vinegar

1 - 2 teaspoons hot pepper oil

1 teaspoon grated gingerroot

1/3 cup water

To make stir-fry:

Heat wok or large skillet over medium heat. Add oil to heated skillet. Add onion and salt, stirring continuously until onion is soft. Add broccoli first, then carrot, then cabbage, then pepper, letting each one cook 1-2 minutes before adding the next. Keep vegetables moving in the pan. Drain water off the arame. Sprinkle arame over vegetables and stir in.

To make drizzle:

Place all ingredients in a small saucepan on low heat. Stir with a whisk until mixture is smooth and warm. Serve stir-fry over your favorite grain with sauce drizzled on top.

For new eaters: Cut up an extra carrot, steam, and puree it. If you're serving the dish over rice, puree the carrot with some cooked rice.

For children: Some may prefer plain rice or noodles with a few of the stir-fried vegetables on the side. Children may enjoy dipping vegetables in a small bowl of the almond drizzle.

Preparation time: 15-20 minutes

Servings: Makes 4 servings of stir-fry and 1 cup sauce

One of the quickest meals you can make is stir-fried vegetables over your favorite whole grains. The addition of Nutty Ginger Drizzle makes the dish one your family will ask for again and again.

Mom's Marvelous Veggie Loaf

1/2 cup hazelnuts (filberts)

2 teaspoons extra-virgin olive oil or butter

1 onion, chopped

1/2 teaspoon sea salt

2 cloves garlic, minced

1 cup grated carrots

2 Tablespoons chopped parsley

1 teaspoon cumin

1 teaspoon oregano

2 1/2 cups cooked millet

1 cup cooked black beans or kidney beans

Sea salt and freshly ground pepper

Preheat oven to 350 degrees F. Place hazelnuts in a small baking dish and roast in the oven for 7-10 minutes. Heat oil in a skillet over medium heat. Add onion, salt, and garlic; sauté until onion is soft. Add grated carrots, parsley, cumin, and oregano to onion mixture; sauté briefly.

Place cooked millet in a large mixing bowl. Add onion-carrot-herb mixture and mix together well. Grind the roasted hazelnuts in a small electric grinder or food processor. Puree the cooked beans. Add ground nuts and pureed beans to millet mixture; blend well. Use your hands if necessary. Add salt and pepper to taste.

Line the long sides and bottom of a loaf pan with parchment paper or brown paper. Oil the paper and short sides of loaf pan. Put the loaf mixture in the pan. Tap the pan on the counter several times to even out contents. Bake 1 hour. Loaf will lift out easily when you pull the sides of the paper. Allow loaf to cool some before slicing.

For new eaters: Reserve some cooked millet and blend with water or breast milk.
For experienced eaters: Mash some extra beans and serve with pureed millet.

Preparation time: 90 minutes
Servings: Makes 1 loaf or 8 slices

Veggie loaf is an excellent way to recycle whole grains and beans. It is easy to make two of these loaves and freeze one for later. This loaf makes a homey dinner and a fabulous sandwich.

Arame and Black-Eyed Peas with Cilantro

2 cups dried black-eyed peas
4 cups water
1 cup arame, soaked in cold water
2 Tablespoons tamari or shoyu
2 Tablespoons brown-rice syrup or maple syrup
1/2 Tablespoon grated gingerroot
1 teaspoon brown-rice vinegar

Garnish:
1/4 - 1/3 cup chopped cilantro

Put peas and water in a pot; bring to a boil. Lower heat and simmer until tender (30-35 minutes). Add arame, tamari, syrup, and gingerroot. Gently stir and simmer mixture 10 more minutes. Add vinegar just before serving and garnish with cilantro.

For experienced eaters: Remove some black-eyed peas when tender and puree with a little water.

Preparation time: 45-50 minutes
Servings: Makes 6-8 servings

This dish, created by my talented friend Minx Boren, delights the taste buds with its unique combination of flavors. It goes well with Summer Corn Bread (page 214) and Susan's Succulent Supper Salad (page 199).

2 cups dried red beans or kidney beans, soaked
2 cloves garlic
1 teaspoon cumin
1 dried red chile pepper
1 2- to 3-inch piece of kombu,
    soaked in cold water 5 minutes
1/3 cup chopped onion
4 cups water
Sea salt

Sassy Red Beans

Drain soaking water from beans. Put beans, garlic, cumin, chile pepper, kombu, onion, and water in a pressure cooker.[29] Bring up to pressure. Lower heat and simmer 40-45 minutes. Remove from heat and let pressure come down (this can be done quickly by placing pot under cold running water). Remove lid, stir, and add salt to taste.

For experienced eaters: Cook beans without garlic, cumin, pepper, or onion. Omit salt. Remove plain beans for baby. Then sauté onion with spices and salt; add to beans for the rest of the family.

Preparation time: 50 minutes
Servings: Makes 8 servings

By just adding a few subtle flavorings to beans, you can create distinctive dishes such as this one. Make extra Sassy Red Beans and use to make Red Bean and Quinoa Chili (page 163) another day.

---

29 Pressure-cooking beans gives them a creamy texture and aids digestibility. However, if you don't own a pressure cooker, boil beans with spices, kombu, and onion for 1 hour. Use 6 cups water instead of 4.

Three Sisters Stew[30]

1 cup dried Christmas lima beans[31], soaked

3 cups water

2 cloves garlic

2 Tablespoons chopped fresh oregano
   (or 2 teaspoons dried)

1 teaspoon cumin seeds

1/2 teaspoon cinnamon

1 Tablespoon extra-virgin olive oil or ghee

1 medium onion, chopped

1/2 teaspoon sea salt

2 - 3 cloves garlic, minced

2 - 3 cups winter squash, cut into chunks
   (peel if not organic)

1 14-ounce can chopped tomatoes

1 Tablespoon chile powder

1 1/2 cups fresh or frozen corn

Optional garnish:

8 - 10 Tablespoons grated cheese

Drain soaking water off beans. Place beans, water, and garlic in a large pot; bring to a boil. Cover and simmer until beans are tender (50-60 minutes). Drain beans and set aside, reserving cooking liquid.

In a large pot, quickly toast oregano, cumin seeds, and cinnamon for about 30 seconds. Add oil, onion, salt, and minced garlic; sauté until onion is soft (5 minutes).

---

30   Native Americans grew corn and planted beans at the base. The corn stalks served as bean poles. They used the ground space between the stalks to grow squash. The three sisters (corn, beans, and squash) lived harmoniously.

31   Kidney, pinto, black, or Swedish brown beans can be substituted.

Add squash, tomatoes, and chile powder; cook until squash is soft (20 minutes). Use reserved bean liquid if mixture is dry. Add cooked beans and corn; simmer until corn is tender. Adjust seasoning to your taste. Serve hot, with grated cheese garnish if desired.

For new eaters: Reserve some peeled squash cubes, steam well, and puree.
For experienced eaters: Reserve some cooked Christmas limas before adding to stew and puree with steamed squash cubes.

Preparation time: 60 minutes for beans,
    25-30 minutes for stew
Servings: Makes 6-8 servings

My colleague Jackie Williams shared this incredible stew with me. It exemplifies the harmony of the three sisters — corn, beans, and squash — and is an excellent dish for the holidays or chilly winter nights.

Mexican Bean and Corn Casserole

1 cup dried pinto beans, soaked
1 clove garlic
1 teaspoon cumin seeds
3 cups water

1 teaspoon extra-virgin olive oil
1 onion, chopped
1/2 teaspoon sea salt
1 clove garlic, minced
1/2 red or green pepper, chopped
1 cup shredded green cabbage
2 teaspoons ground cumin
1 teaspoon oregano
1/2 cup organic tomato sauce
1/4 cup water

2 cups water
1 cup polenta
1 teaspoon sea salt
1 Tablespoon butter
1 Tablespoon parmesan cheese

Drain soaking water off the beans. Place beans in a large pot with garlic, cumin seeds, and 3 cups water; bring to a boil. Then simmer over low heat, covered, until tender (50-60 minutes). Heat oil in a large skillet. Add onion, salt, and garlic; sauté until soft. Add red or green pepper, cabbage, ground cumin, and oregano; continue sautéing 5 more minutes. Add cooked beans to the vegetables with tomato sauce and 1/4 cup water. In a separate pot, bring 2 cups water to a boil. Add polenta, salt, and butter. Stir constantly with a whisk until mixture becomes thick. Preheat oven to 350 degrees F. In a lightly oiled casserole dish, spread the bean-and-vegetable mixture across the bottom. Spread the polenta on top. Sprinkle top with parmesan cheese. Bake, covered, for 25 minutes at 350 degrees F. Remove cover and bake 5 minutes more at 400 degrees F.

For experienced eaters: Omit parmesan. Remove pieces of the baked polenta on top and serve.

Preparation time: 60 minutes for cooking beans,
*   40 minutes for casserole*
Servings: Makes 8 servings

Pinto beans and coarsely ground corn (polenta) make this satisfying one-dish meal the "most popular" in my class on beans. Make two casseroles and freeze one for a busy day.

Curried Lentils and Cauliflower

1 cup dried lentils
1 bay leaf
2 cups water

2 teaspoons extra-virgin olive oil
1 onion, chopped
1 clove garlic, minced
1/4 teaspoon sea salt
1 teaspoon coriander
1 teaspoon cumin
1 teaspoon turmeric
1/4 teaspoon cinnamon
1 small head cauliflower, cut into flowerets
1/2 - 1 cup tomato sauce
1 teaspoon grated gingerroot
3/4 - 1 cup water

Optional garnishes:
1/4 cup roasted cashews
1/4 cup plain yogurt

Wash and drain lentils. Place lentils in pot with bay leaf and water; bring to a boil. Lower heat, cover, and let simmer 25-30 minutes, until lentils are soft.

While lentils are cooking, heat oil in a large pot. Add onion, garlic, and salt; sauté until onion is soft. Add coriander, cumin, turmeric, and cinnamon. Add cauliflower, tomato sauce, gingerroot, and water; stir well. Cover and let simmer until cauliflower is tender (10-15 minutes).

Stir cooked lentils into cauliflower-tomato mixture, discarding the bay leaf. Serve over whole grains and garnish with roasted cashews or plain yogurt if desired.

For experienced eaters: Set aside some plain cooked lentils and puree them, or steam a bit of extra cauliflower and puree it with some water.
For children: Some may prefer plain lentils served with plain cooked rice and a few roasted cashews on the side.

Preparation time: 30-35 minutes
Servings: Makes 4 servings

My friend Joy Taylor made this dish for me many years ago. I jotted down the recipe and adapted it over time. Try serving it over basmati brown rice, which is prepared the same as boiled brown rice (page 83).

Black Bean Tostadas

1 teaspoon extra-virgin olive oil or ghee

1 onion, chopped

2 - 4 cloves garlic, minced

1 teaspoon cumin seeds

2 cups dried black beans, soaked

4 - 6 cups water

Sea salt

1/4 cup chopped cilantro

1/2 cup chopped tomatoes (optional)

12 - 14 flat corn tortillas

Optional garnishes:

Salsa

Cooked brown rice

Leaf lettuce, thinly sliced

Grated red cabbage

Grated zucchini

Grated red radish

Sprouts

Grated cow, goat, or soy cheese

Plain yogurt

Black olives

Avocado slices or guacamole

We often set out black beans, brown rice, salsa, guacamole, and other favorite toppings and let guests create their own tostadas or burritos or whatever. It's a crowd pleaser.

Heat oil in a large pot. Sauté onion, garlic, and cumin seeds in oil until onion is soft. Drain soaking water off beans. Add beans and 6 cups water to onion and spices; bring to a boil. Turn down to simmer and cook, covered, until beans are tender (50-55 minutes). Or pressure-cook 45 minutes with 4 cups water. Salt to taste after the beans are cooked. Stir in cilantro and tomatoes.

Bake or heat tortillas (read the instructions on the package). Serve tortillas, beans, and garnishes in separate bowls. Let diners create their own tostadas.

Preparation time: 1-2 hours,
    20 minutes if beans are precooked
Servings: Makes 6-7 cups beans or 12-14 tostadas

Nut Burgers

3/4 cup sunflower seeds

3/4 cup walnuts

1 teaspoon cumin

1 teaspoon oregano

1/8 teaspoon cayenne

2 cloves garlic, finely chopped

1 small carrot (or 1/2 large one), grated finely

1 cup cooked brown rice

2 Tablespoons tomato sauce

1 - 2 teaspoons cold-pressed canola oil

4 whole-grain hamburger buns

Grind seeds and nuts to a fine meal in a small electric grinder or food processor. Pour into a bowl. Add cumin, oregano, cayenne, garlic, and carrot; mix well. Fold in cooked brown rice. Add tomato sauce a little at a time until you get a stiff but workable texture. Form mixture into patties with moist hands. Refrigerate patties for a few hours if possible.

Lightly coat a skillet with canola oil and brown patties on both sides. Serve on whole-grain buns with your favorite fixings.

For new eaters: Puree extra cooked brown rice with water or breast milk to make a simple cereal.

*Preparation time: 15-20 minutes
    (excluding refrigeration time)
Servings: Makes 4 burgers*

This delicious burger recipe lets you pile up a bun with mustard, pickle, tomato, or other burger condiments and chow down without bothering a single cow.

Tempeh and Red Pepper Stroganoff

1 Tablespoon extra-virgin olive oil
1 large onion, chopped
1 - 2 cloves garlic, minced
1/2 teaspoon sea salt
1/2 teaspoon oregano
1/2 teaspoon thyme
1 large carrot, cut into large matchsticks
1 red pepper, cut into thin strips
1 8-ounce package tempeh, cut into 1/4-inch strips
4 Tablespoons whole-wheat pastry flour

2 Tablespoons mirin
3 Tablespoons tamari or shoyu
1 - 1 1/2 cups water

Garnish:
1/2 cup chopped parsley

Heat oil in a large skillet. Add onion, garlic, salt, and herbs; sauté until onion softens. Add carrot, then pepper, then tempeh, letting each cook a few minutes before adding the next. When tempeh starts to get golden, add flour; stir it in, coating the ingredients well.

In a separate bowl, mix mirin, tamari, and water together. Add slowly to tempeh, stirring as you go, to make a nice gravy. Simmer on low heat for 15-20 minutes, or place in a casserole and bake at 300 degrees F. for 30 minutes for deeper flavors. Serve over your favorite whole grains or noodles garnished with parsley.

For new eaters: Puree some of the cooked carrot.
For experienced eaters: Serve some of the cooked carrot in chunks with cut-up plain noodles or grains.

Preparation time: 35 minutes
Servings: Makes 4 servings

This mouth-watering tempeh recipe is quick to make. Served over quinoa, whole-wheat couscous, or udon noodles, it is a beautifully balanced meal.

2 teaspoons extra-virgin olive oil

1 onion, chopped

2 cloves garlic, minced

1/2 teaspoon sea salt

3 - 4 ounces tempeh,
     crumbled or cut into small chunks

1 cup chopped vegetables (broccoli, green pepper,
     zucchini, mushrooms, and summer squash are
     all good choices)

1 Tablespoon chopped fresh basil leaves
     (or 1 teaspoon dried)

1 Tablespoon chopped fresh oregano
     (or 1 teaspoon dried)

1 15-ounce jar of organic tomato or pasta sauce

1/2 - 1 cup water

1/8 teaspoon extra-virgin olive oil

8 ounces whole-wheat spaghetti

Flash Spaghetti

Bring a large pot of water to a boil for the spaghetti. In a separate 3-quart pot or 10-inch skillet, heat oil. Add onion, garlic, and salt; sauté until soft. Add tempeh to onion mixture and brown on all sides. Add chopped vegetables, herbs, tomato sauce, and water. Stir, cover, and let simmer 10-15 minutes.

Meanwhile, drop oil in the boiling water, then add spaghetti. Let spaghetti boil 12-15 minutes (whole-wheat pastas take longer than refined flour pastas). Rinse and drain spaghetti well in a colander. Serve spaghetti topped with tempeh-vegetable-tomato sauce.

For new eaters: Reserve some zucchini, steam, and puree it.
For experienced eaters: Cut some plain noodles into smaller pieces.

Preparation time: 20 minutes
Servings: Makes 4 servings

Hard-pressed for time? Whip up Flash Spaghetti with fresh vegetables and tempeh for a quick, well-rounded dinner, or plop some in a wide-mouth thermos for a hot lunch.

Szechuan Tempeh

1/4 cup cold-pressed canola oil
1 8-ounce package tempeh, cut into 1/4-inch strips
2 Tablespoons light or white miso
1/4 - 1/3 cup water
2 Tablespoons tamari or shoyu
2 Tablespoons mirin
2 Tablespoons balsamic vinegar
2 Tablespoons brown-rice syrup
2 teaspoons toasted sesame oil or hot pepper oil

Garnish:
1 scallion, thinly sliced

Heat 2 Tablespoons of the oil in a 10-inch skillet. Place half the tempeh strips in the skillet and let them quick-fry, turning them so that both sides brown. Remove fried tempeh onto a paper towel and REPEAT the process with the other half of the tempeh strips, using the other 2 Tablespoons of oil.

In a small bowl, mix miso and water with a whisk until miso is dissolved. Add tamari, mirin, vinegar, syrup, and oil to miso; whisk again. Lower heat on skillet. Place fried tempeh back in the skillet and pour sauce over the top. Garnish with scallion and serve immediately.

Preparation time: 15 minutes
Servings: Makes 3 servings

Our friends Brad and Margaret introduced us to this tasty way to make tempeh. The sweet and salty qualities of Szechuan Tempeh are nicely balanced when it's served atop plain brown rice, quinoa, or whole-wheat couscous.

2 teaspoons extra-virgin olive oil

1 onion, chopped

1 green pepper, chopped

1 clove garlic, minced

1/4 teaspoon sea salt

1 8-ounce package tempeh

2/3 cup fruit-sweetened, organic catsup

2 teaspoons whole-grain mustard

1 Tablespoon brown-rice vinegar

1/2 teaspoon cloves

4 whole-grain hamburger buns

Optional garnishes:

Lettuce

Pickles

Sprouts

Sloppeh Joes

Heat oil in a 10-inch skillet. Add onion, pepper, garlic, and salt; sauté until soft. Crumble tempeh with fork or by hand; add to onion mixture. Let the tempeh brown. Mix catsup, mustard, vinegar, and cloves together in a small bowl. Add to tempeh mixture, mixing well. Warm buns in oven if desired. Spoon tempeh mixture onto buns and serve with your favorite garnish.

For experienced eaters: Serve a warmed bun with a little apple butter or squash butter (page 208).

Preparation time: 20 minutes
Servings: Makes 4 servings

Can you tell I was raised in the 1950s and 1960s? This vegetarian version of the familiar classic was styled from one of my mother's recipes.

Tofu Kale Supper Pie

Crust:
2 cups whole-wheat pastry flour
1/3 cup water
1/3 cup cold-pressed vegetable oil
1/4 teaspoon sea salt

Filling:
2 teaspoons extra-virgin olive oil
1 onion, chopped
Pinch of sea salt
2 carrots, thinly sliced into half-moons
1 bunch kale leaves
Pinch of sea salt
1 pound firm tofu
1 Tablespoon umeboshi vinegar
1 Tablespoon extra-virgin olive oil
1 Tablespoon mustard
2 teaspoons tamari or shoyu
1 Tablespoon fresh dill (or 1 teaspoon dried)

To make crust:

Preheat oven to 350 degrees F. Put flour in a bowl. In a separate bowl, whisk water, oil, and salt together. Slowly pour liquid into flour, blending with a fork. Gather dough into a ball; it should be moist and pliable. Roll out into a crust on a floured surface or a piece of waxed paper. Transfer to an 8- or 9-inch pie pan. Trim edges. Prebake for 10 minutes in the oven.

To make filling:

Heat oil in a large skillet. Add onion, salt, and carrots; sauté until onion is soft. Set aside.

Bring a large pot of water to a boil. Wash kale and remove stems. Add kale leaves and salt to water; boil 5-7 minutes. Remove boiled kale, squeeze out water, and chop fine.

Blend tofu, vinegar, oil, mustard, tamari, and dill in a blender or food processor until smooth. If using firm tofu, you may need to add a little water.

To assemble pie:

Put the onion-and-carrot mixture in the bottom of the prebaked crust. Separate the kale and arrange it on top of the onion-and-carrot mixture. Pour the tofu mixture over the top, covering the vegetables. Bake 30 minutes until the top of the pie begins to turn beige at the edges. Cut and serve.

For new eaters: Steam some extra carrot slices and puree.
For experienced eaters: Make Tofu Mash or Tofu Cubes (page 102) with some extra tofu and serve with carrot puree.

Preparation time: 55 minutes
Servings: Makes 8 slices

Tofu Kale Supper Pie
is an adaptation
of the wonderful tofu quiche
found in Annemarie Colbin's
book "The Natural Gourmet."
This version uses
supernutritious
kale and carrots.

Hiziki Pâté

1 cup hiziki
1 - 1 1/2 cups water or apple juice[32]
1 teaspoon tamari or shoyu

1/4 cup sesame seeds, toasted, then ground
1/2 pound firm tofu, crumbled with a fork
2 Tablespoons light or white miso
1/2 bunch parsley, chopped fine
2 scallions, thinly sliced

Soak hiziki in water for 5 minutes and chop fine. Put hiziki in a medium-size pan and add 1 - 1 1/2 cups water to cover; bring to a simmer. Cover pan and cook until water is absorbed, about 20 minutes. Toward the end of the cooking time, season hiziki with tamari.

While hiziki is cooking, prepare other ingredients. Sesame seeds can be toasted in a skillet on the stove for several minutes, then ground. Gently mix tofu, sesame seeds, miso, parsley, and scallions together in a bowl. Let the hiziki cool and then add to the mixture. Serve with whole-grain crackers, bread, or as a side dish. Will keep 3 days in the refrigerator.

For experienced eaters: Serve cubes of plain tofu and strands of cooked, chopped hiziki.

Preparation time: 30-40 minutes
Servings: Makes 2 1/2 - 3 cups

A very creative friend, Mim Collins, and her teacher, Roberta Lewis, came up with this scrumptious way to use hiziki. I have seen several 2-year-olds, as well as meat-and-potato eaters, gobble it up with glee.

32   Using apple juice cuts the fishy taste of sea vegetables, making the pâté more palatable to newcomers.

2-3 pounds salmon filet[33]

Dr. Bruce's Awesome Grilled Salmon

Marinade:

2/3 cup tamari or shoyu

1/2 cup extra-virgin olive oil

2 teaspoons toasted sesame oil

2 Tablespoons grated gingerroot

Juice of 1 large lime

4 cloves garlic, minced

4 scallions, finely chopped

Garnish:

2 red peppers, cut into big slices

To marinate salmon:

Put tamari, oils, gingerroot, lime juice, garlic, and scallions in a small mixing bowl; whisk together. Place fish in a shallow pan and pour marinade over the top. Allow to marinate one hour in the refrigerator.

To grill salmon:

When the coals in your grill are just becoming white, remove fish from pan and place fish on the grill, skin side down. Brush the top with part of the marinade and grill the fish for about 5 minutes.[34] Turn the fish over and remove the skin; it should come off easily. Brush the top with marinade again and grill for 3-5 minutes more, until the fish is tender at the thickest part. Flip it over and serve grilled side up. Roast chunks of red pepper on grill while cooking fish and serve as a garnish.

Preparation time: 60 minutes for marinating,
*   10-15 minutes for cooking*
Servings: Makes 6 servings,
*   more if used as a side dish*

Dr. Bruce Gardner, a family practitioner, prepared this mouth-watering delicacy for us and I have never forgotten it. The ginger-lime marinade makes this dish awesome.

33   Fresh filet of halibut works well also.
34   The rule of thumb for cooking fish is 10 minutes of cooking time per inch of thickness. This is true for grilling, poaching, baking, or broiling.

Thea's Greek Shrimp Stew

1 Tablespoon extra-virgin olive oil
2 onions, chopped
1/2 teaspoon sea salt
4 cloves garlic, minced
3 cups chopped or diced organic tomatoes
1 cup organic tomato sauce
2 teaspoons wet whole-grain mustard
3 Tablespoons fresh dill (or 1 Tablespoon dried)
1 teaspoon brown-rice syrup
1 pound cooked shrimp
1/4 pound feta cheese, crumbled
1 cup chopped parsley

In a large soup pot, heat oil, then add onions, salt, and garlic; sauté until soft. Add tomatoes, tomato sauce, mustard, dill, and syrup; simmer 20 minutes. About 5 minutes before serving, add shrimp, feta, and parsley. Stir well and serve.

Preparation time: 30 minutes
Servings: Makes 6 servings

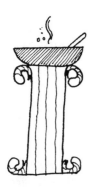

We serve this rich, scrumptious stew to company for a special treat.

1 pound fish steak (shark, cod, salmon, tuna . . .)

Marinade:
2 Tablespoons tamari or shoyu
1 Tablespoon mirin
1 teaspoon brown-rice vinegar
1 teaspoon toasted sesame oil

Whisk tamari, mirin, vinegar, and oil together in a small bowl. Pour over fish and marinate 1-2 hours in the refrigerator. Broil in the oven or cook on the grill. Follow the 1-inch rule: Cook fish 10 minutes for each inch of thickness.

Preparation time: 1-2 hours for marinating,
*   10 minutes for cooking*
Servings: Makes 4 servings if used as a side dish

Japanese Marinated Fish Steak

Any firm fish cut into steaks will work with this marinade. It's especially tasty grilled over mesquite coals.

Baked Chicken with Mushrooms and Rosemary

8 - 10 whole mushrooms
1/2 cup wine, stock, or water
2 Tablespoons tamari or shoyu
3/4 - 1 pound chicken breasts
    (from organically raised chickens)
1 3-inch sprig of fresh rosemary (or 1 teaspoon dried)

Preheat oven to 350 degrees F. Wipe mushrooms clean with a damp towel or rag. Put wine and tamari in an 8-inch baking dish. Place chicken breasts and cleaned mushrooms in the dish. Lay the rosemary sprig on top of the chicken. If using dried rosemary, sprinkle on top. Cover the dish and bake for one hour. Remove cover and broil for a minute or 2 before serving, if desired.

Preparation time: 65-70 minutes
Servings: Makes 4 side-dish-size servings

Occasionally, I bake this tasty chicken dish and use it as a side dish with a large amount of brown rice, steamed vegetables, and salad. Mushrooms are heavenly when you bake them whole.

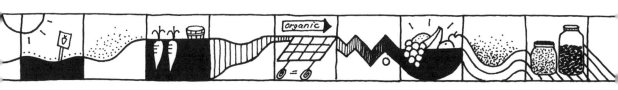

Vital Vegetables

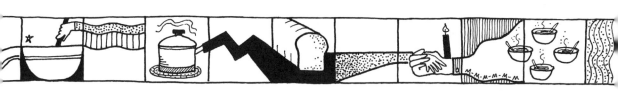

Quick-Boiled Greens

Choose 8 cups of one or more:
Beet greens
Bok choy
Broccoli
Chinese cabbage (napa)
Collard greens
Dandelion greens
Endive
Escarole
Kale
Mustard greens
Swiss chard
Turnip greens
Watercress

2 quarts water or soup stock

Optional Garnishes:
Freshly squeezed lemon juice
Brown-rice vinegar or umeboshi plum vinegar

For greens with tough stems, tear the leaves away from the stem before washing. Wash greens carefully. An easy way is to fill your sink with cold water and submerge the greens. If the water has sediment, drain the sink and REPEAT.

Bring water to a boil. Submerge greens. Boil tender young greens (such as watercress or escarole) for about 30 seconds. Tougher leaves (such as mature collards or kale) need to be cooked for 5-10 minutes. Pour cooked greens into a colander in the sink. Let cool. Squeeze out excess water with your hands. Chop greens into bite-size pieces. Serve with a few drops of lemon juice or vinegar. Reserve cooking water for watering your plants.

Preparation time: 10 minutes
Servings: Makes 2 cups or 4 servings

Vitamin A, vitamin C, folic acid, calcium, iron, and even protein are found in most dark leafy greens. These powerful vegetables should be a daily part of the diet. Quick-boiled greens are also excellent served chilled atop crisp green salads.

2 cups Quick-Boiled Greens (page 190)
1 teaspoon brown-rice syrup
1 - 2 teaspoons brown-rice vinegar
1 teaspoon toasted sesame oil
1 teaspoon hot pepper oil
2 Tablespoons toasted sesame seeds (page 133)

Prepare greens. Mix syrup, vinegar, and oils together. Pour dressing over greens; add seeds and toss well. Serve warm, cold, or at room temperature.

Preparation time: 15 minutes
Servings: Makes 2 cups or 4 servings

Sesame Greens

Sesame greens make a tasty and impressive side dish for any meal.

2 cups Quick-Boiled Greens (page 190)
1/4 cup cashew butter
1 Tablespoon Homemade Curry Paste (page 226)
1 Tablespoon tamari or shoyu
3/4 cup water

Prepare greens. Combine cashew butter, curry paste, tamari, and water in a blender; blend until creamy. Combine greens and blended sauce in a pan. Gently heat before serving.

Preparation time: 15 minutes
Servings: Makes 4 servings

Cashew-Curry Greens

Cashew-Curry Greens are sinfully delicious served over cooked rice or quinoa. For extra decadence, top with a few whole, roasted cashews.

Garlic Sautéed Greens

8 cups chopped raw greens
1 Tablespoon extra-virgin olive oil or ghee
1 Tablespoon minced garlic
1/3 cup water

Garnish:
1 Tablespoon freshly squeezed lemon juice

For greens with tough stems, tear the leaves away from the stem before washing. Wash greens carefully. An easy way is to fill your sink with cold water and submerge the greens. If the water has sediment, drain the sink and REPEAT.

Heat oil in a 10-inch skillet. Add garlic and sauté a minute or so. Add greens and keep them moving in the skillet. When greens start to become a brighter shade and wilt, add water, cover pan, and let steam 5 minutes.[35] Remove lid and cook off any water. Garnish with lemon juice and serve.

Preparation time: 15 minutes
Servings: Makes 2 cups or 4 servings

These are delicious served with black-eyed peas and corn bread.

---

35   Tougher greens like kale or collards require steaming. If using tender greens such as watercress or bok choy, omit the water and steaming.

Dark Greens Salad with Creamy Ginger-Garlic Dressing

Salad:

2 cups Quick-Boiled Greens (page 190)

1/2 head red leaf lettuce

1 bunch watercress, tough stems removed

1/2 cucumber, peeled and thinly sliced

Dressing:

1/2 pound tofu

1 teaspoon grated gingerroot

2 cloves garlic, minced

2 Tablespoons extra-virgin olive oil

2 Tablespoons freshly squeezed lime juice

2 teaspoons tamari or shoyu

1/3 - 1/2 cup water, to desired consistency

Prepare Quick-Boiled Greens and set aside in the refrigerator. Wash lettuce and watercress by placing leaves in a sink full of cold water. Drain and REPEAT. Spin or pat dry. Tear greens into bite-size pieces. Place lettuce and watercress in a large salad bowl. Add Quick-Boiled Greens and cucumber; toss together and set aside.

Place all ingredients for dressing in a blender; blend until smooth. Serve salad with about 2 Tablespoons of dressing per serving on top. Leftover dressing will keep in the refrigerator for about a week.

For experienced eaters or children: Make Tofu Mash or Tofu Cubes (page 102) with leftover tofu.

Preparation time: 15 minutes
Servings: Makes 4 servings salad
*   and more than 1 cup dressing*

This is a delicious way to add dark greens to your diet — just plop them into your favorite salad.

Romaine Radicchio Salad with Lemon-Olive Oil Dressing

Salad:

1/2 head romaine lettuce

1 small head radicchio[36]

1/2 cup alfalfa sprouts

3 thin rounds of red onion

2 Tablespoons crumbled feta cheese (optional)

Dressing:

Juice of 1/2 lemon

2 Tablespoons extra-virgin olive oil

1 teaspoon tamari or shoyu

1 clove garlic, peeled and split in half

1/4 teaspoon freshly ground pepper

In the bottom of a salad bowl, whisk together lemon juice, oil, and tamari with a fork. Add the garlic clove and pepper; let rest.

Wash and dry romaine and radicchio by placing leaves in a sink full of cold water. Drain and REPEAT. Spin or pat dry. Tear lettuce and radicchio into bite-size pieces. Place greens and radicchio in salad bowl on top of dressing. Add sprouts, onion rounds, and feta cheese on top. Before serving, remove garlic clove. Toss salad and dressing together and serve.

Preparation time: 10 minutes
Servings: Makes 6 servings

Sometimes simple is best. The simplest lemon and olive oil dressing can turn flavorful, fresh greens into an elegant salad.

36   Use 1 cup chopped red cabbage if radicchio is unavailable.

Salad:

1/2 large head green cabbage, shredded (8-10 cups)
1 carrot, cut into matchsticks
1/2 red pepper, cut into small strips
1/4 cup toasted sesame seeds[37]

Dressing:

1 teaspoon grated gingerroot
1 clove garlic, minced
2 Tablespoons brown-rice vinegar
2 Tablespoons mirin
2 Tablespoons toasted sesame oil
2 Tablespoons tamari or shoyu
1 Tablespoon hot pepper oil
1 Tablespoon maple syrup

Bring a large pot of water to a boil. Keep cabbage, carrot, and pepper in separate piles. Drop shredded cabbage into boiling water and cook for 30-45 seconds. Add carrot and pepper; cook 15 seconds more. Pour cooked vegetables into a colander and rinse with cold water to stop cooking. Let drain.

Place all dressing ingredients in a small bowl; whisk together and set aside. Gently squeeze the water out of the cooked vegetables and put vegetables into a salad bowl. Add sesame seeds and dressing; toss gently and serve immediately.

For new eaters: Steam and puree an extra carrot.
For experienced eaters: Reserve some plain cooked cabbage and carrot; serve as finger food.

Preparation time: 15 minutes
Servings: Makes 8 servings

Cooked Cabbage Salad with Sweet Sesame Dressing

A colorful winter salad that rounds out any meal. Try it with Peasant Kasha and Potatoes (page 164). The dressing is also excellent on noodles.

---

37   For instructions on toasting sesame seeds, see Rice Balls Rolled in Sesame Salt (page 133).

Mustard Green Salad with Tofu-Dill Dressing

Salad:

1/2 bunch mustard greens[38]

1/2 head green leaf lettuce

1/2 bunch red radishes, sliced

1 handful alfalfa sprouts

Dressing:

1/2 pound tofu

2 Tablespoons brown-rice vinegar

1 Tablespoon fresh dill (or 1 teaspoon dried)

1/2 cup water

Wash mustard greens and lettuce by placing leaves in a sink full of cold water. Drain and REPEAT. Spin or pat dry. Tear greens into bite-size pieces and place in a large salad bowl with radishes and sprouts on top. Set aside.

Place all ingredients for dressing in a blender and blend until smooth and creamy. Dress salad with about 3/4 cup of the dressing before serving and toss well. The leftover dressing will keep in the refrigerator for about a week.

For experienced eaters: Cut up chunks of leftover tofu and make Tofu Cubes (page 102).

Preparation time: 10 minutes
Servings: Makes 6 servings salad
and 1 1/2 cups dressing

The sharp taste of calcium-rich mustard greens goes well with an easy-going tofu dressing. If you use less water in making the dressing, you can create a creamy sauce for pasta or grains.

38   Buy mizuna mustard greens if possible; they are the tenderest.

Salad:

1 bunch watercress, tough stems removed

1/2 head red leaf lettuce

1 cucumber, thinly sliced

Vinaigrette:

1/3 cup unrefined sesame oil

1/4 cup brown-rice vinegar

2 teaspoons toasted sesame oil

1 teaspoon tamari or shoyu

1 teaspoon chopped fresh oregano
   (or 1/4 teaspoon dried)

Wash watercress and lettuce by placing leaves in a sink full of cold water. Drain and REPEAT. Spin or pat dry. Tear greens into bite-size pieces and place in a large salad bowl. Add cucumber and set aside.

Place all ingredients for vinaigrette in a small jar, cover, and shake well. Pour half of the vinaigrette on the salad and toss. The remainder of the vinaigrette will keep in the refrigerator for at least a week.

Preparation time: 10 minutes
Servings: Makes 6 servings salad
   and 2/3 cup vinaigrette

Watercress Salad with Sesame Vinaigrette

This salad is quick, light, and nutritious. Watercress is rich in minerals and is usually free of pesticides as it grows easily and abundantly. Use leftover vinaigrette to dress grain or bean salads for lunchboxes.

Creamy Cole Slaw

Salad:

3 cups green cabbage, shredded (about 1/4 head)

1 cup red cabbage, shredded

1 carrot, grated

1 scallion, chopped finely

Dressing:

3 Tablespoons mayonnaise

2 Tablespoons freshly squeezed lemon juice

1 teaspoon brown-rice syrup

1 teaspoon tamari or shoyu

Freshly ground pepper

Combine cabbages, carrot, and scallion in a bowl; toss together and set aside. Combine all dressing ingredients in a small bowl and blend with a whisk or fork until mixed well. Pour dressing over vegetables and toss again.

For experienced eaters and children: Serve separate little piles of the grated or shredded vegetables without dressing.

Preparation time: 5-10 minutes
Servings: Makes 6 servings

over the meadow and through the woods

This dish has the familiar look and taste of traditional cole slaw, but with about half the mayonnaise and, therefore, half the fat.

Susan's Succulent Supper Salad

Salad:

1/2 head romaine lettuce

1 bunch spinach

1/2 bunch arugula or rocket

1 cup chopped red cabbage

1 tart apple, cut into bite-size pieces

1 ripe avocado, cut into bite-size pieces

1/4 cup raisins

1/4 cup toasted pumpkin seeds

3 scallions, finely sliced

1 or 2 fresh tomatoes, cut into wedges

1 cup alfalfa sprouts

2/3 cup cooked chick-peas

Dressing:

1/4 cup extra-virgin olive oil

3 Tablespoons balsamic vinegar

2 teaspoons Dijon mustard

2 teaspoons maple or brown-rice syrup

1 clove garlic, minced

1/8 teaspoon paprika

1/4 teaspoon tamari or shoyu

Wash lettuce and greens by placing leaves in a sink full of cold water. Drain and REPEAT. Spin or pat dry. Tear greens into bite-size pieces and place in a large salad bowl. Add all other salad ingredients and set aside.

Put all ingredients for dressing in a small bowl or jar. Whisk together or shake vigorously. Dress salad just before serving and toss well.

For new eaters: Reserve a slice or two of avocado, mash or blend, and serve.

For experienced eaters: Steam a few apple slices and serve with a Tablespoon of raisins.

For children: Serve separate piles of raisins, apples, pumpkin seeds, sprouts, and avocado.

Preparation time: 20 minutes

Servings: Makes 8 servings or 4 if used as a main course

My friend Susan Wilson made up this feast of a salad, which gets raves in my classes. It is easy to make.

Grilled Vegetable Salad with Sweet Poppyseed Dressing

Grilled Vegetables:

1 eggplant, cut into 1/2-inch rounds
1 red pepper, cut into large wedges
1 onion, cut into large wedges
1 summer squash, cut into long, thick strips
1 zucchini, cut into long, thick strips
10 big mushrooms
Extra-virgin olive oil

Salad:

8 cups salad greens (any combination of red leaf
    lettuce, mustard greens, watercress, arugula,
    spinach, radicchio, romaine, or Bibb)
1 - 2 ounces feta cheese, crumbled

Dressing:

4 Tablespoons extra-virgin olive oil
3 Tablespoons brown-rice vinegar
2 Tablespoons brown-rice syrup
1 Tablespoon Dijon mustard
2 teaspoons poppyseeds
1 Tablespoon fresh dill (or 1 teaspoon dried)

Light the coals in your grill (a small hibachi works fine). While coals are heating, wash and cut vegetables for grilling. Brush both sides of each vegetable piece with a light coat of oil. When coals are white-hot, place vegetable pieces on grill and cook a few minutes on each side, until the vegetables start to brown. Set aside grilled vegetables.

Wash salad greens by placing leaves in a sink full of cold water. Drain and REPEAT. Spin or pat dry. Tear greens into bite-size pieces and place in a large salad bowl. Cut grilled vegetables into bite-size pieces and add them to salad greens. Crumble feta on top.

Whisk all ingredients for dressing together or shake in a small jar. Dress and toss salad before serving.

For children: You may want to serve grilled vegetables on a shish kebab instead of in a salad. Grilled vegetables can also be served with a dip. (Lemon-Tahini Sauce, page 222, and Tofu-Dill Dressing, page 196, work well.)
For adults: Save leftover grilled vegetables to make sandwiches the next day.

Preparation time: 30 minutes
Servings: Makes 8 servings salad and 2/3 cup dressing

Vegetarians, take heart! Summer grilling is for you, too! Grilled vegetables are delicious whether served over rice, in a pocket pita, or in this incredible salad. Thanks to Susan Wilson for the inspiration.

Salad:
1-2 bunches spinach
1/4 cup walnuts, roasted and chopped
1/2 small red onion, sliced into thin rounds

Vinaigrette:
3 Tablespoons extra-virgin olive oil
2 Tablespoons balsamic vinegar
3/4 teaspoon Dijon mustard
1/4 teaspoon freshly ground pepper

Spinach Salad with Balsamic Vinaigrette

This hearty salad, served with whole-grain bread and a spread such as Gingered Lentil Sandwich Spread (page 136), can be a light summer meal. Leftover vinaigrette works well on grain or bean salads for lunchboxes.

Wash spinach by placing leaves in a sink full of cold water. Drain and REPEAT. Spin or pat dry. Remove stems and tear spinach into bite-size pieces. Place in a large salad bowl; add walnuts and red onion. Place all vinaigrette ingredients in a jar and shake well. Dress salad just before serving. Leftover vinaigrette will keep in the refrigerator for at least a week.

Preparation time: 10 minutes
Servings: Makes 6 servings salad and 1/3 cup vinaigrette

Dulse Salad with Lemon-Tahini Dressing

Salad:

1 cup dried dulse

1 red onion, sliced into thin rounds

1 - 2 stalks celery, cut into bite-size pieces

1 Tablespoon brown-rice vinegar

Pinch of sea salt

4 red leaf lettuce leaves

Dressing:

1/4 cup tahini

1 clove garlic

2 - 3 Tablespoons freshly squeezed lemon juice

1/2 teaspoon tamari or shoyu

1/2 cup water

Soak the dulse in cold water. Meanwhile, cut the other vegetables for the salad. Clean the soaked dulse well, removing any pebbles. Pat dulse dry. Combine dulse, red onion, and celery with vinegar and salt; refrigerate for an hour or so.

Combine all ingredients for dressing in a blender and blend until smooth. Serve the salad on a lettuce leaf with 1 Tablespoon dressing on top. Leftover dressing will keep in the refrigerator for a week.

Preparation time: 15 minutes for making salad,
*   60 minutes for marinating*
Servings: Makes 4 servings salad and 3/4 cup dressing

If you're looking for added iron in your diet, search no more. Dulse, a dark red sea vegetable, contains 11 grams of iron per 1/4 cup. Serve this salad to your favorite pregnant or nursing mom.

6 red potatoes, quartered
2 - 3 carrots, sliced at an angle into chunks
3 Tablespoons extra-virgin olive oil
2 teaspoons cumin
1/4 teaspoon cayenne
1/8 teaspoon cinnamon

Preheat oven to 350 degrees F. Scrub potatoes and carrots. Remove eyes from the potatoes and peel vegetables if not organic. Cut up vegetables and place in an 8-by-8-inch baking dish. Mix oil and spices together in a small bowl. Drizzle over top of the vegetables. Mix vegetables with a wooden spoon so they are evenly coated. Cover pan and bake 1 hour.

For new eaters: Remove a little potato and carrot before adding oil and spices. Bake in a separate dish. Blend baked vegetables with a little water.

Preparation time: 70 minutes
Servings: Makes 4 servings

Variation: Sweet Potato Roast

Substitute 4 sweet potatoes, scrubbed and cut into chunks, for the red potatoes.

organic Produce →

The spices are subtle, so children love these succulent, roasted vegetables. The dish requires slow baking in the oven, but very little time for you in the kitchen.

Potato Gratin

2 teaspoons extra-virgin olive oil
1 red pepper, sliced thin
1 large onion, sliced thin
2 cloves garlic, minced
4 - 6 red potatoes, sliced 1/4-inch thin,
    steamed 10 minutes until edges are limp
2 Tablespoons parmesan cheese (optional)
Freshly ground pepper

Heat oil in a skillet. Add pepper, onion, and garlic; sauté for a few minutes. Preheat oven to 350 degrees F. Layer steamed potatoes and vegetables in a casserole. Cover and bake 30-40 minutes. Uncover the casserole and top with parmesan and pepper. Turn oven up to 400 degrees F. and bake until the top is brown, approximately 10 minutes.

For new eaters: Put some of the steamed potatoes in a separate baking dish and bake 30-40 minutes. Remove and puree with water or breast milk.

Preparation time: 50 minutes
Servings: Makes 4-6 servings

This recipe was inspired by one in a book called "Gourmet Underway" by the Resource Institute in Seattle. Traditional potatoes au gratin are loaded with milk and cheese, but this lighter version is equally satisfying.

Shopping for Winter Squash

Just about everyone loves the taste of sweet vegetables. I returned to Kansas one Thanksgiving and prepared Baked Winter Squash (page 206) and sweet potatoes mashed together for the family gathering. Several relatives praised the offering and asked for the recipe. I repeated many times that it was simply baked buttercup squash and sweet potatoes. My grandmother insisted that there must be brown sugar, pineapples, marshmallows, or all three in the dish.

The autumn harvest brings pumpkins and a wide variety of winter squashes, each with its own unique and unbelievably sweet flavor. These vegetables not only score high in taste, but are rich in vitamin A, vitamin C, fiber, and trace minerals. Here are some varieties to shop for:

Acorn squash, shaped like a large acorn with prominent ridges; comes in dark green, yellow, or orange; sweet, light flesh

Buttercup squash, shaped like a pumpkin but smaller; green or gold skin; meat is dark orange, moist, and creamy

Butternut squash, gourd-shaped with a neck and a bulbous base; buff-colored skin; flesh is orange and firm

Delicata squash, small, oblong shape; yellow skin with green stripes; particularly sweet, golden-colored flesh

Golden turbans, distinctive turban shape, like a double-decker pumpkin; comes in hues of green, gold, orange, and red; mild, pleasant flavor

Hubbard, large, smooth-skinned squash; gray-green color; classic flavor

Kabocha, pumpkin-shaped; dark green with gray-brown nubs; dark orange flesh

Spaghetti squash, large, oval-shaped squash; yellow skin; insides become long, thin, golden strands when cooked

Sugar pie pumpkins, small, dark orange pumpkins; perfect for pie-making

Basic Baked Winter Squash

1 winter squash (any variety)[39]

Preheat oven to 350 degrees F. Small squashes can be washed and baked whole. Larger squashes can be cut in half. Be sure to use a strong, sharp knife. Scoop out the pith and seeds; lay squash flat on a lightly oiled baking sheet or dish. Bake until tender. Test by inserting a fork; it should slide in easily and feel soft.

Small squashes such as delicata take only 35-45 minutes to bake, while a squash weighing 3 pounds may take up to 90 minutes. Another option is to cut the squash into chunks and place in a lightly oiled, covered casserole. Bake for 20-30 minutes.

For new or experienced eaters: Reserve some baked squash and puree with a little breast milk or water.

Preparation time: Depends on size of squash
Servings: 2 1/2 pounds of squash makes 2-3 cups
cooked squash or 4 servings

My very favorite vegetable dish. It soothes the soul.

39   See list of squashes on page 205.

1 garnet yam
1 or 2 delicata squashes
1/4 cup soy milk or coconut milk
1/2 teaspoon cinnamon
1/4 teaspoon nutmeg

Sweet Autumn Bake

Preheat oven to 400 degrees F. Wash yam and cut in half. Place yam face down on an oiled cookie sheet and put in oven. Cut squash in half and scoop out seeds. After 20 minutes, put the squash face down on the cookie sheet with the yam halves and bake both for 40 minutes more or until tender.

Let the vegetables cool until you can comfortably handle them. Scoop out the insides of the yam and the squash. Blend the insides with milk and spices in a food processor, with a hand mixer, or by hand using a potato masher. Put mixture in a baking dish, cover, and keep warm in a low-temperature oven until served. For a beautiful touch, pipe the puree onto plates through a pastry bag.

For new eaters: Puree some of the baked squash and yam before adding milk and spices.

Preparation time: 60 minutes
Servings: Makes 6 servings,
   depending on size of vegetables

This dish will be gobbled down
by toddlers and
grandparents alike.
Its beautiful color and
delectable taste
go well with any meal.

Winter Squash Variations

- Spices and herbs can enhance flavor. Cinnamon, nutmeg, cardamom, and allspice add to the familiar sweetness. Savory tastes can be created by adding a bit of rosemary, oregano, or thyme to your winter squash dish.

- Add leftover cooked and mashed winter squash, or grated, raw squash to muffins, hot cereal, pancakes, and quick breads for extra sweetness and nutrition. Leftover cooked winter squash freezes well for later use. See "Recycling Food Using Leftovers" (page 73) for more ideas.

- Use leftover baked and pureed winter squash to make a delicious alternative to butter — Squash Butter. Add 1 teaspoon tahini and 1 teaspoon miso to 1 cup pureed winter squash; mix well and spread on bread or muffins.

- Simmer 2 - 3 cups peeled winter squash chunks in 4 - 6 cups water with 1 chopped onion, 1 chopped apple, and 1 Tablespoon curry powder for 1/2 hour and puree it for a luscious soup.

- You can add bite-size chunks of winter squash to beans, stews, and soups to make hearty autumn fare. See Three Sisters Stew (page 172).

- Pureed Basic Baked Winter Squash (page 206) is excellent baby food.

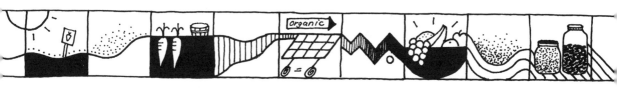

Fresh Breads and Muffins

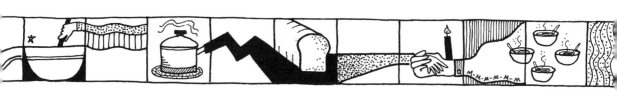

Homemade Whole-Grain Breads

Starter Dough:

2 cups cooked whole grains

2 cups water

1/4 cup cold-pressed vegetable oil

1 Tablespoon sea salt

1 Tablespoon dry yeast

1 cup whole-wheat flour (more or less)

Blend grains and water in a blender or food processor until creamy; pour into a large mixing bowl. Mix in oil, salt, and yeast. Add enough flour to make the mixture look like thick cooked cereal. Cover the bowl with plastic wrap or a damp towel; leave for 12-24 hours at room temperature.[40]

To make the bread:

Starter Dough

1/4 cup sweetener

   (such as barley malt or maple syrup)

2 cups whole-wheat flour

3 - 4 cups unbleached white flour or whole-wheat flour

After Starter Dough has set for 12-24 hours, add sweetener to Starter Dough and stir with wooden spoon. Begin adding whole-wheat flour, stirring it in. As you add white flour, the mixture will be too difficult to stir. Knead it by hand in the bowl and continue to add white flour. When dough is less sticky, transfer it to a floured surface and knead 10-15 minutes or until dough is soft and springy, but not sticky. Wash and dry mixing bowl; then oil it. Place dough in bowl, cover, and let rise in a warm place 1 1/2 - 2 hours.[41]

To make loaves:

Lightly oil 2 loaf pans. Divide dough in half. Punch down and loaf the dough in the following way (children love to help with this part):

---

40   You can refrigerate the fermented Starter Dough for up to a week and make the bread another day.

41   You can freeze all or half the dough after the first rising. Place dough in a sealed plastic bag, label, and put in the freezer. Thaw dough, form loaf, and bake it another day.

- Flatten half the dough into a square on your working surface. Press all the air out of the dough by vigorously slapping the dough with the palms of both hands. Cover the entire area of the dough.
- Fold the flattened dough into a triangle and press it down again.
- Fold 2 corners into the center and press again.
- Fold the top point into the body of the dough and press it down again.
- Pick up the dough with both hands and begin rolling it into itself. This stretches the outside of the dough and creates a tight roll with no air pockets. Seal the seam by flattening it with the heel of your hand.
- Shape the dough into a nice loaf and place in the pan seam side down.
- Punch down and shape the other half of the dough.

To bake the bread:
1 teaspoon water
1 teaspoon barley malt or maple syrup
1 teaspoon cold-pressed vegetable oil
Pinch of sea salt

Mix water, syrup, oil, and salt in a small cup or bowl. Coat the top of each loaf with this mixture. Cover and let rise in pans for 45-60 minutes until the loaves have doubled in size.

Test the bread for readiness. If you press the dough and it wants to stay in, but still has a little spring, it's ready to bake.

Preheat oven to 350 degrees F. Bake 45-50 minutes. Bread will come out of pans after 5 minutes of cooling. Let it cool 30 minutes before slicing (if you can wait!).

Preparation time: Each step of actual work takes only 5-15 minutes, over a period of 2 days. The fermenting, rising, and baking take time.
Servings: Makes 2 loaves

Whole-Grain Bread Variations

Rice Bread

Starter Dough:
2 cups cooked brown rice

2 cups water

1/4 cup cold-pressed vegetable oil

1 Tablespoon sea salt

1 Tablespoon dry yeast

1 cup whole-wheat flour (more or less)

To make the bread:
Starter Dough

1/4 cup barley malt

2 cups whole-wheat flour

3 - 4 cups unbleached white flour or whole-wheat flour

Quinoa Garlic Herb Bread

Starter Dough:
2 cups cooked quinoa

2 cups water

1/4 cup extra-virgin olive oil

1 Tablespoon sea salt

1 Tablespoon yeast

1 cup whole-wheat flour (more or less)

To make the bread:
Starter Dough

6 cloves garlic, minced very fine

1 Tablespoon chopped fresh basil leaves
    (or 1 teaspoon dried)

2 Tablespoons chopped fresh parsley

2 Tablespoons chopped fresh cilantro

2 teaspoons chopped fresh rosemary
    (or 1/2 teaspoon dried)

2 cups whole-wheat flour

3 - 4 cups unbleached white flour or whole-wheat flour

Orange Millet Raisin Bread

Here are four delicious versions of Jeff's bread. Follow directions for Homemade Whole-Grain Breads with these specific ingredients.

Starter Dough:

2 cups cooked millet

2 cups orange juice

1/4 cup cold-pressed vegetable oil

1 Tablespoon sea salt

1 Tablespoon yeast

1 cup whole-wheat flour (more or less)

To make the bread:

Starter Dough

1/4 cup barley malt or maple syrup

2 cups raisins

1 teaspoon cinnamon

2 cups whole-wheat flour

3 - 4 cups unbleached white flour or whole-wheat flour

Bean Apple Rye Bread

Starter Dough:

2 cups cooked beans

    or 1 cup cooked beans

    and 1 cup Basic Baked Winter Squash (page 206)

1 1/2 - 2 cups water

1 Tablespoon yeast

1 Tablespoon sea salt

1 cup whole-wheat flour

1/4 cup cold-pressed vegetable oil

To make the bread:

Starter Dough

1/3 cup apple butter

2 Tablespoons Sucanat or date sugar

2 cups whole-wheat flour

1 cup rye flour

2 - 3 cups unbleached white flour or whole-wheat flour

Summer Corn Bread

1 cup cornmeal
1 cup whole-wheat pastry flour
2 teaspoons nonaluminum baking powder
1/4 teaspoon sea salt
1 Tablespoon dulse flakes (optional)

1/4 cup cold-pressed vegetable oil
1/4 cup sorghum or maple syrup
1 egg
1/2 cup plain soy milk
1/2 cup water
1 cup fresh or frozen corn kernels

Preheat oven to 375 degrees F. Mix cornmeal, flour, baking powder, salt, and dulse flakes in a large bowl; set aside.

In a separate bowl, mix oil, sorghum, egg, milk, and water. Add wet ingredients to dry mixture and mix well. If using fresh corn kernels, remove kernels from cooked ear of corn with a knife and add. Two ears usually yield one cup of corn. Frozen corn can be added as is. Add corn to batter and fold in.

Lightly oil an 8-by-8-inch pan. Pour batter into pan. Bake 25-30 minutes. Top will crack slightly, and bread will begin to pull away from the sides when done.

For experienced eaters: Quickly boil some extra fresh or frozen corn. Puree in a blender with a little water until smooth.

Preparation time: 40 minutes
Servings: Makes 16 2-inch squares

Fresh corn kernels freshen up this old favorite, and the added dulse gives a mineral boost. Children love corn bread served with apple butter. This is an adaptation of a recipe by Nancy Rankin.

2 cups cornmeal

2 cups whole-wheat pastry flour or barley flour

4 teaspoons nonaluminum baking powder

1/4 teaspoon sea salt

3 Tablespoons dulse flakes

1/2 cup cold-pressed vegetable oil

1/2 cup maple syrup

2 eggs

1 1/2 - 2 cups water

3/4 cup leftover Basic Baked Winter Squash
   (page 206) (buttercup, butternut, and delicata
   squashes work well, or use baked sweet potato)

Topping:

1/3 cup pumpkin seeds

Preheat oven to 375 degrees F. Lightly oil muffin tins or line with paper muffin cups. Mix cornmeal, flour, baking powder, salt, and dulse flakes together in a large bowl; set aside.

In a separate bowl, whisk together oil, syrup, eggs, water, and squash until smooth. Combine wet ingredients with dry mixture and mix with a minimum of strokes. Spoon into muffin cups. Decorate top of each muffin with pumpkin seeds. Bake 20 minutes. Top of muffin should crack slightly when done.

For new or experienced eaters: Reserve a portion of the Basic Baked Winter Squash or sweet potato; puree or mash.

Preparation time: 30 minutes
Servings: Makes 18 regular muffins or 24 minimuffins

Sweet Squash Corn Muffins

These corn muffins, developed by Nancy Rankin and me, are rich in taste and nutrition. The winter squash imparts vitamin-rich sweetness, and the dulse flakes add iron.

Applesauce Muffins

1 cup whole-wheat pastry flour
1 cup barley flour
1 Tablespoon nonaluminum baking powder
1/2 teaspoon cinnamon
1/4 teaspoon nutmeg

1/4 cup cold-pressed vegetable oil
1/4 cup apple butter
1/4 cup sorghum
    (barley malt or maple syrup can be substituted)
1 cup applesauce
1 egg
1/4 cup water or milk

Preheat oven to 400 degrees F. Lightly oil muffin tins or line with paper muffin cups. Mix together flours, baking powder, and spices in a large bowl; set aside.

In a separate bowl, whisk together oil, apple butter, sorghum, applesauce, egg, and water. Add wet ingredients to dry mixture and fold gently until mixed, using a minimum of strokes. Fill 12 baking cups with the batter. Bake 15-20 minutes.

For new or experienced eaters: Use organic applesauce and serve some plain.

Preparation time: 25 minutes
Servings: Makes 12 regular muffins

Applesauce muffins are easy to pack in a lunchbox, serve as snacks at school, or grab for a quick breakfast. Their not-too-sweet flavor makes them a perfect accompaniment to soups or salads.

1 1/2 cups whole-wheat pastry flour
1 1/2 cups unbleached white flour
1 Tablespoon baking powder
1 teaspoon baking soda
1 teaspoon sea salt
1 teaspoon cinnamon
1/2 teaspoon cloves
1/2 teaspoon cardamom

12 dates, pitted and chopped
1 cup hot water
15-ounce can pumpkin
    or 2 cups Basic Baked Winter Squash (page 206)
3/4 cup soy milk
1/3 cup cold-pressed vegetable oil
1/3 cup maple syrup
2 teaspoons vanilla extract
2 eggs
1/3 cup walnuts, chopped

Pumpkin Muffins

Preheat oven to 350 degrees F. Lightly oil muffin tins or line with paper muffin cups. Mix together flours, baking powder, baking soda, salt, and spices in large mixing bowl; set aside.

Put dates and hot water in a blender; blend until smooth. Add pumpkin, soy milk, oil, maple syrup, and vanilla extract; blend again. Add eggs and pulse briefly. Add wet ingredients to dry mixture and fold gently, using a minimum of strokes. Gently fold walnuts into batter. Fill muffin cup to top with batter. Bake 40-45 minutes. Test for doneness with toothpick; muffin is done if toothpick comes out cleanly from the center.

Preparation time: 60 minutes
Servings: Makes 18 muffins

Canned pumpkin or leftover Basic Baked Winter Squash is delicious in this recipe. Winter squash renders a sweeter muffin.

Poppyseed Muffins

1 1/2 cups whole-wheat pastry flour
3/4 cup unbleached white flour
3/4 cup cornmeal
1 Tablespoon baking powder
1 teaspoon baking soda
1 teaspoon sea salt
1 teaspoon cinnamon
2/3 cup poppyseeds

12 dates, pitted and chopped
1 cup hot water
1/2 cup orange juice
1/2 cup plain yogurt
2 ripe bananas
1/2 cup maple syrup or concentrated fruit sweetener
1/3 cup cold-pressed vegetable oil
1 teaspoon vanilla extract
2 eggs

Preheat oven to 350 degrees F. Lightly oil muffin tins or line with paper muffin cups. Put flours, cornmeal, baking powder, baking soda, salt, cinnamon, and poppyseeds in large mixing bowl; stir and set aside.

Place dates and hot water in a blender; blend until smooth. Add juice, yogurt, bananas, syrup, oil, and vanilla extract; blend again. Add eggs and pulse briefly. Add wet ingredients to dry mixture and mix together, using a minimum of strokes. Fill muffin cups to top with batter. Bake 40-45 minutes.

Preparation time: 55-60 minutes
Servings: Makes 18 muffins

Variation: Blueberry Muffins

Omit poppyseeds and add 2 cups of blueberries to batter.

Variation: Poppyseed Cake

Pour batter into two 8-inch round cake pans and bake as above. Spread Apricot Glaze (page 248) or Banana Cream Frosting (page 252) between layers and on top.

Using various sweet fruits lowers the need for concentrated sweeteners in a recipe. Dates, ripe bananas, and orange juice marry well with poppyseeds to make a wonderful muffin.

Banana Date Nut Bread

1 1/2 cups whole-wheat pastry flour
1/2 cup unbleached white flour
2 teaspoons nonaluminum baking powder
1/2 teaspoon sea salt

2 ripe bananas[42]
1/4 cup cold-pressed vegetable oil
   or melted, unsalted butter
10 - 12 dates, pitted and chopped
Juice of 1 orange plus enough water to equal 1 cup
1 teaspoon vanilla extract
1 egg
1/4 cup chopped walnuts
1/4 cup raisins

Preheat oven to 375 degrees F. Mix flours, baking powder, and salt together in a bowl; set aside.

Put bananas, oil, dates, juice, water, and vanilla extract in a blender; blend until smooth. Add egg to blender and pulse briefly. Add wet ingredients to dry mixture and mix well. Fold in chopped nuts and raisins. Put mixture in a lightly oiled loaf pan and bake for 45 minutes or until a clean knife inserted in the center comes out clean.

Preparation time: 60 minutes
Servings: Makes 1 loaf or 8 1-inch slices

This moist, sweet dessert bread uses various fruits for flavor. Enjoy this bread at your next tea party.

---

42   To get extra sweetness from bananas, peel overripe ones and freeze them. Thaw before using.

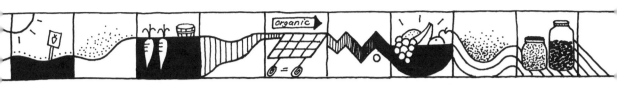

Sauces and Stuff

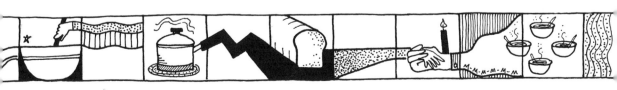

Lemon-Tahini Sauce

This sauce is so versatile you may want to keep a batch on hand all the time. It is excellent on rice, noodles, salads, and more.

1/2 cup tahini
4 - 6 Tablespoons freshly squeezed lemon juice
1 - 2 cloves garlic
1 teaspoon tamari or shoyu
1/16 teaspoon (just a pinch) cayenne
3/4 cup water

Place all ingredients in a blender; blend until smooth. Allow mixture to set for a half hour if possible to allow flavors to meld. Sauce will keep in the refrigerator for 10-14 days.

Preparation time: 5 minutes
Servings: Makes 1 1/4 cups

Tahini Oat Sauce with Scallions

This creamy, simple-to-make sauce is just the thing to serve over brown rice or whole-grain noodles.

1/4 cup rolled oats
1 cup water
Pinch of sea salt
2 Tablespoons tahini
1 Tablespoon tamari or shoyu
1 Tablespoon water
1 scallion, finely chopped

Put oats, water, and salt in a small pan; bring to a boil. Lower heat, cover, and simmer 10-12 minutes. Put oat mixture in a blender with tahini, tamari, and water; blend until smooth. Return to small pan, adding chopped scallion. Gently reheat, if necessary, before serving.

For new eaters: Cook oats without salt and puree some for your baby before adding other ingredients.

Preparation time: 15 minutes
Servings: Makes 1 cup

1/4 cup almond butter
2 teaspoons maple syrup
2 Tablespoons tamari or shoyu
1 Tablespoon brown-rice vinegar
1 teaspoon grated gingerroot
1 - 2 teaspoons hot pepper oil
1/3 cup water

Put all ingredients in a small pan on low heat. Using a whisk, mix ingredients until smooth and warm. Serve immediately over grains, beans, or cooked vegetables.

Preparation time: 5 minutes
Servings: Makes 1 cup

Nutty Ginger Sauce

A sensuous topping for grains or vegetables. I especially like it served over kasha. You can substitute different nut butters to create slight variations in taste.

1/2 pound tofu
1 teaspoon grated gingerroot
2 cloves garlic, minced
2 Tablespoons extra-virgin olive oil
2 Tablespoons lime juice
2 teaspoons tamari or shoyu
1/4 cup water

Place all ingredients in a blender; blend until smooth. Will keep in the refrigerator 4-5 days.

Preparation time: 5 minutes
Servings: Makes 1 cup

Creamy Ginger-Garlic Dressing

This lively sauce is delicious served on whole-grain pastas, rice, kasha, cooked greens, steamed vegetables, and green salads.

Mushroom-Wine Gravy

2 teaspoons butter
1/4 pound mushrooms, cleaned and sliced
Pinch of sea salt
1 cup water
1 Tablespoon tamari or shoyu
1 Tablespoon cashew butter
1 Tablespoon arrowroot
2 Tablespoons white wine

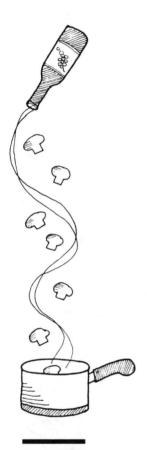

In a small pan, melt butter. Add mushrooms and salt; sauté until mushrooms are soft. Whisk in water, tamari, cashew butter, arrowroot, and wine. Heat until gravy becomes thick (a few minutes).

Preparation time: 10 minutes
Servings: Makes 1 1/2 cups of gravy

Mashed potatoes and gravy,
vegetarian style.
Use this gravy on
Mom's Marvelous Veggie Loaf
(page 169) or on
simple cooked grains.

1/2 pound unsalted butter
1 clean 8-ounce jar with lid

Ghee[43]

Put butter in a saucepan. Heat butter until it begins to boil, then turn heat to low. White foam (from the milk solids) will accumulate on the top. Use a small strainer and begin gently skimming solids off the top without disturbing the bottom. As you continue this process, the liquid in the bottom of the pan will begin to appear clear and golden. When all the water is boiled out of the butter, the cooking will sound like hissing and the bubbling will stop. Remove from heat and let cool a moment or two. Pour the ghee into the jar. It will solidify as it cools. Store in the refrigerator.

Preparation time: 15 minutes
Servings: Makes about 1 cup

Thought in the East to have many virtues, ghee is said to take on and magnify the properties of the food with which it is combined, making the food more nutritious.

43   Ghee will tolerate a higher heat than whole butter and will not scorch.

Homemade Curry Paste

1 cup extra-virgin olive oil
1 pound onions, chopped fine
1/4 cup cumin seeds
1 teaspoon fenugreek
1 teaspoon whole cloves
2 teaspoons whole black pepper

2 Tablespoons whole mustard seeds
2 teaspoons allspice
1 teaspoon cardamom
4 teaspoons cinnamon
1/4 cup turmeric
1/4 cup coriander
2 teaspoons cayenne

1/4 cup fresh gingerroot, peeled and chopped fine

Heat oil in a skillet on low heat. Add onions and sauté until very soft. While onions are cooking, grind cumin, fenugreek, cloves, and pepper to a fine powder.

Mix the newly ground spices with mustard seeds (whole), allspice, cardamom, cinnamon, turmeric, coriander, and cayenne; set aside.

Add gingerroot to soft onions and oil; let it cook a few minutes. Add spices to onions and gingerroot; cook 5 more minutes. Store in a sealed jar in the refrigerator where it will keep for several months.

Preparation time: 20-25 minutes
Servings: Makes 2 cups

Jeff Basom created this multiuse flavoring for soups, beans, and all sorts of vegetable dishes. This handy product for busy cooks will keep for a month or more in the refrigerator. It also makes a great gift.

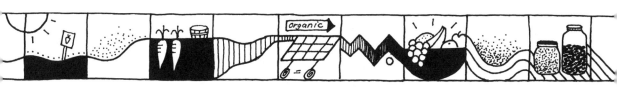

Wholesome Desserts

Adapting Recipes that Contain Sugar

For more nutritious desserts, you can replace 1 cup of white or brown sugar with 1 cup of any of the alternative sweeteners listed below. Instructions for balancing dry and wet products are on page 229. These alternative sweeteners are fairly interchangeable; for instance, if a recipe calls for 1 cup of honey, you could use 1/2 cup brown-rice syrup and 1/2 cup date puree.

These sweeteners vary in sweetness, so you can pick the ones that suit your needs. The "sweeter" alternatives are at the top of each list; the less sweet ones toward the bottom. For more information on some of these products, see the "Glossary of Ingredients" in the Appendix.

Dry Sweeteners:
Sucanat (dried organic cane juice)
Fruitsource (granulated rice syrup and grape juice concentrate)
ground date sugar

Thick Liquid Sweeteners:
maple syrup
sorghum
concentrated fruit sweetener
Fruitsource (liquid form)
barley malt
brown-rice syrup (rice syrup)
pureed dates (Winter Fruit Puree, page 100)
pureed ripe bananas
apple butter
frozen fruit juice concentrate
fruit juice
amasake

- When using any wet concentrated sweetener in place of dry sugar, reduce liquid content in the recipe by 1/4 cup. If the recipe calls for no liquid, add 3-5 Tablespoons flour for each 3/4 cup of concentrated sweetener.

- Heating thick syrups before using makes them more pourable. To heat, set the jar in hot water for 5-10 minutes. Be sure to oil measuring utensils used with the thick syrups.

- Because they contain a natural starch-splitting enzyme, some malted sweeteners (brown-rice syrup and barley malt) may liquefy the consistency of a mixture, especially if eggs are in the recipe. Boiling the malt syrup for 2-3 minutes before using can prevent this. Let it cool slightly before adding to recipe.

- You can also reduce fats and sugars in traditional recipes by partly replacing them with juice or water. For example, if a recipe calls for 1/2 cup honey and 1/2 cup oil, substitute 1/3 cup brown-rice syrup, 1/3 cup apple juice, and 1/3 cup oil.

Some of the better alternative sweeteners are expensive. This can help us keep sweets in perspective: Desserts and goodies are not daily bread.

Gingerbread People

1/4 cup unsalted butter, softened
1/4 cup Sucanat or date sugar
1/4 cup brown-rice syrup
1/4 cup blackstrap molasses
1 Tablespoon grated gingerroot

2 1/2 cups whole-wheat pastry flour
1/2 cup unbleached white flour
1 teaspoon baking soda
1/4 teaspoon cloves
1/2 teaspoon cinnamon
1/2 teaspoon sea salt
1/4 - 1/2 cup orange juice

Decorations:
Dried cranberries
Papaya bits
Peanuts
Raisins

Preheat oven to 350 degrees F. In a large mixing bowl, blend butter and Sucanat until creamy. Add syrup, molasses, and gingerroot; mix well.

In a separate bowl, combine flours, soda, cloves, cinnamon, and salt. Add dry mixture to wet ingredients a little at a time, alternating with orange juice as needed. Work in the last of the flour mixture with your hands.

Lightly oil a cookie sheet and roll the dough directly onto it. Cut out figures with a cookie cutter or make up your own shape. Remove scraps of dough between cutouts to make more cookies. Add decorations before baking. Bake 8 minutes or longer according to thickness of dough.

Preparation time: 15-20 minutes
Servings: Makes 8-15 cookie people,
   depending on thickness

**Children love making
and decorating these
tasty little cookie people.**

2 cups whole-wheat pastry flour
1 cup almonds (ground into 1 1/2 cups meal)
2 teaspoons baking powder
1/4 teaspoon sea salt

1/3 cup cold-pressed vegetable oil
      or melted, unsalted butter
1/3 cup apricot or apple juice
1/3 cup maple syrup or concentrated fruit sweetener
1 1/2 teaspoons almond extract
1/4 teaspoon vanilla extract
Apricot preserves (fruit-sweetened)

Preheat oven to 350 degrees F. Combine flour, almonds, baking powder, and salt in a mixing bowl; set aside.

In a separate bowl, mix oil, juice, syrup, and extracts together. Add wet ingredients to dry and mix well, kneading a little. Form dough into circles and place on lightly oiled cookie sheet. Indent each cookie with your thumb or your child's thumb; put 1/2 teaspoon preserves in the imprint. Bake 15 minutes, until edges turn golden.

Preparation time: 30 minutes
Servings: Makes 24 cookies

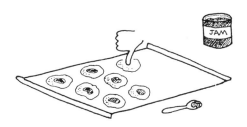

These delicious and fun-to-make thumbprint cookies are perfect with afternoon tea.

Cynthia's Oatmeal Cookies

2 cups rolled oats
1 cup whole-wheat pastry flour
1/4 teaspoon sea salt
1 teaspoon cinnamon

1/3 cup concentrated fruit sweetener,
    brown-rice syrup, or maple syrup
1/4 cup cold-pressed vegetable oil
    or melted, unsalted butter
1/2 - 3/4 cup apple juice
1 teaspoon vanilla extract
1/4 cup chopped walnuts
1/4 cup raisins or unsweetened
    or malt-sweetened carob chips
1/4 cup shredded, unsweetened coconut

Preheat oven to 350 degrees F. Mix oats, flour, salt, and cinnamon together in a bowl; set aside.

In a separate bowl mix together sweetener, oil, juice, and vanilla extract. Add wet ingredients to dry mixture and mix well. Stir in nuts, raisins or carob chips, and coconut. Drop by teaspoon onto a lightly oiled cookie sheet. Bake for 12-15 minutes, until golden on edges.

Preparation time: 20 minutes
Servings: Makes 24 cookies

These are yummy and quick —
my primary requirements
for a great dessert.

1 cup barley flour
1 cup spelt flour
1/2 teaspoon baking soda
1 teaspoon cinnamon
1/2 teaspoon ginger
1/4 teaspoon nutmeg
1/4 teaspoon allspice

3/4 cup pureed, cooked pumpkin, winter squash,
   or sweet potato
3/4 cup Sucanat or date sugar
1/2 cup apple butter or plain yogurt
2 Tablespoons cold-pressed vegetable oil

Preheat oven to 350 degrees F. Combine flours, soda, cinnamon, ginger, nutmeg, and allspice in a mixing bowl; set aside.

In a separate bowl, combine pumpkin, Sucanat, apple butter, and oil. Add wet ingredients to dry mixture. Lightly oil a cookie sheet and drop mixture by Tablespoons onto cookie sheet. Bake 15 minutes.

Preparation time: 25-30 minutes
Servings: Makes 24 cookies

Halloween Cookies

(wheat-free)

The children at the Briar Rose Kindergarten in Seattle happily devoured these Halloween cookies with a swirl of Yummy Yam Frosting (page 252) on top, a healthy harvest treat designed by Rita Carey.

Carob
Carob-Chip
Cookies

1 1/2 cups whole-wheat pastry or barley flour
1 cup carob powder, sifted
1/8 teaspoon sea salt
1/4 cup unsweetened carob chips
1/4 cup raisins

1/3 cup concentrated fruit sweetener
    or brown-rice syrup
1/3 cup cold-pressed vegetable oil
    or melted, unsalted butter
1/3 cup water
1 Tablespoon almond butter
1 teaspoon vanilla extract

Garnish:
12 almonds, sliced in half

Preheat oven to 350 degrees F. In a large mixing bowl, combine flour, carob powder, salt, carob chips, and raisins; set aside.

In a separate bowl, whisk together sweetener, oil, water, almond butter, and vanilla. Add wet ingredients to dry mixture and mix well. The batter is quite thick. Using your hands to knead it together works well. Form 2-inch round cookies with moist hands and place on a lightly oiled cookie sheet. Place half an almond in the center of each cookie. Bake 12 minutes.

Preparation time: 20 minutes
Servings: Makes 24 cookies

These are fudgy and fast.
Make a lot.
They get eaten up quickly!

Brown-Rice Crispy Treats

1 teaspoon unrefined sesame oil
1 cup brown-rice syrup
2 Tablespoons almond butter or tahini
2 teaspoons vanilla extract[44]
6 cups dry natural brown-rice crispy cereal

Optional additions:
1/2 cup peanuts
1/2 cup raisins or currants
1/2 cup unsweetened carob chips
1/2 cup chopped almonds

Put oil into a large pot and heat. Add rice syrup and nut butter. Stir and heat until bubbles form. Turn off heat and add vanilla extract. Add cereal and mix well with a spatula. Stir in optional items and mix lightly.

Press into a 9-by-13-inch pan. With slightly wet hands, press mixture flat. Let mixture set to room temperature. Slice and serve. Lasts a week in an airtight container.

Preparation time: 5-8 minutes
Servings: Makes 24 squares

The kids at Decatur Elementary School in Seattle did a swell job of making and devouring these quick-to-fix treats during an after-school cooking class I conducted. This is an adaptation of a recipe from Nancy Rankin.

44   I sometimes substitute 1/4 teaspoon butterscotch flavoring for the vanilla extract for a slightly different flavor.

Nutty Carmelcorn

1/4 cup almonds
1/4 cup peanuts
1/4 cup walnuts or hazelnuts

1/2 cup brown-rice syrup
8 cups popped corn (1/2 cup yields 10 cups popped)
1/4 cup raisins or currants

Preheat oven to 350 degrees F. Place nuts on cookie sheet and toast in oven until they begin to turn golden and give off a nutty aroma (8-10 minutes). (If using hazelnuts, remove skin after toasting.) Set aside.

Heat jar of rice syrup in a pan of boiling water to soften it. Place popped corn, raisins, and nuts in a large bowl; pour syrup over them. With moistened hands, mix well so syrup lightly covers all. This is a sticky business, so keep remoistening hands and work quickly.

Transfer mixture to an oiled baking sheet and spread out in a single layer. Bake for 8-10 minutes and not a minute more. Let cool 5 minutes before removing with spatula. Soak baking sheet in hot water to remove crusty sweetener.

Preparation time: 20 minutes
Servings: Makes 5-7 servings

This recipe comes from "Fresh from a Vegetarian Kitchen" by Meredith McCarty. Nutty Carmelcorn became a popular snack at my daughter's preschool.

1/2 cup brown-rice syrup
3/4 cup almond butter
1/4 teaspoon vanilla extract
3/4 cup carob powder, sifted

Carob Almond Fudge

Warm rice syrup in a pan of hot water. Put almond butter in a small mixing bowl. Blend in syrup and vanilla extract. Slowly add carob powder. When it becomes hard to stir, pick up the whole mixture with your hands and knead a few times until mixed well and smooth. Press mixture into a small square dish (a plastic sandwich container works well). Refrigerate about 1 hour, then cut into 1-inch squares.

Preparation time: 10 minutes for making fudge,
    60 minutes for setting
Servings: Makes 25 1-inch pieces

This treat is rich and mouth-watering, just as fudge should be, but without the cooking usually required. I make carob fudge for a special holiday candy at Christmas or Valentine's Day.

Fruitsicles

Juicesicles

1 cup juice (raspberry, grape, cherry, apple, tropical)

Pour juice into holders and freeze.

Creamy Orange-Vanilla Pops

3/4 cup orange juice
1/4 cup vanilla yogurt
1 teaspoon vanilla extract

Blend all ingredients in a blender, pour into holders, and freeze.

Banana-Raspberry Pops

1 banana
1/3 cup raspberries
1/2 cup water

Blend all ingredients in a blender, pour into holders, and freeze.

Melonsicles

2 cups melon chunks
  (cantaloupe, honeydew, watermelon)
1/4 cup water

Blend all ingredients in a blender, pour into holders, and freeze. If using watermelon, remove seeds and omit water.

You can buy Popsicle holders in the summertime at most stores that carry toys or kitchenware. Dream up an endless variety of frozen treats to delight sun-soaked children and adults.

Maltsicles

8 ounces malted soy milk

Pour commercially made malted soy milk, in any flavor you like, into Popsicle holders and freeze.

Note how much liquid it takes to fill your Popsicle holders. Each of these recipes makes one cup of liquid, which fills four of the common cylindrical-style holders. Freeze for at least 2 hours. Run warm water over the outside of the holder until the pop pulls out easily. You can also use ice-cube trays to make iced fruit cubes for children to suck.

Preparation time: 5 minutes for making pops,
  2 hours for freezing
Servings: Makes 4 fruitsicles,
  depending on size of holders

Apricot Kuzu Custard

A sweetly soothing dessert or snack that is easy to prepare. With a little granola sprinkled on top, it's fit for company.

2 Tablespoons kuzu
2 cups apricot nectar or juice
2 teaspoons tahini
1 teaspoon vanilla extract

Dissolve kuzu in cold or room-temperature juice. Put mixture in a small pan over medium heat, stirring constantly. As mixture simmers, it becomes clear and thick. Once this happens, remove from heat. Add tahini and vanilla extract; mix well. Serve immediately; custard will get rubbery if allowed to cool to room temperature.

For experienced eaters: Cool slightly before serving.

Preparation time: 5-10 minutes
Servings: Makes 4 servings

Raspberry Pudding Gel

I admit an occasional desire for Mom's pudding-from-a-box, so I invented this healthier, sugar-free version. It's creamy, smooth, yummy, and sweet.

1 quart raspberry juice
1/3 cup agar flakes
1 Tablespoon kuzu dissolved in 1/4 cup water
2 Tablespoons concentrated fruit sweetener
1 teaspoon vanilla extract
1 Tablespoon tahini

Garnish:
Fresh raspberries

Put juice and agar in a 2-quart saucepan over medium heat; bring to a boil. Lower heat and simmer 10 minutes. Add dissolved kuzu, stirring mixture constantly until smooth and clear. Remove from heat. Add sweetener and vanilla extract; stir again. Pour into a 9-by-13-inch pan and let gel at room temperature or in the refrigerator (an hour or more).

Put gelled mixture in a blender or food processor with the tahini; blend for a few seconds until smooth. Pour into individual serving cups. Serve with fresh raspberries on top.

Preparation time: 20 minutes for making,
*   60 minutes for setting*
Servings: Makes 6-8 servings

1 cup soy milk

1 cup amasake

2 Tablespoons agar flakes

1 Tablespoon kuzu dissolved in 1/4 cup water

2 Tablespoons maple syrup or brown-rice syrup

1/2 teaspoon vanilla extract

Optional garnishes:

4 teaspoons fruit-sweetened jam

Grated nutmeg

Vanilla Amasake Pudding

Pour soy milk and amasake into a pan. Sprinkle agar over the top. Heat to a simmer without stirring. Simmer 10 minutes or until flakes have dissolved. Add dissolved kuzu. Stir briskly with a whisk until mixture thickens. Add syrup and stir again. Remove from heat. Stir in vanilla extract. Pour into an 8-by-8-inch pan and let set at room temperature or in the refrigerator (about an hour).

Once set, run the mixture through a blender or food processor for a few seconds to create a creamy pudding texture. Pour into individual serving cups and garnish with a teaspoon of jam or a sprinkle of nutmeg.

Preparation time: 10-15 minutes for making,
*   60 minutes for setting*
Servings: Makes 4 servings

Variation: Butterscotch Amasake Pudding

Use 1/4 teaspoon butterscotch flavoring in place of vanilla extract.

Amasake is a naturally sweet, thick rice drink that makes great dairy-free puddings.

Winter Fruit Compote with Nut Milk

Compote:
1/4 cup dried apricots
1/4 cup dried cherries
1/4 cup pitted prunes
1 apple, sliced
1 pear, sliced
1 cinnamon stick
1/8 teaspoon nutmeg
1 cup apple juice

Nut Milk: [45]
2 Tablespoons ground almonds
2 Tablespoons ground cashews
1 cup water
1 teaspoon maple syrup
1/2 teaspoon vanilla extract

Place apricots, cherries, prunes, apple, pear, cinnamon stick, nutmeg, and juice in a medium-size pan; bring to a boil. Lower heat and simmer, covered, for 20-30 minutes, until all the fruit is soft. Remove cinnamon stick.

Put ground nuts, water, maple syrup, and vanilla extract in a blender; blend until smooth to make Nut Milk.

Put fruit compote in individual serving bowls and top with 1/4 cup Nut Milk. Nut Milk will keep 2 days in the refrigerator, but may separate and need reblending.

Preparation time: 35 minutes
Servings: Makes 4 servings

Here's a tummy-warming treat that's perfect for cold weather.

---

45   For other versions of nut milk, see Nut Milks (page 97).

Pear-Plum Crisp

1 cup rolled oats
1/2 cup whole-wheat pastry flour
1/2 teaspoon sea salt
1/4 cup cold-pressed vegetable oil
1/4 cup maple syrup or concentrated fruit sweetener
1/3 cup chopped nuts

2 Tablespoons water
2 Tablespoons maple syrup
    or concentrated fruit sweetener
1 teaspoon cinnamon
1/4 teaspoon nutmeg
2 teaspoons vanilla extract
5 cups sliced pears and plums
    (about 3 pears and 5 plums)

Preheat oven to 350 degrees F. Mix oats, flour, and salt together in a bowl. Add oil and sweetener; mix well. Stir in nuts and set aside.

In a small bowl combine water, syrup, spices, and vanilla extract; set aside. Slice fruit and place in a lightly oiled pie pan or an 8-by-8-inch baking dish. Pour the liquid mixture over the fruit and toss gently. Spoon the oat-nut mixture evenly on top of the fruit. Cover and bake 45 minutes. Uncover and bake 15 minutes more to crisp the topping.

Preparation time: 80 minutes
Servings: Makes 8 servings

Variation: Apple Crisp

Substitute 5 cups sliced apples for plums and pears. Add 1 teaspoon lemon juice to water, syrup, spices, and vanilla extract. Bake 1 hour and 15 minutes.

Variation: Peach-Blueberry Crisp

Substitute 1 pint blueberries and 3 cups sliced peaches for plums and pears. Sprinkle 1-2 Tablespoons arrowroot over the fruit before adding liquid mixture and tossing. Bake 50-60 minutes.

This wonderful autumn dessert uses the fruits of the season and is easy to double for a large family.

Tofu Cheesecake with Hazelnut Crust and Raspberry Topping

Crust:

1 1/4 cups rolled oats

1/3 cup hazelnuts, ground

1/2 cup whole-wheat pastry or barley flour

1/4 cup cold-pressed vegetable oil

2 Tablespoons maple syrup

1 - 2 Tablespoons water

Filling:

2 packages of silken tofu (10 ounces)

1/2 teaspoon sea salt

2 - 3 Tablespoons freshly squeezed lemon juice

6 - 8 Tablespoons maple syrup

3 Tablespoons tahini

2 teaspoons vanilla extract

1/4 teaspoon almond extract

1/2 teaspoon rice vinegar

1 Tablespoon kuzu dissolved in 1/4 cup water

Raspberry Topping: [46]

1/2 cup fruit-sweetened raspberry jam

2 Tablespoons kuzu or arrowroot
     dissolved in 1/2 cup water

To make crust:

Preheat oven to 350 degrees F. Grind oats and nuts in a small electric grinder or food processor. Blend ground oats and nuts with flour in a mixing bowl.

In a separate bowl, mix oil and syrup together. Add wet ingredients to dry mixture and work in, adding 1-2 Tablespoons water if necessary. Press mixture into the bottom of a lightly oiled 9-inch springform pan or pie pan. Bake for 10-12 minutes. Remove crust from oven and lower temperature to 300 degrees F.

---

46   This pie is also beautiful without the Raspberry Topping, garnished only with fresh strawberry and kiwi slices.

To make filling:

Place tofu, salt, lemon juice, syrup, tahini, vanilla extract, almond extract, vinegar, and dissolved kuzu in a blender or food processor; blend until smooth. Pour into prebaked pie crust. Bake for 25 minutes. Turn off oven and let pie rest in oven for 25 minutes. Cool, cover, and refrigerate.

To make topping:

Place jam and dissolved kuzu in a pan. Stir with a whisk. Heat, stirring constantly until thick and clear. Let topping cool slightly before pouring on cheesecake. Topping can be added before or after refrigeration.

Preparation time: 90 minutes
Servings: Makes 8 servings

This dessert looks like a traditional cheesecake but has half the fat and calories. Use silken tofu for the smoothest texture.

---

1 quart cherry juice or cherry cider
1/3 cup agar flakes

Pour juice into a medium-size pan. Sprinkle agar on top; bring to a boil. Lower heat and simmer for 10 minutes or until agar flakes are completely dissolved. Remove from heat and pour mixture into a 9-by-13-inch pan. Let set in the refrigerator (about an hour), then jiggle some down your throat.

Preparation time: 15 minutes for making,
   60 minutes for gelling
Servings: Makes 8 servings

Variation: Cherry-Banana Jiggle

Cut up banana slices in individual serving bowls, pour simmered cherry-agar mixture on top of bananas, and let set.

Cherry Jiggle

Gelatin is a product manufactured from animal hooves. The same gelling action can be obtained from agar, a sea vegetable rich in fiber and minerals.

Blueberry-Strawberry Tart

1 1/4 cups rolled oats
1/4 cup almonds, ground
1/4 cup walnuts, ground
1/4 cup whole-wheat pastry flour
Pinch of sea salt
2 Tablespoons maple syrup
2 Tablespoons cold-pressed vegetable oil
2 Tablespoons water

1 cup strawberries or raspberries
1 cup apple or berry juice
2 Tablespoons kuzu or 1/4 cup arrowroot
1 cup blueberries
1 Tablespoon concentrated fruit sweetener
    or brown-rice syrup

Preheat oven to 350 degrees F. Combine oats, ground nuts, flour, and salt together in a bowl. Add syrup, oil, and water; mix well. Press the mixture into an 8-by-8-inch pan with wet hands. Bake 10-12 minutes. Remove from oven and let cool.

Wash and trim strawberries; cut in half. (If using raspberries, use full-size.) Mix juice and kuzu together in a small pan until kuzu is dissolved. Add blueberries and sweetener; heat mixture on medium heat, stirring constantly until thick and clear, about 5 minutes. Remove from heat; add strawberries or raspberries. Pour mixture on top of prebaked oat-nut crust. Cool at room temperature or in the refrigerator before serving.

Preparation time: 25 minutes
Servings: Makes 9 servings

A cheerful dessert,
this tart gets its beauty and
sweet taste from the lovely
berries of summertime.

1 1/2 cups unbleached white flour
1/2 cup whole-wheat pastry flour
1 Tablespoon nonaluminum baking powder
1/4 teaspoon sea salt

1 1/2 cups cooked millet
1 cup orange juice
1/2 cup water
1/2 cup cold-pressed vegetable oil
1/3 cup maple syrup
2 eggs

Gracie's Yellow Birthday Cake

Preheat oven to 350 degrees F. Lightly oil and flour two 8-inch cake pans. Sift flours, baking powder, and salt together in a large mixing bowl; set aside.

Put millet and juice in a blender and blend until smooth. Add water, oil, syrup, and eggs to the millet puree in the blender; pulse briefly. Add wet ingredients to dry mixture and mix well.

Pour into cake pans. Bake 30-40 minutes, until cake begins to pull away from edge of pan. Let cool in pans for 10 minutes before removing. Wait until completely cool before icing.

For new eaters: Cook some extra millet and puree with water. Warm slightly before serving.

Preparation time: 50-55 minutes
Servings: Makes an 8-inch 2-layer cake or 18 cupcakes

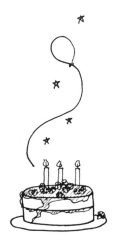

Cooked millet gives this cake its moist texture and its happy yellow color. I made this cake for my daughter, Gracie's, birthday, using apricot jam between the layers and Carob Butter Icing (page 251) on top.[47] Divine!

47   Blueberry Sauce (page 116) and Raspberry Topping (page 244) are scrumptious on this cake, too.

Carrot Cake with Apricot Glaze

Cake:

1 cup whole-wheat pastry flour

1 cup unbleached white flour

1 Tablespoon nonaluminum baking powder

1/8 teaspoon sea salt

1 teaspoon cinnamon

1/4 teaspoon nutmeg

1/2 cup concentrated fruit sweetener

1/2 cup cold-pressed vegetable oil

1/2 cup water

1 cup apple or apricot juice

2 eggs

3 large carrots, finely grated

1 Tablespoon grated lemon peel

1/3 cup chopped walnuts

1/3 cup raisins or currants

Apricot Glaze:

1 Tablespoon kuzu

1 cup apricot juice or nectar

1 Tablespoon freshly squeezed lemon juice

1 Tablespoon concentrated fruit sweetener

To make cake:

Preheat oven to 350 degrees F. Lightly oil a 10-inch tube pan or 2 round 8-inch cake pans. Sift together flours, baking powder, salt, and spices in a mixing bowl; set aside.

Put sweetener, oil, water, juice, and eggs in a separate bowl; whisk together. Add wet ingredients to dry mixture and mix well. Fold in carrots, lemon peel, nuts, and raisins. Pour batter into pan(s); tap pans on counter to release air bubbles and bake for 50-60 minutes or until knife inserted in center of cake comes out clean. Remove and let cool.

To make glaze:

Dissolve kuzu in juice in a small pan. Heat mixture on medium heat, stirring constantly, until it becomes clear and thick (5 minutes). Remove from heat, add lemon juice and sweetener; stir well. Spread over the top of tube cake or between layers and on top of layer cake.

Preparation time: 90 minutes
Servings: Makes 12 servings

This familiar cake looks quite elegant when you decorate the top with fresh raspberries or with a few fresh flowers and date halves.

Dark Sweet Carob Cupcakes

1 cup whole-wheat pastry flour
1/2 cup unbleached white flour
1/2 cup carob powder
1 Tablespoon nonaluminum baking powder

1 1/2 cups cooked millet
1 cup hot water + 1 Tablespoon grain "coffee"
    (Cafix or another brand)
1/2 cup cold-pressed vegetable oil
1/3 cup concentrated fruit sweetener or maple syrup
1 teaspoon vanilla extract
2 eggs

Preheat oven to 350 degrees F. Lightly oil muffin tins or line with paper muffin cups. Sift flours, carob powder, and baking powder together into a mixing bowl; stir and set aside.

Put millet, water, and grain coffee in a blender; blend until smooth. Add oil, sweetener, and vanilla extract to millet mixture; blend again. Add eggs and pulse briefly. Add wet ingredients to dry mixture and mix well. Pour batter into muffin cups, filling 3/4 full. Bake 30-35 minutes[48] or until toothpick inserted in center of cupcake comes out clean.

For new eaters: Cook some extra millet and puree with water. Warm slightly before serving.

Preparation time: 35-40 minutes
Servings: Makes 18 cupcakes

Children love these little cakes. The cooked millet adds moistness and extra nutrition. Use colored or patterned muffin cups for extra appeal.

48   For an 8-inch 2-layer cake, bake 40-45 minutes.

Carob Butter Icing

1/2 cup concentrated fruit sweetener
    or brown-rice syrup
1/2 cup carob powder, sifted
1/4 cup creamy almond butter
1/8 teaspoon sea salt
2 - 3 Tablespoons apple or orange juice
2 teaspoons vanilla extract

Heat fruit sweetener in a small saucepan. Stir in carob powder and heat, stirring constantly, until mixture begins to a simmer. Add nut butter, salt, and juice; stir again. Remove from heat and add vanilla extract; stir until creamy. Add a bit more juice if too thick so cake will ice easily. Ice cooled cake immediately.

Preparation time: 10 minutes
Servings: Makes 1 1/2 cups icing[49]

This sinfully delicious icing is an adaptation of the carob icing found in Marcea Weber's book "The Sweet Life," a trailblazer in creative uses of alternative sweeteners.

49   1 1/2 cups will ice the top and sides of 2 8-inch layers of cake or 1 9-by-13-inch cake.

Banana Cream Frosting

Using tofu and banana as a base, you can create sweet creamy icings that children love to lick. This icing works well on Dark Sweet Carob Cupcakes (page 250), Poppyseed Cake (page 219), and Pumpkin Muffins (page 217).

6 ounces tofu
1/2 ripe banana
2 Tablespoons concentrated fruit sweetener
2 teaspoons almond or cashew butter
1/2 teaspoon vanilla extract
1 - 2 Tablespoons pineapple juice or water

Blend tofu, banana, fruit sweetener, almond or cashew butter, and vanilla extract in a blender or food processor. Add enough juice or water to get a smooth consistency. Refrigerate frosting if not using right away. Store leftover goodies topped with frosting in refrigerator.

Preparation time: 10 minutes
Servings: Makes about 1 cup[50]

Yummy Yam Frosting

This naturally sweet, beautiful, golden-orange frosting comes from the creative mind of Rita Carey. Use it to top cookies, cupcakes, quick breads, graham crackers, or Gingerbread People.

1 cup mashed baked yams
2 ounces or 1/4 cup softened cream cheese
2 teaspoons melted unsalted butter
2 Tablespoons maple syrup or brown-rice syrup
1/2 teaspoon lemon or orange juice

Place yams, cream cheese, butter, syrup, and juice in a bowl; cream together. Puree this mixture in a blender, food processor, or with a hand mixer to a smooth, spreadable consistency.

Preparation time: 5 minutes
Servings: Makes about 1 1/2 cups frosting[50]

---

50   1 1/2 cups frosting is plenty for 2 dozen cookies, muffins, or a 2-layer cake.

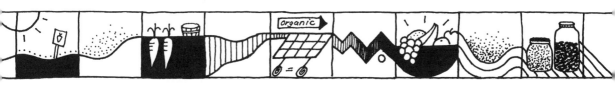

What's to Drink?

Drink Water

When I was growing up, I drank soda pop when I was thirsty, and I had a choice of six different kinds. But our bodies require simple water. You can save both money and calories by quenching your family's natural thirst with "plain" water. Cold drinks may halt the stomach's warm digestive process, so avoid ice water with food.

Some parents habitually give juice or soda to a thirsty child. Try offering water first, especially if your child drinks juice and then won't eat. It's important to keep the attention at mealtime on eating, not drinking. Save juices, teas, milks, and other drinks for between-meal snacks. For everyday meals, serve water or no drinks with dinner.

Warm Weather Drinks

Sparkling Fruit Juice

2 cups fruit juice
2 cups sparkling water

Combine fruit juice and sparkling water.

Servings: Makes 1 quart

Cold Herbal Tea

4 tea bags of herbal tea (the fruitier flavors work well)
3 cups boiling water

Brew tea in boiling water. Pour into a pitcher filled with ice cubes.

Servings: Makes 1 quart

Lemon Water

1/2 lemon, sliced
1 quart water

Put lemon slices in a pitcher of water and refrigerate.

Servings: Makes 1 quart

Bubbly Fruit Tea

1 cup herb tea (pick a fruity flavor with hibiscus
    or rose hips and sweet spices)
1 1/2 cups fruit juice
1 1/2 cups sparkling water

Brew and cool tea. Combine with juice and sparkling water; serve cold.

Servings: Makes 1 quart

Banana Milk

1 ripe banana
2 cups soy, nut, or cow's milk
1 teaspoon vanilla extract

Blend all ingredients in a blender and serve.

Servings: Makes 2 1/2 - 3 cups

Cold Weather Drinks

Cranberry Ginger Cider

2 cups cranberry juice
2 cups apple cider
8 1/4-inch slices fresh gingerroot
1/2 teaspoon orange zest

Place all ingredients in a pan and simmer 15 minutes; serve warm.

Servings: Makes 4 cups

Hot Mocha Milk

1/2 teaspoon Cafix or other grain beverage
1/2 teaspoon carob powder
1/2 cup boiling water
1/2 teaspoon brown-rice syrup or maple syrup
1/3 - 1/2 cup soy or other milk

Put Cafix and carob powder in a cup. Fill cup halfway with boiling water. Stir in syrup. Fill cup to top with milk.

Servings: Makes 1 cup

Yogi Tea

4 cups water
10 whole cloves
12 whole cardamom pods
12 whole black peppercorns
2 sticks of cinnamon
3 slices fresh gingerroot, 1/4-inch thick
1 cup soy or cow's milk
Maple syrup to taste

Bring water, spices, and gingerroot to a boil in a pot. Lower heat and simmer 15-20 minutes. Add milk. If using cow's milk, bring to a boil again. Turn heat off. Strain and serve with a touch of maple syrup to sweeten.

Traditionally, a small amount of black tea is added to the brew. I've omitted it because most of us don't need the caffeine; children certainly do not.

Servings: Makes 4-5 cups

Ginger Tea

2 cups water
1-inch fresh gingerroot, sliced thin
Freshly squeezed lemon juice
Maple syrup to taste

Simmer water and gingerroot 10-20 minutes. Strain and pour into cups. Add a squeeze of fresh lemon to each cup. Sweeten with a touch of maple syrup if desired.

Servings: Makes 2 cups

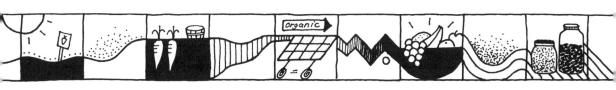

Appendix
and
Index

Glossary of Ingredients

Agar, a sea vegetable, is a natural gelling agent that can be used in place of animal gelatin. Agar thickens at room temperature, unlike gelatin, which must be chilled. One-quarter cup of agar gels a quart of liquid. Agar is sold in bars and flakes; flakes are easier to measure. Store in a sealed container in a cool, dark place.

Amaranth, a tiny seed, was an important food source for the Aztecs. Amaranth is rich in iron and, when cooked, it has the texture of cornmeal mush. Amaranth can also be sprouted like alfalfa seeds. Store amaranth and other whole grains in airtight containers where they will keep for 6-9 months.

Amasake, a traditional Japanese product, is made by fermenting sweet brown rice into a thick sweet liquid. Sold in the refrigerated section of natural foods stores or in aseptic packages on the shelf, amasake can replace not only sweeteners but also dairy products in natural desserts.

Arame, a sea vegetable, is finely shredded, cooked, and then naturally sun-dried. When reconstituted, it looks like small, black threads. Its milder flavor makes it a good introductory sea vegetable. Store in a sealed container in a cool, dark place, where it will keep indefinitely.

Arrowroot powder comes from a tropical plant whose tuberous root is dried and ground into a fine powder. Arrowroot, a natural thickener, can be substituted for cornstarch, in equal measure. Whole foods cooks prefer arrowroot's or kuzu's natural method of preparation over cornstarch, which is bleached and chemically treated during processing. You can substitute 2 Tablespoons of arrowroot for 1 Tablespoon of kuzu. Arrowroot keeps indefinitely in a sealed container on the shelf.

Baking powder, nonaluminum, is described under "nonaluminum baking powder."

Balsamic vinegar is an Italian red-wine vinegar with a lower-than-average acidity. Its sweet, mellow flavor comes from being aged in wood, making it a distinctive addition to dressings and marinades. Vinegars store on the shelf indefinitely.

Barley malt is a complex carbohydrate sweetener made by sprouting barley in water. It is dark and thick and has a maltlike taste. Sorghum or rice syrup can be substituted for barley malt. Refrigerate after opening.

Basmati brown rice is a long slender grain with a distinctly aromatic flavor. Basmati rice is popular in Indian and Pakistani cultures.

Brown-rice syrup, a naturally processed sweetener, is made by sprouting brown rice in water, applying heat to stop the sprouting, then drying out the rice malt. Rice syrup has a lighter, more delicate flavor than barley malt. Substitute rice syrup in equal amounts for honey, maple syrup, or barley malt. To enhance pouring, place rice syrup in a pan of hot water before using. Refrigerate after opening.

Brown-rice vinegar is a mild, delicate vinegar made from fermented brown rice. It is less acidic than most vinegars; you can substitute apple cider vinegar for brown-rice vinegar. Vinegars store on the shelf indefinitely.

Bulgur is parboiled, dried, and cracked whole wheat. Store whole grains in airtight containers for 6-9 months.

Cafix, a powder made from grains, figs, and other natural ingredients, is stirred into hot water for a coffee substitute. Cafix and similar products, such as Pero and Inka, are interchangeable and can be stored on the shelf.

Carob is an evergreen tree with edible pods, also known as Saint John's bread. The powder made from the pods is naturally sweet, low in fat, high in calcium, and caffeine-free. **Carob powder** can be stored on the shelf in an airtight container for 6-12 months. Sift before using if lumpy. **Carob chips** come unsweetened and malt-sweetened. Some chips contain dry milk and most contain palm kernel oil, which has unhealthfully high saturated fat levels. Look for carob products made without palm kernel oil, or use it sparingly.

Chipotle chiles are smoked, dried jalapeño peppers. Store on the shelf.

Concentrated fruit sweetener is a commercial syrup made from peach, pineapple, pear, and other fruit juices that have been cooked down. Look for it in the refrigerated section of natural foods stores or on the shelf with other sweeteners. Concentrated fruit sweetener can be used in a recipe in place of honey, barley malt, rice syrup, or maple syrup in equal measure. Refrigerate after opening.

Couscous is actually a tiny pasta made from coarsely ground and steamed wheat. It is usually made from refined wheat, though whole-wheat couscous is becoming more commonly available. Store whole grains in airtight containers for 6-9 months.

Date sugar is simply dried, ground dates. Substitute cup-for-cup for white sugar. While date sugar works well in baked goods, it does not dissolve well and is not recommended for use as a sweetener in hot beverages. Store it in a sealed container in a cool, dry place.

Dulse is a sea vegetable extremely high in iron (14 milligrams per 1/4 cup) and other minerals. The dried leaves can be soaked for 5 minutes and added to soups or salads. Dried dulse is also sold broken into tiny bits as **dulse flakes.** Sprinkle onto most any food for a nutritional boost. Dulse stores indefinitely in an airtight container in a cool, dark place.

Essene bread is a naturally sweet, moist, flourless bread. Sprouted grains are crushed, hand-shaped, then slowly baked at low temperatures. Sprouted wheat bread comes in several flavors and is found in the refrigerated section of most natural foods stores.

Extra-virgin olive oil comes from the first pressing of the olives. I use extra-virgin olive oil for dressings and light sautéing. Purchase oils in small bottles and use them within a few months to avoid spoilage. Most cooks recommend refrigeration for oils. Hold bottle under warm water for 30 seconds to restore free-flowing qualities.

Flour. See "spelt," "unbleached white flour," "whole-wheat flour," and "whole-wheat pastry flour." Store flours, including barley flour, buckwheat flour, brown-rice flour, and spelt flour, in a cold, dry place for 1-2 months, in the refrigerator for 6 months, or in the freezer for up to 12 months.

Fruit sweetener is described under "concentrated fruit sweetener."

Fruitsource is the brand name of a granular product made from grape juice concentrate and whole-rice syrup. Substitute Fruitsource for white sugar in equal amounts. When you use Fruitsource, mix it with liquid ingredients first and allow it to set 2-3 minutes before mixing with dry ingredients. Store on the shelf in an airtight container. Fruitsource is also available in a syruplike form that can be substituted in equal amounts for maple syrup or honey. Store the syrup form in the refrigerator after opening.

Ghee is clarified butter used in traditional Indian cooking. The milk proteins in the butter are removed and only the fat remains. Unlike butter, ghee can hold high heat without scorching. For more information and instructions on how to make ghee, see page 225. Refrigerate homemade ghee.

Hiziki, of all the sea vegetables, is the richest in calcium. Its thick, black strands have a firm texture and look striking with other colors. As with several other sea vegetables, soak in cold water before using. The strong taste can be moderated by cooking hiziki in apple juice or by combining it with other vegetables. Store hiziki in a sealed container in a cool, dark place, where it will keep indefinitely.

Kasha is roasted buckwheat groats. Buckwheat is actually the seed of a plant related to rhubarb that originated in Russia. Store whole grains in airtight containers for 6-9 months.

Kombu is a dark green sea vegetable sold in thick strips. It contains glutamic acid, which acts as a tenderizer when added to cooking beans. As with other sea vegetables, kombu is mineral-rich. Store kombu in a sealed container in a cool, dark place, where it will keep indefinitely.

Kuzu, from the root of the kuzu (or kudzu) plant, looks like broken chalk. Kuzu can be dissolved in cold or room-temperature liquid and used as a thickener. In macrobiotic practice, kuzu is recommended for its soothing effects on the digestive system. You can substitute 2 Tablespoons arrowroot for 1 Tablespoon of kuzu. Kuzu keeps indefinitely in a sealed container on the shelf.

Maple syrup is made from the boiled sap of sugar maple trees. About 40 gallons of sap (from nine trees) make 1 gallon of syrup. Maple syrup is available in three grades, A, B, or C, determined by the temperature used and length of time cooked. The lighter the color, the better the quality (and the more expensive). Store in a cool location to prevent fermentation and crystallization. During hot weather, refrigerate. Freezing maple syrup may damage its flavor.

Millet is a small, round, golden grain that continues to be a major food source in Asia, North Africa, and India. Store whole grains in airtight containers for 6-9 months.

Mirin, a versatile sweet cooking wine, is made from sweet brown rice and contains no additives. Dry sherry may be substituted for mirin. Store mirin in a closed container in a cool, dry place.

Miso is a salty paste made from cooked and aged soybeans. The soybeans are mixed with various grains and other ingredients to produce different flavors. The longer miso is aged and the darker its color, the stronger and saltier the taste. Miso is traditionally used as a soup base, but can also be used in spreads, dressings, and dips, or as a substitute for salt. Unpasteurized miso contains beneficial enzymes and organisms that aid digestion. Refrigerated miso keeps indefinitely.

Mochi is made from sweet brown rice that has been cooked, pounded into a paste, and then compressed into dense bars. Mochi requires cooking. When broken into squares and baked at 400 degrees F. for 10 minutes, it puffs up and gets gooey inside. It can also be grated and melted into foods. Refrigerate opened packages and eat within a week. Extra packages can be stored in the freezer and thawed in about 2 hours.

Molasses, a by-product of sugar refinement, has a strong bittersweet flavor. Only blackstrap molasses has appreciable amounts of iron and calcium. Barley malt or sorghum can be substituted for molasses. Molasses keeps for up to 6 months in a sealed container in a cool place; however, refrigeration is safest.

Nonaluminum baking powder is recommended for use as a leavening agent in nonyeasted baked goods. Stored in a closed container in a cool, dry place, nonaluminum baking powder keeps indefinitely.

Nori, a dried and rolled sea vegetable, resembles dark green or black paper. While nori is most commonly used in making sushi, it can also be eaten directly from the package after lightly toasting or crumbled onto foods. Store in the freezer in a zip-lock bag to preserve freshness.

Oils. See "extra-virgin olive oil," "toasted sesame oil," and page 38 of "Shopping and Storing Whole Foods."

Quinoa (*keen-wah*) was cultivated in Peru for thousands of years. This staple food of the Incas has been rediscovered and is now grown in the United States. Store whole grains in airtight containers for 6-9 months.

Radicchio is a small, burgundy-and-white-colored head of lettuce leaves. The leaves have a slightly sharp taste.

Ramen is a dry block of quick-cooking pasta. The cooked noodles are curly. Ramen is made from a variety of flours and usually comes packaged with a packet of dry seasonings to be used in cooking.

Rice syrup is described under "brown-rice syrup."

Sea salt is refined sodium chloride from seawater. Although the potassium iodide in commercial table salt is helpful for people with no access to seafood or sea vegetables, dextrose (a type of sugar), sodium bicarbonate, and other unwanted substances are also added in processing of commercial salt. [51] High-quality sea salt contains none of these additives. Salt can be eliminated from any recipe if desired.

Shoyu is made from soybeans, wheat, water, and sea salt, but unlike commercial soy sauces shoyu does not contain sugar, monosodium glutamate, and other additives. Both shoyu and tamari are naturally brewed and aged and used to flavor dishes. Tamari is similar to shoyu but contains little or no wheat. Store shoyu or tamari in a sealed container on the shelf indefinitely.

Soba is a traditional type of Japanese noodle made principally from buckwheat. For more information, see "Whole-Grain Noodles and Pastas," page 84.

Sorghum is a syruplike sweetener with a rich, dark taste. It is made by concentrating the juice of crushed and boiled sorghum stems. The sorghum plant is a relative of millet. Barley malt can be substituted for sorghum. Refrigerate after opening.

Soy beverage or soy milk, best known by commercial names such as WestSoy and Edensoy, is a high-protein alternative to cow's milk. Manufacturers of soy beverages have succeeded in producing delicious "milks" from soybeans in many flavors. Do not substitute soy milk for infant formula as it does not contain all of the necessary nutrients for growing babies. Soy beverage usually comes in aseptic packages that require refrigeration after opening.

Spelt was a staple grain in Biblical times. Easier to digest than whole wheat, spelt makes a suitable substitute in flour products. It is sold in flour, flakes, and whole form. Store whole grains in airtight containers for 6-9 months.

Sucanat is the brand name for dried, organic sugar cane juice. Sucanat resembles brown sugar in appearance and taste, though less sweet, and it's less refined than white sugar. Substitute Sucanat for white or brown sugar.

Tahini is a creamy paste made of crushed, hulled sesame seeds. Seeds used for tahini are either raw, toasted, or lightly toasted, each giving the tahini a slightly different flavor. Sesame is uniquely resistant to rancidity; perhaps that's why it has been enjoyed by many cultures over the centuries. Refrigerate after opening.

Tamari is a naturally brewed soy sauce made from soybeans, water, and sea salt. Tamari and shoyu are interchangeable. Also see "shoyu."

---

51   Janice Fillip, "Salt, with a Grain of," *Whole Foods* (April 1980)

(Glossary of Ingredients, continued)

Tempeh, originally an Indonesian food, is made from soybeans that have been cooked and split to remove the hull. A culture is added to the cooked beans, which age for several days before forming into a solid piece which can be cut and sliced. This high-protein food can be baked, boiled, fried, or steamed. Store tempeh in the refrigerator and use within 1 week. Tempeh can also be frozen for up to 6 months; allow 1 hour to thaw.

Toasted sesame oil has a darker appearance and nuttier taste than plain sesame oil and delivers a lot of flavor in small amounts. Store in the refrigerator.

Tofu is soybean curd made from the "milk" of soybeans. Tofu's low calories, relatively high protein, and bland flavor make it a versatile ingredient. A variety of textures are available: firm, soft, and silken. Soft or silken tofu works well for dressings and desserts, while firm tofu holds its shape in stir-frys and marinated dishes. Tofu can be purchased in bulk or in packages. Be sure to note the expiration date on packages. Cover bulk tofu and packaged tofu that has been opened in fresh water and store in the refrigerator. Change the water daily and use tofu within a week. To freshen tofu, drop it in boiling, salted water for a few minutes; remove and use.

Udon noodles are traditional Japanese noodles made from a combination of whole-wheat, brown-rice, and white flours. See "Whole-Grain Noodles and Pastas," page 84, for more information.

Umeboshi plum paste is a puree made from pitted umeboshi plums. Plums and paste keep indefinitely when stored in a sealed container on the shelf. A pinch of sea salt in 1 Tablespoon of lemon juice can be substituted for 1 plum or 2 teaspoons of paste, although it doesn't produce quite the same flavor.

Umeboshi plum vinegar is the leftover juice from the plum-pickling process. The taste gives a lift to soups and salad dressings and eliminates the need for salt in a recipe. The vinegar stores indefinitely in a sealed container in a cool, dry place.

Umeboshi plums come from Japanese apricots that are picked green and pickled in sea salt with shiso leaves. Their unique salty-sour taste adds zip to recipes.

Unbleached white flour has had the bran and germ removed in a refining process. But unlike regular white flour, it has not been bleached. When used in combination with whole-grain flours, this flour gives muffins, crusts, and cakes a lighter texture. Store in an airtight container in a cool, dry place for up to a year.

Wakame is a green, leafy sea vegetable high in calcium and other minerals. A small amount expands when soaked; after soaking, remove the main rib or stem and cut leaves into small pieces. Often used in soups, wakame can also be toasted and ground into a condiment. Store in a sealed container in a cool, dark place indefinitely.

Wheat berries are whole-wheat kernels. They can be purchased as soft red winter wheat or hard winter wheat berries. Store whole grains in airtight containers for 6-9 months.

Whole-wheat flour is ground from hard winter wheat and contains more gluten than whole-wheat pastry flour, making a suitable choice for yeasted breads. Store flour in a cold, dry place for 1-2 months, in the refrigerator for 6 months, or in the freezer for up to 12 months.

Whole-wheat pastry flour is ground from soft spring wheat and has less gluten, making it better for whole-grain cakes, crusts, and unyeasted breads. Store flours in a cold, dry place for 1-2 months, in the refrigerator for 6 months, or in the freezer for up to 12 months.

Bibliography

Abrahamson, E.M., M.D., and A.W. Pezet. *Body, Mind & Sugar.* New York: Pyramid Publications, 1951.

Ballantine, Rudolph, M.D. *Diet and Nutrition,* pp. 55, 59, 128-130. Honesdale, PA: Himalayan International Institute, 1978.

Breastfeeding Abstracts (Spring 1987), cited in the *Doctor's People* (October 1991): p. 3.

Caughlin, Goldie. "What's a Mother to Do?" *PCC (Puget Consumers' Co-op) Sound Consumer,* no. 228 (March 1992): p. 11.

Chow, Marilyn P., Barbara A. Durand, Marie N. Feldman, and Marion A. Mills. *Handbook of Pediatric Primary Care.* New York: John Wiley & Sons, 1984.

Colbin, Annemarie. *Food and Healing.* New York: Ballantine Books, 1986.

Dorfman, Kelly. "All about Feeding Babies" *Mothering Magazine* (Fall 1987): pp. 33-39.

Dufty, William. *Sugar Blues.* New York: Warner Books, 1975.

Ensminger, Audrey H., M.E. Ensminger, James E. Konlande, and John R.K. Robson, M.D. *Food and Nutrition Encyclopedia,* vol. 2, pp. 1460-67. Clovis, CA: Pegus Press, 1983.

Fillip, Janice. "Salt, with a Grain of" *Whole Foods* (April 1980).

Firkaly, Susan Tate. *Into the Mouths of Babes.* White Hall, VA: Betterway Publications, 1984.

Gardner, Joy. *Healing Yourself during Pregnancy,* pp. 28-37. Freedom, CA: Crossing Press, 1987.

Goldsmith, Judith. *Childbirth Wisdom.* Brookline, MA: East West Books, 1990.

Guthrie, Helen. *Introductory Nutrition.* St. Louis: Times Mirror/Mosby College Publishing, 1986.

Haas, Elston, M.D. *Staying Healthy with the Seasons,* p. 112. Millbrae, CA: Celestial Arts, 1981.

Harnett-Robinson, Roy, M.D., pediatrician practicing in New York City. Interview, August 1988.

Infact Newsletter (Fall 1991), 2, cited in *Mothering Magazine,* no. 63 (Spring 1992): p. 26.

Kenda, Margaret Elizabeth, and Phyllis S. Williams. *The Natural Baby Food Cookbook.* New York: Avon Books, 1982.

"Kiddie Fat" *Nutrition Action Health Letter,* vol. 18, no. 5 (June 1991): p. 3.

King, Jonathan. "Is Your Water Safe to Drink?" *Medical Self Care* (November-December 1985): p. 44-57.

La Leche League International. *The Womanly Art of Breastfeeding,* pp. 288-89. New York: Plume, New American Library, 1981.

The Lancet, no. 337 (April 1991), 929-33, cited in *Mothering Magazine,* no. 63, (Spring 1992): p. 26.

Leach, Penelope. *Your Baby and Child.* New York: Knopf, 1989.

Liebman, Bonnie. "Baby Formulas: Missing Key Fats?" *Nutrition Action Health Letter,* vol. 17, no. 8 (October 1990): pp. 8-9.

McDougall, John A., M.D. "The Best Foods for the Expectant Mother" *Vegetarian Times* (January 1985): pp. 54-57.

McDougall, John A., M.D. *A Challenging Second Opinion,* pp. 183-84. Piscataway, NJ: New Century, 1985.

Mohrbacher, Nancy, and Julie Stock. *The Breastfeeding Answer Book.* Franklin Park, IL: La Leche League International, 1991.

Mohrbacher, Nancy, and Judy Torgus. *The New La Leche League Leaders Handbook.* Franklin Park, IL: La Leche League International, 1989.

Morningstar, Amadea, and Urmila Desai. *The Ayurvedic Cookbook,* pp. 260-61. Santa Fe, NM: Lotus Press, 1990.

(Bibliography, continued)

Murray, Michael, N.D., and Joseph Pizzorno, N.D. *Encyclopedia of Natural Medicine*, pp. 63, 229, 459. Rocklin, CA: Prima Publishing, 1990.

Murray and Pizzorno cite these references in particular to support their information about sugar:

Bernstein, J., Alpert, S., Nauss, K., and Suskind, R. "Depression of lymphocyte transformation following oral glucose ingestion," *American Journal of Clinical Nutrition*, no. 30 (1977): p. 613.

Mann, G. "Hypothesis: the role of vitamin C in diabetic angiopathy," *Perspectives in Biology and Medicine*, no. 17, (1974): pp. 210-17.

Mann, G., and Newton, P. "The membrane transport of ascorbic acid," *Annals of the New York Academy of Sciences*, no. 258 (1975): pp. 243-51.

Ringsdorf, W., Cheraskin, E., and Ramsay, R. "Sucrose, neutrophil phagocytosis and resistance to disease," *Dental Survey*, no. 52, (1976): pp. 46-48.

Sanchez, A., Reeser, J., Lau, H., et al. "Role of sugars in human neutrophilic phagocytosis" *American Journal of Clinical Nutrition*, no. 26, (1973): pp. 46-48.

Oski, Frank, M.D. *Don't Drink Your Milk!*, pp. 24-27. Syracuse, NY: Mollica Press, 1983.

Palmer, Gabrielle. *The Politics of Breastfeeding*, pp. 42-48. London: Pandora Press, 1988.

Pearce, Joseph Chilton. *Evolution's End.* San Francisco: Harper & Row, 1992.

Pearce, Joseph Chilton. *Magical Child Matures.* New York: E.P. Dutton, 1985.

Petrulis, Nina, La Leche League International leader in Seattle, WA. Interview, January 1992.

Physicians Committee for Responsible Medicine. "The New Four Food Groups." Washington, DC: Physicians Committee for Responsible Medicine.

Physicians Committee for Responsible Medicine. "PCRM Update" (May-June 1991). Washington, DC: Physicians Committee for Responsible Medicine.

Pipes, Peggy, R.D., M.P.H. *Nutrition in Infancy and Childhood*, p. 145. St. Louis: C.V. Mosby, 1981.

Pope, Sharon. "Good Nutrition for the Very Young" *PCC (Puget Consumers' Co-op) Sound Consumer*, no. 181 (April 1988): pp. 1, 3, 6.

Price, Weston, M.S., D.D.S., F.A.C.D. *Nutrition and Physical Degeneration: A Comparison of Primitive and Modern Diets and Their Effects.* La Mesa, CA: Price-Pottenger Nutrition Foundation, 1945.

Pryor, Karen. *Nursing Your Baby*, pp. 52-53. New York: Pocket Books, 1973.

Robbins, John. *A Diet for a New America*, pp. 97-121, 189, 266-67, 309-13. Walpole, NH: Stillpoint, 1987.

Robertson, Laurel, Carol Flinders, and Brian Ruppenthal. *The New Laurel's Kitchen*, pp. 415-16, 461-87. Berkeley, CA: Ten Speed Press, 1986.

Schardt, David. "The Problem with Protein" *Nutrition Action Health Letter*, vol. 20, no. 5 (June 1993).

Smith, Lendon, M.D. *Feed Your Kids Right*, p. 36. New York: McGraw-Hill, 1979.

Weed, Susun S. *Wise Woman Herbal for the Childbearing Year.* Woodstock, NY: Ash Tree Publishing, 1986.

Yudkin, John, M.D. *Sweet & Dangerous.* New York: Bantam Books, 1972.

Recommended Reading

These are a few of the books that have been inspiring and helpful to me.

Food and Health

Ballantine, Rudolph, M.D. *Diet & Nutrition.* Honesdale, Pa: Himalayan International Institute, 1978.

Colbin, Annemarie. *Food and Healing.* New York: Ballantine Books, 1986.

Goldbeck, Nikki and David. *The Goldbecks' Guide to Good Food.* New York: Penguin, 1987.

Haas, Elston M., M.D. *Staying Healthy with the Seasons.* Millbrae, CA: Celestial Arts, 1981.

Price, Weston A., M.S., D.D.S., F.A.C.D. *Nutrition and Physical Degeneration.* La Mesa, CA: Price-Pottenger Nutrition Foundation, 1945.

Robbins, John. *A Diet for a New America.* Walpole, NH: Stillpoint, 1987.

Cooking

Colbin, Annemarie. *The Book of Whole Meals.* New York: Ballantine Books, 1983.

Colbin, Annemarie. *The Natural Gourmet.* New York: Ballantine Books, 1989.

Estella, Mary. *The Natural Foods Cookbook.* Tokyo and New York: Japan Publications, 1985.

Greene, Karen. *Once upon a Recipe.* New Hope, PA: New Hope Press, 1987.

Levitt, JoAnn, Linda Smith, and Christine Warren. *Kripalu Kitchen.* Summit Station, PA: Kripalu Publications, 1980.

McCarty, Meredith. *Fresh from a Vegetarian Kitchen.* Eureka, CA: Turning Point Publications, 1989.

Resource Institute. *Gourmet Underway.* Seattle: Resource Institute, 1990.

Robbins, John. *May All Be Fed.* New York: William Morrow, 1992.

Robertson, Laurel, Carol Flinders, and Brian Ruppenthal. *The New Laurel's Kitchen.* Berkeley, CA: Ten Speed Press, 1986.

Rombauer, Irma S., and Marion Rombauer Becker. *Joy of Cooking.* New York: Bobbs-Merrill Company, 1975.

Turner, Kristina. *The Self-Healing Cookbook.* Vashon Island, WA: Earthtones Press, 1987.

Wagner, Lindsay, and Ariane Spade. *The High Road to Health.* New York: Prentice-Hall, 1990.

Warrington, Janet. *Sweet and Natural Desserts.* Freedom, CA: Crossing Press, 1982.

Weber, Marcea. *Naturally Sweet Desserts.* Garden City Park, NY: Avery Publishing Group, 1990.

Weber, Marcea. *The Sweet Life.* Tokyo and New York: Japan Publications, 1981.

Breastfeeding, Babies, and Children

Firkaly, Susan Tate. *Into the Mouths of Babes.* Whitehall, VA: Betterway Publications, 1984.

Gardner, Joy. *Healing Yourself during Pregnancy.* Freedom, CA: Crossing Press, 1987.

Goodwin, Mary T., and Gerry Pollen. *Creative Food Experiences for Children.* Washington, DC: Center for Science in the Public Interest (CSPI), 1974.

Kenda, Margaret Elizabeth, and Phyllis S. Williams. *The Natural Baby Food Cookbook.* New York: Avon Books, 1982.

Kitzenger, Sheila. *Breastfeeding Your Baby.* New York: Knopf, 1991.

La Leche League International. *The Womanly Art of Breastfeeding.* New York: Plume, New American Library, 1981.

Mendelsohn, Robert S., M.D. *How to Raise a Healthy Child in Spite of Your Doctor.* Chicago: Contemporary Books, 1984.

Mothering Magazine, a quarterly periodical, published by Peggy O'Mara, P.O. Box 1690, Santa Fe, NM 87504.

Palmer, Gabrielle. *The Politics of Breastfeeding.* London: Pandora Press, 1988.

Weed, Susun S. *Wise Woman Herbal for the Childbearing Year.* Woodstock, NY: Ash Tree Publishing, 1986.

Yntema, Sharon. *Vegetarian Baby.* Ithaca, NY: McBooks Press, 1980.

Nutritional Information for Recipes

Each piece of food that Nature provides is unique. The nutritional elements of broccoli grown in your garden may be different from those of broccoli bought at the supermarket. Laboratories and equipment vary, and even the most reliable resources differ in their nutritional analysis of food. The numbers on this chart reflect data from the best available resources under these circumstances.

Optional ingredients are not included in the chart. When a recipe gives a choice of 2 ingredients or 2 amounts, only the first choice is analyzed.

The following data are to be used as a guide for composing menus to meet your needs. I urge you to let smell, taste, and common sense prevail over numerical measures of milligrams or calories when making your food choices.

Recipe Title (Data for 1 serving unless otherwise indicated) **Bustling Breakfasts**		Calories	Protein (g)	Fat (g)	Cholesterol (mg)	Carbohydrates (g)	Calcium (mg)	Iron (mg)	Sodium (mg)	Vit A (IU)	Vit C (mg)
Ancient Grain Raisin Cereal	p. 108	200	6.4	3.2	0	37.7	36	4.22	200	4	.3
5-Grain Morning Cereal	p. 109	163	5.46	1.5	0	32.4	12	1.89	112	3	0
Steel-Cut Oats w/Dates & Cinn.	p. 110	175	6.7	2.7	0	32.1	28	2.04	69	5	.1
Peaches 'n Millet 1 serv w/ 1 T. apple butter	p. 110	174	4.44	1.7	0	35.9	8	1.26	70	133	3.2
Orange Hazelnut Museli 1 serv w/o toppings	p. 111	280	8.17	8.7	0	44.8	55	2.5	5	139	31.6
Nut & Seed Granola 1/4 cup	p. 112	133	3.99	7.9	0	13	18	1.44	12	19	0
Kasha for Breakfast	p. 113	179	5.43	3.5	0	34.3	24	1.43	75	20	7.1
Jam-Filled Mochi 1 serv w/ 1 tsp. jam	p. 114	156	3	1.3	0	33	*	*	2	*	0
Sprouted Essene Bread 1 one-inch slice w/ 1 c. blueberries	p. 114	248	8	3	0	47	29	2	11	150	19
Warming Miso Soup	p. 115	51	4	2	0	5.2	40	.9	522	136	1.3
Goldie's Whole-Grain Pancakes 1 pancake	p. 116	81	2.89	.6	1	16.8	85	.51	85	15	.1
Blueberry Sauce 1/3 cup	p. 116	70	.25	.2	0	17.3	7	.27	3	25	3.9
Tofu Vegetable Scramble	p. 117	86	6.48	4.9	0	5.5	92	2.35	182	407	18.9
Abby's Healthy Home Fries	p. 118	151	3.75	.1	0	33.9	10	.57	140	79	22.6
Tempeh Bacon	p. 119	163	9.93	11.6	0	5.4	17	.98	211	28	.2

∗ = data unavailable

The following resources were used to compute the data reflected on the chart:

Diet Simple Plus for IBM and Compatible Computers. Salem, OR: N-Squared Computing.

Pennington, Jean A.T., Ph.D., R.D., rev. *Bowes and Church's Food Values of Portions Commonly Used.* 15th ed. Philadelphia: Lippincott, 1989.

Michael Jacobson's *Nutrition Wizard.* Public Interest Software. Washington, DC: Center for Science in the Public Interest.

Robertson, Laurel, Carol Flinders, and Brian Ruppenthal. *The New Laurel's Kitchen.* Berkeley, CA: Ten Speed Press, 1986.

Information was also gathered from manufacturers of some food products.

(Nutritional Information for Recipes, continued)

Recipe Title *(Data for 1 serving unless otherwise indicated)* **Lively Lunchboxes**		Calories	Protein (g)	Fat (g)	Cholesterol (mg)	Carbohydrates (g)	Calcium (mg)	Iron (mg)	Sodium (mg)	Vit A (IU)	Vit C (mg)
Karen's Sesame Noodles	p. 122	318	10.69	9.7	0	45.9	76	3.8	530	8	.9
Lunchbox Noodles 1 serv using corn pasta	p. 123	243	4.43	8	0	40.4	24	.65	525	10	.1
Confetti Rice Salad	p. 124	294	5.37	18	0	29.9	44	2	53	3154	31.2
Dilled Rice & Kidney Beans	p. 125	294	7.97	11.4	0	41.6	52	2.44	270	5	1.1
Santa Fe Black Bean Salad	p. 126	136	5.69	5.1	0	18.1	36	2	185	770	25.9
Lemon Basil Potato Salad	p. 127	192	3.34	7.2	0	29.3	42	1.03	183	132	24.1
Aunt Cathy's Crunchy Cole Slaw	p. 128	173	3.42	14.3	0	10.2	31	1.15	53	1861	18.3
Tabouli	p. 129	205	4.25	10.8	0	24.5	34	1.71	273	332	16
Mad Dog Rice Salad 1 cup	p. 130	277	9.38	9.4	0	40.5	78	2.5	103	3613	11.6
Asian Noodle Salad	p. 131	350	10.9	16.5	0	46.5	61	2.07	794	48	.5
Quick Quinoa Salad	p. 132	300	9.23	14.5	0	35.2	74	5.47	506	2934	13.2
Rice Balls w/Sesame Salt 1 rice ball	p. 133	59	1.86	2.4	0	7.7	10	.49	78	6	0
Tempeh Club Sandwiches 1 plain sandwich	p. 134	285	18	9.5	0	32.7	42	2.74	361	*	.3
Gingered Lentil Sandwich Spread 1/4 cup	p. 136	88	4.19	3.9	0	9.9	17	1.14	164	73	0
Hummus 1/4 cup	p. 137	124	4.3	7.5	0	10.9	33	1.31	95	6	3.7
Tofu-Chive Spread 1/4 cup	p. 138	86	5.75	6.3	0	3.8	64	1.5	139	148	3.8
Tamari-Roasted Nuts 1/4 cup	p. 139	219	7.89	18.3	0	9.5	59	2.9	267	33	.1
Savory Sandwiches to Go 1 sand. w/ black bean and rice filling	p. 140	269	10.15	4.5	0	47.5	41	2.83	28	28	.8
Miso-Tahini & Rasp. Jam Sandwich 1 sandwich	p. 143	341	11.1	15	0	44.4	76	3.18	470	17	1.6
Apple-Miso Almond-Butter Sandwich 1 sandwich	p. 143	252	8.11	9.8	0	35	79	2.6	396	15	1.8
Carrot Flowers	p. 146	30	.83	.1	0	7.2	19	.45	21	16,876	6

∗ = data unavailable

(Nutritional Information for Recipes, continued)

Recipe Title (Data for 1 serving unless otherwise indicated)		Calories	Protein (g)	Fat (g)	Cholesterol (mg)	Carbohydrates (g)	Calcium (mg)	Iron (mg)	Sodium (mg)	Vit A (IU)	Vit C (mg)
Soothing Soups											
Cynthia's Hearty Veg-Miso	p. 148	82	4.39	1.5	0	13.7	49	.99	539	5773	13.8
Cream of Asparagus	p. 149	60	2.68	2.1	0	8.7	21	.65	181	335	14
Dean Street Split Pea	p. 150	97	4.82	2.1	0	15.8	33	1.37	291	5095	5.8
Rosemary Red	p. 151	83	3.66	2.5	0	12.4	29	1.13	169	8702	5.9
White Beans & Fresh Herbs	p. 152	141	7.26	3	0	23	102	3.42	279	5306	8.1
Dark Beans & Sensuous Spices	p. 153	137	7.11	3.1	0	22	53	2.15	275	5135	6.3
Indian Red Lentil	p. 154	119	5.79	3.3	6	17.7	54	2.61	283	841	16.1
Golden Mushroom-Basil	p. 155	150	4.42	5.1	0	22.5	63	1.68	655	3695	16.2
Creamy Broccoli	p. 156	134	5.54	3.7	0	23.8	129	1.62	207	1971	82.7
Thick Potato Caulif. & Dulse	p. 157	156	6.24	3.6	0	26.4	85	3.7	675	3448	50.3
Nina's Famous Spring Beet	p. 158	94	4.63	1.5	0	18.5	140	2.54	554	8775	45.3
Chipotle Navy Bean	p. 159	202	11.93	2.5	0	34.5	86	4.16	367	0	3.3
Substantial Suppers											
Indian Rice & Lentils 1 serv w/ 1 T. topping	p. 162	204	6.86	3.7	1	36.4	76	1.79	200	32	4.9
Red Bean & Quinoa Chili	p. 163	241	11.45	3.4	0	43.3	69	5.19	451	418	20.5
Peasant Kasha & Potatoes	p. 164	84	4.6	2.4	0	11.3	18	1.39	96	0	7.2
Polenta Pizza 1 slice	p. 165	252	7.45	5.5	5	45.5	93	3.13	713	827	23.4
Millet Croquettes 2 croquettes w/ 1/4 c. gravy	p. 166	378	8.36	15.8	0	51	66	2.8	935	5155	12
Mixed-Veg. Stir-Fry w/Nutty Ginger 1 serv w/ 1/4 c. sauce	p. 168	231	7.23	14.6	0	20.8	202	2.56	704	6703	83.2
Mom's Marv. Veg. Loaf 1 slice	p. 169	191	6.06	6.7	0	27.7	41	1.59	140	2558	4.7
Arame & Black-Eyed Peas	p. 170	100	5.34	.4	0	19.9	76	2.02	424	68	*
Sassy Red Beans	p. 171	163	10.59	.8	0	30	60	3.43	274	14	.8
Three Sisters Stew	p. 172	175	7.71	3	0	31.9	73	2.96	157	3093	19.5
Mexican Bean & Corn Casserole	p. 174	200	8.54	3.3	5	34.8	77	3.22	584	425	16.1
Curried Lentils & Cauliflower	p. 175	119	6.1	2.8	0	18.8	53	2.29	192	170	41.8

* = data unavailable

(Nutritional Information for Recipes, continued)

Recipe Title *(Data for 1 serving unless otherwise indicated)* **Substantial Suppers** (cont.)		Calories	Protein (g)	Fat (g)	Cholesterol (mg)	Carbohydrates (g)	Calcium (mg)	Iron (mg)	Sodium (mg)	Vit A (IU)	Vit C (mg)
Black Bean Tostadas *1 plain bean tostada*	p. 176	190	9.77	2	0	35.2	97	3.44	188	102	1.9
Nut Burgers *1 burger w/ bun*	p. 177	516	14.9	31.5	0	48.7	158	4.79	336	5203	4.1
Tempeh & Red Pepper Stroganoff	p. 178	239	15.8	8	0	24.8	82	2.82	1068	6176	51.5
Flash Spaghetti	p. 179	336	16.15	5.1	0	54.7	97	4.81	443	1103	32.5
Szechuan Tempeh	p. 180	401	18.43	27.7	0	20.1	40	1.59	1042	88	.9
Sloppeh Joes *1 serv on a bun*	p. 181	317	19.10	8.6	0	43	62	3.22	781	98	33.9
Tofu Kale Supper Pie *1 slice*	p. 182	295	9.04	15.2	0	35.1	107	2.8	198	7468	17.5
Hiziki Pâté	p. 184	85	5.48	4.5	0	6.5	100	5.16	373	259	9.6
Dr. Bruce's Grilled Salmon	p. 185	396	33.25	26.5	103	4.8	80	1.93	950	1574	58
Thea's Greek Shrimp Stew	p. 186	226	23.5	7.4	131	15	244	3.22	540	1280	31.7
Japanese Marinated Fish Steak *1 serv using cod steak*	p. 187	160	27.88	2.6	66	2	54	.91	782	18	1.9
Baked Chicken w/ Mush. & Rosemary	p. 188	131	15.73	3.9	42	2.7	33	1.19	562	45	.9
Vital Vegetables											
Quick-Boiled Greens (examples)	p. 190										
1/2 c. cooked kale		21	2.5	.25	0	3.5	103	.9	23	4500	50
1/2 c. cooked collards		31	3.4	.7	0	4.7	170	.7	18	7410	72
1/2 c. cooked broccoli		17	2.4	.25	0	4.5	86	.7	13	1940	70
1/2 c. cooked bok choy		12	1.2	.15	0	2	175	.47	15	2535	13
Sesame Greens *1 serv using kale*	p. 191	67	3.52	4.6	0	5	109	1.22	25	4570	51
Cashew-Curry Greens *1 serv using collards*	p. 191	150	6.95	9.5	0	11	202	1.89	283	7414	72.6
Garlic Sautéed Greens *1 serv using collards*	p. 192	66	3.52	4.2	0	5.7	181	.78	19	7411	74.3
Dark Greens Salad *1 serv w/ 2 T. dressing*	p. 193	82	6.57	3.6	0	8.7	248	2.02	115	8513	84.3
Romaine Radicchio Salad *1 serv w/ dressing*	p. 194	56	.94	4.8	0	3.2	31	.55	63	541	17.1
Cooked Cabbage Salad *1 serv w/ 1 T. dressing*	p. 195	103	2.6	7.4	0	8.4	56	.99	281	2890	42.9

✳ = data unavailable

(Nutritional Information for Recipes, continued)

Recipe Title (Data for 1 serving unless otherwise indicated) Vital Vegetables (cont.)		Calories	Protein (g)	Fat (g)	Cholesterol (mg)	Carbohydrates (g)	Calcium (mg)	Iron (mg)	Sodium (mg)	Vit A (IU)	Vit C (mg)
Mustard Green Salad 1 serv w/ 2 T. dressing	p. 196	25	2.52	.9	0	2.7	58	1.06	10	1243	12.9
Watercress Salad 1 serv w/ 1 T. dressing	p. 197	70	.81	7.1	0	2.1	36	.52	37	1069	10.2
Creamy Cole Slaw	p. 198	71	.98	5.6	4	5	31	.44	111	3488	27.1
Susan's Succulent Supper Salad	p. 199	218	6.1	14.7	0	19.8	81	3.53	66	3481	29.7
Grilled Vegetable Salad 1 serv w/ 1 T. dressing	p. 200	142	4.44	9.5	6	13	120	2.11	132	3120	35.8
Spinach Salad 1 serv w/ 1 T. dressing	p. 201	112	2.97	10.3	0	4.7	65	1.76	52	3696	16.6
Dulse Salad 1 serv w/ 1 T. dressing	p. 202	135	8.67	3	0	20.1	103	11.55	690	420	10.5
Roasted Potatoes & Carrots	p. 203	333	5.71	11	0	55.1	40	3.64	29	10145	29.7
Potato Gratin	p. 204	153	3.73	1.8	0	31	19	.72	6	703	45.1
Basic Baked Winter Squash 1 cup	p. 206	130	3.7	.82	0	31	57	1.43	2	8610	27
Sweet Autumn Bake	p. 207	119	3.45	.9	0	25.2	52	1.27	9	7279	22.8
Fresh Breads and Muffins											
Rice Bread 1 thick slice	p. 212	197	5.33	3.4	0	36.9	15	1.9	323	0	0
Quinoa Garlic Herb Bread 1 thick slice	p. 212	189	5.65	3.6	0	33.8	20	2.39	323	11	.7
Orange Millet Raisin Bread 1 thick slice	p. 213	258	6.37	3.6	0	51.8	25	2.34	325	52	12.9
Bean Apple Rye Bread 1 thick slice	p. 213	195	6.45	3.5	0	36.1	22	2.19	322	6	.5
Summer Corn Bread 1 square	p. 214	118	2.69	4.5	13	18	40	.56	83	81	.3
Sweet Squash Corn Muffins 1 muffin	p. 215	212	4.29	8.6	24	31.9	71	1.6	136	473	1.2
Applesauce Muffins 1 muffin	p. 216	156	2.64	5.6	18	25.1	70	.55	87	33	.9
Pumpkin Muffins 1 muffin	p. 217	171	4.45	6.5	24	25.6	66	1.53	234	6039	1.2

＊ = data unavailable

(Nutritional Information for Recipes, continued)

Recipe Title *(Data for 1 serving unless otherwise indicated)* **Fresh Breads and Muffins** (cont.)		Calories	Protein (g)	Fat (g)	Cholesterol (mg)	Carbohydrates (g)	Calcium (mg)	Iron (mg)	Sodium (mg)	Vit A (IU)	Vit C (mg)
Poppyseed Muffins *1 muffin*	*p. 218*	190	4.45	7.3	24	28.8	135	1.36	235	82	4.7
Banana Date Nut Bread *1 slice*	*p. 220*	289	5.53	10.9	27	45.8	85	1.68	222	103	10.4
Sauces and Stuff											
Lemon-Tahini Sauce *2 Tablespoons*	*p. 222*	74	2.5	6.4	0	3.1	19	.59	39	10	3.7
Tahini Oat Sauce *2 Tablespoons*	*p. 222*	34	1.3	2.1	0	2.7	13	.35	198	34	.6
Nutty Ginger Sauce *2 Tablespoons*	*p. 223*	66	1.6	5.3	0	3.1	33	.43	264	0	.1
Creamy Ginger-Garlic Dressing *2 Tablespoons*	*p. 223*	54	2.25	4.7	0	1.3	30	.58	90	0	1.3
Mushroom-Wine Gravy *1/4 cup*	*p. 224*	41	.92	2.4	3	2.9	11	.37	266	48	.4
Homemade Curry Paste *1 Tablespoon*	*p. 226*	82	.68	7.7	0	3.3	26	1.27	2	18	1.9
Wholesome Desserts											
Gingerbread People *1 cookie person*	*p. 230*	238	4.36	5.4	12	45	77	3.63	201	226	4.4
Apricot Thumbprint Cookies *1 cookie*	*p. 231*	123	2.47	6.3	0	15.7	40	.63	49	46	0
Cynthia's Oatmeal Cookies *1 cookie*	*p. 232*	98	2.02	4	0	14.3	9	.66	26	5	.1
Halloween Cookies *1 cookie*	*p. 233*	78	1.21	1.4	0	15.7	10	.54	18	145	3.1
Carob Carob-Chip Cookies *1 cookie*	*p. 234*	106	1.82	4.7	0	17.8	34	.78	13	0	.4
Brown-Rice Crispy Treats *1 square*	*p. 235*	70	.92	1.3	0	13.9	4	.26	3	0	0
Nutty Carmelcorn	*p. 236*	169	3.94	7.2	0	24.6	22	.66	3	15	.2
Carob Almond Fudge *1 one-inch piece*	*p. 237*	73	1.4	4.6	0	8.6	32	.45	2	0	0

✳ = data unavailable

(Nutritional Information for Recipes, continued)

Recipe Title *(Data for 1 serving unless otherwise indicated)* **Wholesome Desserts** (cont.)		Calories	Protein (g)	Fat (g)	Cholesterol (mg)	Carbohydrates (g)	Calcium (mg)	Iron (mg)	Sodium (mg)	Vit A (IU)	Vit C (mg)
Fruitsicles											
1 Juicesicle (using apple juice)	*p. 238*	29	0	0	0	7.3	4	.22	2	0	.5
1 Creamy Orange-van. Pop	*p. 238*	33	1.06	.3	1	6.9	27	.09	5	100	23.3
1 Banana-rasp. Pop	*p. 238*	35	.33	.3	0	7.9	2	.16	1	36	5.1
1 Melonsicle	*p. 239*	12	.25	.1	0	2.8	4	.08	3	1076	14.1
1 Maltsicle	*p. 239*	80	2.0	3.7	0	9.7	*	.36	47	0	3.0
Apricot Kuzu Custard	*p. 240*	114	1.02	1.4	0	25.6	16	.64	5	1652	1.2
Raspberry Pudding Gel	*p. 240*	99	.54	1.1	0	21.9	9	1.14	1	11	2.1
Vanilla Amasake Pudding	*p. 241*	128	4.55	1.1	0	22.9	40	1.32	32	*	*
Winter Fruit Compote *1 serv w/ 1/4 c. nut milk*	*p. 242*	190	2.53	4.7	0	38.5	45	2	6	1352	5.5
Pear-Plum Crisp	*p. 243*	260	4.09	11.6	0	39.4	41	1.3	136	151	6.7
Tofu Cheesecake	*p. 244*	334	7.12	15.4	0	45	80	2.1	141	9	2.2
Cherry Jiggle	*p. 245*	53	.04	0	0	12.6	4	.95	1	0	0
Blueberry-Strawberry Tart	*p. 246*	184	3.89	8.1	0	25.7	31	1.11	33	33	11.7
Gracie's Yellow Birthday Cake	*p. 247*	238	4.43	10.9	36	31.5	81	1.35	136	85	10.3
Carrot Cake w/ Apricot Glaze	*p. 248*	274	4.69	12.8	36	37.3	85	1.66	120	5392	2.9
Dark Sweet Carob Cupcakes *1 cupcake*	*p. 250*	151	2.74	7.3	24	21.1	58	.86	62	29	*
Carob Butter Icing *2 Tablespoons*	*p. 251*	82	1.18	3.2	0	14.5	31	.57	24	0	0
Banana Cream Frosting *2 Tablespoons*	*p. 252*	42	1.6	1.6	0	5.4	19	.45	1	6	.8
Yummy Yam Frosting *2 Tablespoons*	*p. 252*	47	.56	2.8	8	4.5	12	.17	18	724	2.1
What's to Drink?											
Banana Milk *1 cup*	*p. 255*	112	9.67	3	0	11.7	67	1.33	80	30	3.3
Cranberry Ginger Cider *1 cup*	*p. 256*	130	0	.1	0	33.5	13	.65	9	5	55
Hot Mocha Milk *1 cup*	*p. 256*	48	4.8	1.3	0	5	38	.67	43	*	*

✱ = data unavailable

Index

CYNTHIA LAIR was born and raised in Wichita, Kansas. She graduated magna cum laude with a Bachelor of Arts in Speech/Theatre from Wichita State University. During the following thirteen years in New York City, Cynthia acted in television commercials and studied nutrition. She graduated as a Certified Health and Nutrition Counselor from Gary Null's Health and Nutrition Program and began teaching the "Healthy Child Series" at The Natural Gourmet Cookery School. Since moving to Seattle, Cynthia has been teaching whole foods cooking classes at the Puget Consumers' Co-op, Kitchen Kitchen, The Herbfarm, Cook's World, HIV University, and other places. Cynthia lives with her husband, Michael, and their daughter, Grace.

The Newest and Best from LuraMedia
For Your Family

*For every parent and teacher who wants to end violence
and create a safe, peaceful world for children.*

Raising Peaceful Children in a Violent World
by Nancy Lee Cecil

This action book offers creative and practical ways to teach children peaceful conflict resolution. Includes chapters on family communication, discipline strategies, racial attitudes, gender stereotypes, TV, toys, games, and books.

*For every parent whose days never seem to include enough time
for "quality" family activities.*

Seven Times the Sun:
Guiding Your Child Through the Rhythms of the Day
by Shea Darian

Written by a Waldorf mother and educator, this creative guide helps parents and children turn simple moments into loving, consistent rituals. A one-of-a-kind book weaving songs, stories, and verses throughout, showing how to bring joy to meals, bedtime, chores, naps, and playtime.

Give yourself a bit of "quality" time, too . . .

Finding Stone:
A Quiet Parable and Soul-Work Meditation
by Christin Lore Weber

Enter the ancient meditative practice of standing before life's mysteries. Accompany "Finding Woman" on a journey to discover your Stone of healing, wisdom, and power in the beauty and simplicity of this parable and reflections.

*If you've ever read one of Madeleine L'Engle's fantasy books to your children (or been
captivated by the stories yourself!), you'll want to know more about this fascinating author.*

Madeleine L'Engle, Suncatcher:
Spiritual Vision of a Storyteller
by Carole F. Chase

The first-ever comprehensive study of Madeleine L'Engle's remarkable life, writings, philosophy, and spiritual vision. "Finally, both a well-written biography and discerning overview of the work of one of the greatest creative writers and mystics of our times."—M. Scott Peck. M.D.

And for the child in you . . .

The Woman Who Lost Her Heart:
A Tale of Reawakening
by Susan Delattre and Susan O'Halloran

A delightful fairy tale for grown-ups. A woman awakens one morning to discover that she has, literally, lost her heart. During her quest to recover what is missing, she realizes how she has maimed herself in order to adjust to an increasingly frenetic world.

LuraMedia books are available in bookstores
or call 1-800-FOR-LURA to order.
Ask for our free catalog!